ROMAN WIVES, ROMAN WIDOWS

ROMAN WIVES, ROMAN WIDOWS

The Appearance of New Women
and the Pauline Communities

Bruce W. Winter

WILLIAM B. EERDMANS PUBLISHING COMPANY
GRAND RAPIDS, MICHIGAN / CAMBRIDGE, U.K.

Wm. B. Eerdmans Publishing Co.
255 Jefferson Ave. S.E., Grand Rapids, Michigan 49503 /
P.O. Box 163, Cambridge CB3 9PU U.K.

Printed in the United States of America

08 07 06 05 04 03   7 6 5 4 3 2 1

Library of Congress Cataloging-in-Publication Data

Winter, Bruce W.
Roman wives, Roman widows: the appearance of new women
and the Pauline communities / Bruce W. Winter.
p.   cm.
Includes bibliographical references and index.
ISBN 0-8028-4971-7 (pbk.: alk. paper)
1. Women in Christianity — History — Early church, ca. 30-600.
2. Women — Religious aspects — Christianity —
History of doctrines — Early church, ca. 30-600.
3. Women — Biblical teaching.
4. Sex role — Religious aspects — Christianity.
5 Social classes — Rome.
6. Rome — Social life and customs.   I. Title.

BR195.W6W56   2003
270.1′082 — dc21

2003054330

www.eerdmans.com

Contents

Preface   xi

Abbreviations   xvi

1. **The Search for a Setting**   1

   I. The Connection between Roman Law and Roman Society   2

  II. The Neglected First-Century Women   3

 III. Defining 'Appearance', 'New' and 'Roman'   4

 IV. Perceptions of First-Century Women   6

  V. Proletarian or Socially Diverse Christian Women   7

 VI. Enslaved *v.* Emancipated Women?   8

VII. The Structure of This Book   9

PART I

2. **The Appearance of New Wives**   17

   I. Roman Women   17

    Wives and the Legal Power of Husbands   17

    Wives and the Portrayal of Affectionate Husbands   18

v

CONTENTS

Wives and Unfaithful Husbands 19

II. 'New' Roman Women 21

Change 21

Contemporary Writers 23

The Promotion of Promiscuity by Poets 24

Catullus (*c.* 84-54 B.C.) 25

Propertius (*c.* 48-16 B.C.) 25

Ovid (43 B.C.–A.D. 17) 27

Playwrights and New Roman Comedy 30

III. Roman Social Values in the East 32

Roman Culture 32

Roman Women 34

IV. Conclusions 37

3. New Wives and New Legislation 39

I. Augustus' Marriage Legislation of 17 B.C. 40

II. Reactions to Augustus' Legislation 47

Women's Defiance 47

Equestrians' Revolt 48

Horace on the lex Julia 49

Legal Inequality 50

Julia and *lex Julia* 51

III. The Subsequent Response of Augustus 52

IV. Amendments to the Legislation in A.D. 9 54

V. Conclusions 56

4. New Wives and Philosophical Responses 59

I. Cardinal Virtues and New Roman Wives 60

II. Women Studying Philosophy 63

Self-Control 63

  Justice   64

  Courage   64

 III. 'Headstrong and Arrogant' Women   65

 IV. Educating Daughters   66

  V. Single and Married Men and Sexual Indulgence 68

 VI. Pythagorean Woman to Woman   72

VII. Conclusion   74

PART II

 5. The Appearance of Unveiled Wives in 1 Corinthians 11:2-16 77

  I. The Significance of the Veil in Marriage   78

  II. The Significance of the Removal of the Veil in Public 81

 III. Modest and Immodest Appearances in Roman Law 83

 IV. Official Policing of Dress Codes on Religious Occasions 85

  V. What Was 'Proper' in Roman Corinth?   91

 VI. Appearing to Be Contentious   94

 **6. Deciphering the Married Woman's Appearance,
  1 Timothy 2:9-15**   97

  I. Dress Codes in 1 Timothy 2:9-11   98

  Respectable Apparel   99

  Modesty and Self-Control (2:9a, 15)   101

  Adornment   103

  Hairstyles   104

  Gold   104

  Pearls   105

  Godliness and Good Works   108

CONTENTS

II. Abortion or Child-Bearing? (2:15a)   109

    Avoiding Childbearing   110

III. Submissiveness and Learning, Teaching and Dominating
    (2:11-12)   112

    Submissiveness or Teaching   113

    Speaking and Teaching   115

    To Have Authority or Dominate?   116

IV. Conclusions   119

7. **The Appearance of Young Widows, 1 Timothy 5:11-15**   **123**

  I. The Widows and the Christian Community   124

 II. Inappropriate Behaviour by Young Widows   128

III. To Marry and Have Children   137

8. **The Appearance of Young Wives, Titus 2:3-5**   **141**

  I. The Legal Privileges of Cretan Women   141

    Ancient Rights   141

    The Coming of Roman Culture   144

 II. Cultural Conditioning and Cretan Christianity   145

    Instructors v. Elders   146

    Cretans and Cretanizing   149

III. Drunkenness among Older Married Women   152

IV. Recalling Young Married Women to Their Responsibilities   154

    'Wakeup Calls'   155

    Lovers of Husbands and Children   159

    Household Management   160

    Debauchery among Older Children   163

    The Behaviour of Husbands   164

    Traditional and Christian Values   165

 V. Conclusions   167

PART III

9. **The Appearance of Women in the Public Sphere**   173

   I. Women in Commerce   174

  II. Women in the Courts   176

 III. Women in Politics   180

    Election Propaganda in Pompeii   180

    The Roman Forum and Italy   180

    Woman, Civic Patrons, Magistrates, and Gymnasiarch in the East   181

    Junia Theodora, the Federal Patron in Corinth   183

      Junia Theodora's Benefactions   185

      Junia Theodora's Official Honours   186

      The Stated Purposes for Honouring Junia Theodora   186

      Junia Theodora and the Request of the Lycian Federation   187

    The Limits of Participation   191

  IV. Women in *politeia* and Women in the Church   193

    Junia Theodora and Phoebe, Patron and Deacon   194

    Junia Theodora and Junia   200

   V. Conclusions   204

Appendix: Women in Civic Affairs   205

Iunia Theodora   205

  1. *A Decree of the Federal Assembly of the Lycian Cities*   205

  2. *A Letter from the Lycian City of Myra to Corinth*   206

  3. *A Letter from the Lycian City of Patara*   206

  4. *A Letter of the Federal Assembly to Corinth Introducing a Second Decree in Favour of Iunia Theodora*   208

  5. *A Decree of the Lycian City of Telmessos*   209

Claudia Metrodora from Chios   210

  1. *Claudia Metrodora as Magistrate (stephanephoros)*   210

  2. *Claudia Metrodora and Her Many Other Public Offices*   210

CONTENTS

3. *Claudia Metrodora from Ephesos*   211

Bibliography   212

Index of Subjects   224

Index of Modern Authors   228

Index of Scripture and Other Ancient Sources   231

Preface

⁎

*Roman Wives, Roman Widows: The Appearance of New Women and the Pau-
line Communities* aims to show that where the poets and other literary ob-
servers in the late Republic and early Empire, Augustus in his marriage legislation, the Stoic and the Neo-Pythagorean philosophical schools in their
deliberations and the letters to the Pauline communities discuss the behaviour of a certain type of women, they were all dealing with one and the same
phenomenon. It is what some ancient historians have recently designated the
'new woman' who was contrasted with the modest wife and widow. From ancient literary, legal, and non-literary sources it will be argued that the appearance of the 'new woman' can be identified.

This book does not focus on the authorial views on women in the relevant New Testament texts. It does not discuss the early Christian household
codes nor 1 Corinthians 7 which contains the longest discussion on marriage,
singleness, divorce, remarriage and courtship directed to the Christian communities in the early church.

It was in the midst of teaching a course on hermeneutics called "Text and
Context" at Beeson Divinity School in 2000 that this book had its genesis. A
graduate student requested that a lecture be given on 'being saved through
childbirth' in 1 Timothy 2:15 in its social context. I was at that time completing
the first draft of the chapter "Veiled Men and Wives and Christian Contentiousness (1 Corinthians 11:2-16)" for my book, *After Paul Left Corinth: The Influence of Secular Ethics and Social Change.* What struck me as I began to pre-
pare the material was how apposite the particular cultural setting of the
Corinthian passage was in illuminating aspects of 1 Timothy 2:8-15.

I had assumed that the ancient material would have already been brought
to light in the not inconsiderable secondary literature on 1 Timothy 2:9-15.

However, I discovered from Andreas Köstenberger who has published in this area that was not the case,[1] and was encouraged to publish the evidence for the appearance of the 'new woman' in 1 Timothy 2:9-15 whose existence was unknown to Pauline scholars.[2]

Later that year at the Trans-Pennine Ancient History Seminar at the University of Liverpool, I read a paper on the subject of "The New Roman Wife and the Pauline Churches" as part of the term's seminar theme. I did not pursue its publication in their forthcoming volume on the ancient family although the New Testament material was of interest in that it provided another view in the ancient world that interacted with the 'new women', the other two being the Stoics and the Neo-Pythagorean philosophical schools.

In the discussions that followed the paper I gave on the search for a *Sitz im Leben* of 1 Timothy 2 at the British New Testament conference in September, 2000, my colleagues confirmed the need for a publication. While preparing this paper, it became clear that one could not do justice to all the material in the passage and the issues involved, let alone other New Testament texts.[3] A short monograph which gathered the primary evidence was needed on the appearance of 'new' Roman women in the first century. The extensive secondary discussion by ancient historians on extant sources in the late Republic and early Empire, especially the vast body of Roman law that is not normally brought within the ambit of Pauline studies, also needed to be noted.

These are the circumstances that gave rise to yet another book on a somewhat well trodden, if not overworked, topic. I hope that this monograph will be seen to be a constructive contribution to the important issue of women in the Pauline communities as it seeks to secure as the starting point the *Sitz im Leben* of texts relating to them.

There may be those who remain sceptical about the need to explore these texts yet again. One can also understand that some will have no stomach for any further discussions if this book was being written to re-ignite what has, at times, been something of an acrimonious debate. Those apprehensions are understood, given it would have been expected that discussions

---

1. A. Köstenberger, "A Complex Sentence Structure in 1 Timothy 2:12," in A. J. Köstenberger, T. R. Schreiner, and H. S. Baldwin, eds., *Women in the Church: A Fresh Analysis of 1 Timothy 2:9-15* (Grand Rapids: Baker, 1995), ch. 4; and A. J. Köstenberger, "Ascertaining Women's God-Ordained Role: An Interpretation of 1 Timothy 2:15," *BBR* 7 (1997): 107-44.

2. There is a short discussion by K. E. Corley, *Private Women, Public Meals: Social Conflict in the Synoptic Tradition* (Peabody, Mass.: Hendrickson, 1993), pp. 53-62, whose work I did not discover until I had completed revising this book.

3. A summary of the conference paper was published as "The 'New' Roman Wife and 1 Timothy 2:9-15: The Search for a *Sitz im Leben*," *TynB* 51.2 (2000): 285-94.

on this New Testament subject would have manifested a more courteous treatment of those who have taken different views on this issue. After all, its wider teaching affects the treatment of others — 'show perfect courtesy towards all', Titus 3:2.

However unfortunate the way in which the arguments of others were sometimes handled in the past, that provides no logical reason for not putting forward new material that could help illuminate the New Testament texts by securing their social setting with a greater certainty. To date, almost all of the discussion on women in the Pauline communities has focused on the cultural preconceptions or theological preconditioning of the writer of particular passages; little attention has been given to the setting of the women under discussion. Furthermore, the appropriate semantic fields have not always been carefully scrutinised when making decisions on the apposite rendering of key terms used in New Testament passages about women, wives or widows.

A good deal of the *Angst* that marked the early years of controversy over these passages has now subsided. I judge this to be an apposite time for all to revisit these texts in the light of the ancient social contexts from which they arose.

It is clear that in the past hermeneutical methods have been found wanting. For example, the support invoked from 1 Corinthians 11:2-16 for wearing head coverings in church up until the second half of the last century went unchallenged until women in the wider society ceased wearing hats and gloves in public (except for weddings, gala occasions and royal garden parties). This widespread Western custom was then largely abandoned in church gatherings because society in general ceased to observe it. However, no justification was given from pulpits for this; they can remain conspicuously silent when congregations abandon ecclesiastical directives in favour of changes in social customs in the wider society. Some decades later the same text was invoked in support of male headship in the congregation. I have previously raised my own uncertainties about invoking this text on head coverings for men and women in support of male headship in the congregation. This interpretation arose because insufficient attention seems to have been given to the relationship between the words 'woman' and 'veil' and the social context.[4]

Those who believe that you simply apply the text to the contemporary situation are faced with the need to instruct women praying or prophesying in the congregation to cover their heads or else crop or shave their hair. Young

---

4. See my "Veiled Men and Wives and Christian Contentiousness (1 Corinthians 11:2-16)," in *After Paul Left Corinth: The Influence of Secular Ethics and Social Change* (Grand Rapids: Eerdmans, 2001), ch. 6 and the comment on p. 141, n. 81.

men must also resist the cultural trend of shoulder-length hair that has passed in and out of fashion at least twice in recent decades.[5] This seems to be the logical consequence of simply applying the text from 1 Corinthians 11:2-16.

If the text is to be applied literally then the injunctions in 1 Timothy 2:9 for women not to wear gold or pearls should question our present-day tolerance of the adornment with traditional jewellery, body piercing, and expensive clothing. On what basis can you ignore those injunctions and yet insist on the enforcement of those immediately following in 2:12? The apostolic tradition in 1 Timothy 5:14 that young widows remarry is not enforced, or even taught, in Christian communities today in the West. It was, however, a legal stipulation in legislation introduced by Augustus.

This raises the issue of the criteria for selectivity. What are the grounds on which it is decided to apply or not to apply a text or part thereof? Rigorous hermeneutical considerations have been rightly to the fore in recent decades. In the multicultural settings of worldwide Christianity it is highly appropriate to inquire into the basis on which judgements are made for the application of some texts and not others. Arguments such as common sense will hardly gain acceptance from those who rightly seek to establish careful criteria in the field of hermeneutics. Those interested in biblical interpretation have not always seen the need to pursue the first-century setting of particular texts, before proceeding to locate an identical issue in the contemporary scene and then engaging with it.[6]

Others will want to argue that New Testament authors were the children of their time. Those who do so have to account for the fact that some aspects of New Testament teaching were distinct and consciously ran counter to the cultural norms of the day.[7]

---

5. On the latter issue see my "Veiled Men and Wives and Christian Contentiousness (1 Corinthians 11:2-16)," esp. pp 131-33.

6. The two horizons being referred to here can be mistaken. A. C. Thiselton wrote of a philosophical perspective as his early book made clear, *The Two Horizons: New Testament Hermeneutics and Philosophical Description with Special Reference to Heidegger, Bultmann, Gadamer, and Wittgenstein* (Exeter: Paternoster Press, 1980). His subsequent discussion has taken seriously the first-century horizon, see, e.g., his monumental commentary, *The First Epistle to the Corinthians: Commentary on the Greek Text* (Grand Rapids and Carlisle: Eerdmans and Paternoster, 2000). Not all who have pursued the issue of hermeneutics have been as careful as he is in seeking first to understand the ancient world setting of the text.

7. On this issue see most recently my "Roman Law and Society in Romans 12–15," in P. Oakes, ed., *Rome in the Bible and the Early Church* (Carlisle and Grand Rapids: Paternoster and Baker, 2002), ch. 3, pp. 67-102. A projected volume, *The Pauline Corpus Against Its Environment,* will cover a much wider treatment of texts and demonstrate the counter-cultural nature of substantial teaching on important aspects of the lives of early Christians.

I was recently made acutely aware of the predicament that some Christian women who work in the business and academic world have when it comes to explaining some enigmatic sections in biblical texts on women to their colleagues. The educated Bible reader has difficulties understanding those that deal with women in the Pauline churches because they are texts without social contexts which have been used selectively.

This research is produced under the auspices of the Institute for Early Christianity in the Graeco-Roman World, Cambridge. It is part of on-going work which aims to examine the intersection of documents of early Christianity with the world of its day. This book was written as part of a long-term commitment to harvest the enormous number of extant literary and non-literary sources to illuminate New Testament texts in their first-century settings. Such work seeks to take note of the discussion of those ancient historians, epigraphists, papyrologists and archaeologists, as well as the history of recent scholarly approaches. Given that their discussion is not normally accessible to New Testament scholars, I have not hesitated to quote them *verbatim* where their discussion of the ancient sources has been important for the argument.

I owe an enormous debt to my wife who edited this book in the midst of her own very busy schedule and to Judith Taylor for reading through yet another of my manuscripts. A longstanding friend, Alanna Nobbs, Associate Professor of Ancient History at Macquarie University, very kindly read the manuscript and made helpful suggestions and corrections. It will be clear that I am also indebted to ancient historians who have devoted themselves in recent times to the previously neglected study of women in the ancient world. Without their publications this book could not have been produced.

Roman Wives, Roman Widows had its genesis in lectures given at Beeson Divinity School, Samford University while a visiting research professor in 2000. I wish to dedicate it to the dean, faculty, and staff, as well as the students whose stimulating and persistent questions helped conceive this book.

Abbreviations

AJAH	*Anglo-Jewish Art and History*
ANRW	*Aufstieg und Niedergang der römischen Welt*
BBR	*Bulletin of Biblical Research*
BDF	Blass, Debrunner, Funk
BICS	*Bulletin of the Institute of Classical Studies*
CQ	*Classical Quarterly*
CIL	*Corpus Inscriptionum Latinarum*
CP	*Classical Philology*
Epigrammata Graeca	*Epigrammata Graeca ex Lapidibus Conlecta*
IG	*Inscriptiones Graecae*
IGUR	*Inscriptiones Graecae Urbis Romae*
JbAC	*Jahrbuch für Antike und Christentum*
JRA	*Journal of Roman Archaeology*
JRS	*Journal of Roman Studies*
Liddell & Scott	*A Greek-English Dictionary and Supplement*, 9th ed.
NTS	*New Testament Studies*
PBSR	*Papers of the British School at Rome*
SEG	*Supplementum Epigraphicum Graecum*
TAPA	*Transactions of the American Philological Association*
Thesleff, *Texts*	H. Thesleff, *The Pythagorean Texts of the Hellenistic Period*
TynB	*Tyndale Bulletin*
YCS	*Yale Classical Studies*

Philo of Alexandria

Conf.	*De confusione linguarum*
Congr.	*De congressu eruditionis gratia*
Det.	*Quod deterius potiori insidiari soleat*
Flacc.	*In Flaccum*
Fug.	*De fuga et inventione*
Gig.	*De gigantibus*
Immut.	*Quod Deus immutabilis sit*
Jos.	*De Josepho*
L.A. III	*Legum allegoriae*
Legat.	*De legatione ad Gaium*
Mig.	*De migratione Abrahami*
Prov.	*De providentia*
Vit.	*De virtutibus*

CHAPTER 1

The Search for a Setting

'The potential for more fruitful contact between classical studies and studies of early Christianity [on women] is great, and it provides another opportunity to look at the intersection of Roman, Greek and Near Eastern cultural traditions.'[1] Beryl Rawson, who has herself written extensively on the Roman family, made this observation recently at the end of a helpful critique of the history of recent research on women in the Greek and Roman world by ancient historians. This book takes up her recommendation and explores that contact for the first century. A great deal of light has thereby been shed on texts addressed to women in the Pauline communities.

The research for this book has also shown that the flow of first-century information need not only be from the ancient world to the New Testament *corpus*. The evidence from the latter can provide significant additional material for a fruitful interaction with ancient historians with the movement from *Christentum* to *Antike*, as Rawson herself has suggested.[2]

---

1. B. Rawson, "From 'daily life' to 'demography'," in R. Hawley and B. Levick, eds., *Women in Antiquity: New Assessments* (London: Routledge, 1995), ch. 1, *cit.* p. 18.

2. For N.T. evidence on the due Roman process of criminal law, see my "*Christentum und Antike*: Acts and the Pauline Corpus as Ancient History," in T. W. Hillard, R. A. Kearsley, C. E. V. Nixon and A. M. Nobbs, eds., *Ancient History in a Modern University* (Grand Rapids: Eerdmans, 1998), Vol. 2, pp. 121-30; and on the importance of the Second Sophistic from Philonic and Pauline sources see my *Philo and Paul among the Sophists: Alexandrian and Corinthian Responses to a Julio-Claudian Movement*, 2nd edition (Grand Rapids: Eerdmans, 2002).

I. The Connection between Roman Law and Roman Society

Some see the vast body of extant Roman law as a significant sub-discipline of ancient history, while others see it as independent of its setting and simply an aspect of study of law as a whole. Crook noted that 'legal historians were pursuing the legal history of Roman antiquity, but the general historians were making insufficient use of Roman law in their treatments of social and economic history'.[3] He considers this a deficiency because the central thesis of his early work on *Law and Life of Rome* was that it is impossible to deal with Roman society and Roman law as if they were basically autonomous spheres not only in Rome but also, we might add, in Roman colonies and her provinces of the Empire.[4] Roman public and private law regulated most aspects of life in antiquity.

The legal sources, statutes, juristic opinions, textbooks, documents and reports preserve a wealth of information that helps illuminate or supplement important aspects of Roman society and economy. This is the central concern of the recent book, Speculum Iuris: *Roman Law as a Reflection of Social and Economic Life in Antiquity*.[5] The essential aspects of Roman society were consciously built on Roman law and operated on that basis. Unlike cultures before or after, citizens of Rome and those in Roman colonies scattered throughout the Empire were aware of this important nexus and, therefore, were well informed of their rights, how privileges were grounded in Roman law and how much of life might be determined by it.[6]

It is for this reason that Crook has continued to argue over the decades

---

3. See most recently J. A. Crook, "Legal History and General History," *BICS* 41 (1996): 31-36.

4. J. A. Crook, *Law and Life of Rome, 90 B.C.–A.D. 212* (New York: Cornell University Press, 1967).

5. Crook's approach has recently been evaluated but not in any acknowledged response to his succinct, programmatic essay cited in n. 3. From the legal historian's perspective, see B. Sirks, "Conclusion: Some Reflections," which provides a balanced approach compared with that of J.-J. Aubert's essay "Conclusion: A Historian's Point of View" in J.-J. Aubert and B. Sirks, eds., Speculum Iuris: *Roman Law as a Reflection of Social and Economic Life in Antiquity* (Ann Arbor: University of Michigan Press, 2002), pp. 169-81, 182-92. Aubert remains highly sceptical of the value of any cross-disciplinary approaches between the two overlapping spheres. This volume has some important essays relevant for this monograph, especially T. A. J. McGinn, "The Augustan Marriage Legislation and Social Practice: Elite Endogamy versus Male 'Marrying Down,'" pp. 46-93. For a discussion of a later period see D. A. Lee, "Decoding Late Roman Law," *Journal of Roman Studies* XCII (2002): 185-193, where he reviews three monographs dealing with the period and support the approach of Crook, adding to the discussion in his review article.

6. See Crook, *Law and Life of Rome, 90 B.C.–A.D. 212*, pp. 7-8, for a discussion of the penchant of Roman citizens for a knowledge of legal matters for this very reason.

that there is an urgent need to integrate Roman legal history with the wider discipline of history. His astute observations have proved extremely important for this book because much of the discussion on women and the Pauline communities has neglected critical evidence from Roman law. As with other evidence this has not been taken into account and, as a result, has coloured our understanding of texts dealing with first-century Christian women.

K. Hopwood in a Festschrift essay for J. A. Crook makes this judgement. 'The [Roman] laws passed are an invaluable source for the ideology of their period: they may or may not tell us what people were doing; instead, they tell us what the ruling groups wanted people to be doing and what they wanted them not to be doing.'[7]

However, it will be argued that in the Pauline communities there are reflections of aspects of Roman law which sought to regulate behaviour patterns. It was for this reason that some of the instructions to the Pauline communities appear to have been framed, taking cognisance of those laws. They also prescribed certain patterns of conduct that were endorsed by Roman law. There is also evidence that Christian women and men followed, or were in danger of following, the examples of those who were successfully promoting mores that were outlawed.

II. The Neglected First-Century Women

In a corporate essay, the ancient historians Elaine Fantham, Helen Peet Foley, Natalie Boymel Kampen, Sarah Pomeroy and Alan Shapiro have produced evidence for the existence of what they have designated the 'new woman'.[8] This book argues that, in the midst of extensive and sometimes intense discussions of texts specifically relating to women in the Pauline communities, the late Republican and early Roman Empire evidence has not been brought into that debate. The focus of this book is the *Sitz im Leben* of the recipients and not authorial responses to secular influences on Christian wives and widows.

Part I on this book will present evidence for new mores that had come to determine the social activities of the 'new woman' and, in some cases, endorsed her illicit sexual liaisons with younger, single men. This evidence helps

7. K. Hopwood, "Aspects of Violent Crime in the Roman Empire," in P. McKechnie, ed., *Thinking like a Lawyer: Essays on Legal and General History for John Crook on His Eightieth Birthday*, Mnemosyne Supplements ccxxxi (Leiden: E. J. Brill, 2002), pp. 63-80, *cit.* p. 65.

8. E. Fantham, H. Peet Foley, N. Boymel Kampen, S. B. Pomeroy, and A. H. Shapiro, "The 'New Woman': Representation and Reality," in *Women in the Classical World* (Oxford: Oxford University Press, 1994), ch. 10.

illuminate the settings of the biblical texts, and the focus of the book may cause readers to rethink their interpretation of the texts addressing women in the Pauline communities. These texts will be the subject of our investigation in Part II of this book.

Neglected, but extremely significant, archaeological evidence brings to light the fact that women could undertake important roles in society in the first century. This extant material provides a context for the crucial role some of them played in the spread of early Christianity. While statistical information must be treated with caution, it is not without significance that there are eighteen women mentioned by name in those churches, comprising twenty percent of the total number of men and women specifically named.

Part III focuses on the important contribution that certain women of means made to the spread and support of early Gentile Christianity beyond Palestine. These women were Lydia, Euodia, Syntyche in Philippi; Phoebe in Corinth; Junia in Rome; and Priscilla, who, along with her husband, was in Corinth, Ephesus and in Rome for two periods. It will be argued that the reasons why these women were able to contribute so much were not unrelated to new 'roles' that women undertook in society in the late Republican period and early Empire. There were pivotal legal and social changes that made way for this participation, including a measure of financial independence that facilitated these new roles. There is evidence that women could occupy civic posts and have the title of civic magistrates, and those with wealth (and what was deemed to be rank and status) influenced commercial, civic and provincial affairs.

III. Defining 'Appearance', 'New' and 'Roman'

It is important to note that the terms 'appearance', 'new' and 'Roman' are consciously employed in two quite distinctive ways in this book. The term 'appearance' is used ambiguously because it refers first to the emergence on the scene in the first century of what has come to be seen as a new breed of wives whose lifestyle differed considerably from that of the traditional image of the modest wife. The term was also chosen because of the way that social conventions in the early Empire were grounded in Roman law. This is certainly the case with the dress code of respectable married women in comparison with that of high-class prostitutes and others. Roman jurisprudence distinguished between them by means of their appearance, which was defined in terms of apparel and adornment. McGinn noted something fundamental to understanding men and women in the ancient world. 'In classical antiquity, you

4

were what you wore.'[9] We will demonstrate that this Roman phenomenon belongs to a wider issue — the social engineering by Augustus and the clear identification of classes in Roman society. That was observed not only in the protocol at dinners and in the allocation of seating in the theatres on the grounds of class, but also in the distinctive dress codes for men and women, including wives.

The 'new' wife or widow in the late Roman Republic and early Empire was the one whose social life was reported to have been pursued at the expense of family responsibilities that included the complex running of households. Life beyond their household could involve illicit liaisons that defied the previously accepted norms of marriage fidelity and chastity. The possible influence or impact which that had in the Pauline communities will be traced in Part II. The term 'new woman' may seem to be something of a pejorative one but it has been adopted by some ancient historians in order to describe this latter group of women.[10] For want of another term I have used it to describe the wives and widows who embraced new social mores.

The term 'Roman' and not *romanitas* is used to describe the nature, as well as the origin, of particular values.[11] They spread throughout the empire and promoted the 'modesty' of matrons whose images, styles and values were skilfully exploited and exported in statue types by Augustus. It was all part of the Romanization package for the East and other parts of the Empire. While there were women with Latin names in the Pauline communities, for the purposes of this book 'Roman' is not used to designate citizenship (unless specified) but rather, particular values. They also include the new social mores of unchastity and marriage infidelity which Augustus judged to pose a threat to both the fabric and future of the family and the Roman Empire. He, as its founder, consciously promoted and rewarded traditional Roman values.

The final chapter uses the term 'roles' to describe the new activities that certain women of means engaged in outside the family and in the wider society, both in business and in the public place. The term *politeia* is used of one sphere in the dichotomy adopted in the ancient world to describe the whole

---

9. T. A. J. McGinn, *Prostitution, Sexuality and the Law in Ancient Rome* (Oxford: Oxford University Press, 1998), p. 162.

10. E. Fantham *et al.*, "The 'New Woman': Representation and Reality," in *Women in the Classical World* (Oxford: Oxford University Press, 1994), ch. 10.

11. I have avoided using the term *romanitas* even though it has steadily gained currency in recent time among some ancient historians. The term is not to be found in the *Oxford Latin Dictionary* which cites words occurring in sources up to A.D. 200. It was Tertullian, "On the Pallium," 4, who first used it and did so pejoratively to describe those in Carthage who aped Roman culture.

of life, i.e., private and public. Because of their participation in the latter some Christian women were in a new position to contribute greatly, both in terms of time and resources, to the expansion of the early Pauline mission.

IV. Perceptions of First-Century Women

One unexplored assumption in New Testament scholarship is that wives in the first century were something of a monochrome group; this is also assumed of those in the early Christian communities. Some believe that all women were duly confined to domestic dwellings in order to fulfil the role of a dutiful wife engaged primarily in childbearing and managing the household. Some scholars still perceive them to have been kept away from the public gaze. However, it is known that first-century women, unlike their sisters in the previous Classical Greek and Hellenistic eras, certainly appeared in public. Even in the Classical Greek period cultural mores for women were not always the same as for the Mediterranean as a whole.[12] On reflection, even if there was no material to the contrary, it is very unlikely that one could epitomize all first-century marriages by a single stereotype of restriction to the home and reproductive activity in the vast Roman Empire, any more than it would be possible to do so today in our multicultural world.

Even if this assumption of the first-century situation was correct for those in rural settings in isolated parts of the Empire (where it is hard to verify the situation for lack of evidence), it is certainly not the picture that emerges of women in urban settings where the earliest Christian communities were established.

A recent and important observation was made of female society in the late Roman Republic and early Empire: 'To judge from our sources in the last years of the republic, the more independent women of good family were beginning to decide for themselves what kind of social occasion they enjoyed.'[13]

What gave rise to such a change in the traditional behaviour of married women that was to result, in some cases, in flagrant sexual unfaithfulness to their husbands and which occurred, at times, with immunity? Wives had gained a measure of financial security that provided some independence from husbands, and their property was no longer automatically transferred to their husbands on marriage. Chapters 2-4 will note the explanations and defence in

12. For example, there had long been a considerable difference in laws governing identical property rights of women in Crete and Athens and their participation in society. See pp. 142-43.
13. Fantham *et al.*, "The 'New Woman,'" p. 280.

ancient sources of such behaviour by some women of social status and their advocates; we will also note the legal and philosophical responses to them.

This book will also argue that in response a powerful alternative paradigm was promoted in the late Republican period that greatly influenced first-century urban society. The emperors not only promoted images of themselves for political purposes in cities throughout the Empire, but also used those of their wives for cultural and moral purposes.[14] Roman imperial coins and statues were the first-century 'billboards' and played a critical role in imperial propaganda as important tools for shaping societal values. The imperial clothing and hair styles of wives were meant to make them icons and trend-setters and, it will be argued, were deliberately used to counter influences in society which were judged to be detrimental to its well-being. It is sometimes forgotten that the skilful promotion of fashionable trends is the domain not only of more recent cultures. Augustus and some of his successors used appearance and apparel to promote values to counter what they regarded as promiscuous tendencies in the Empire.

V. Proletarian or Socially Diverse Christian Women

Modern understandings of the social status of early Christians and therefore, by implication, that of women, wives and widows in the early church has been greatly influenced by the work of Adolf Deissmann in the early twentieth century. At the time of his taking the New Testament chair in Berlin he joined the German Workers' Party and recast the status of early Christians as Proletariat, a perception that dominated studies for nearly a century.[15] His eisegesis has subsequently dogged much of the discussion of the status of Christians, including that of women.

In more recent decades ancient historians have sent signals to the contrary. For E. A. Judge and others such a perception of Christians' status is not

14. For a discussion of this see S. E. Wood, *Imperial Women: A Study in Public Images, 40 B.C.–A.D. 69* (Leiden: E. J. Brill, 1999), and more recently a helpful study by P. A. Roche, "The Public Image of Trajan's Family," *Classical Philology* 97.1 (2002): 41-60.

15. A. Deissmann, *Light from the Ancient East: The New Testament Illustrated by Recently Discovered Texts of the Graeco-Roman World* (ET reprint, Grand Rapids: Baker, 1978), p. 8, '. . . the tentmaker's words [1 Cor. 1:26-31] about the origins of his churches in the lower classes of the great towns form one of the most important testimonies, historically speaking that Primitive Christianity gives of itself.' For a response, see my critique of the search for a Vulgärethik in my "Elitist Ethics and Christian Permissiveness," *After Paul Left Corinth: The Influence of Secular Ethics and Social Change* (Grand Rapids: Eerdmans, 2001), ch. 5, esp. pp. 105-9 and p. 158, n. 54.

supported by a careful reading of the New Testament texts. This 'new consensus', as it has become known, has slowly gained ground over the Deissmann thesis. New Testament evidence does not allow us to typecast as 'working class' all Christian women, any more than it has been shown to be an appropriate term to describe the various strata of society from which male converts were drawn. It should be added that the 'new consensus' does not argue that all were from the upper social registers, or even the middle class, which is an inaccurate classification of first-century society. This means that the possibility of some Christian women belonging to, or being influenced by, the upper-class values of the 'new' woman cannot be discounted *a priori*. The New Testament evidence examined in subsequent chapters shows that this influence filtered down from the Senatorial ranks to women in the wider Roman society.

VI. Enslaved *v.* Emancipated Women?

The way to describe the difference in the status and activities of Roman women in the late Republic and early Empire has been a matter of not inconsiderable discussion.[16] McGinn has framed an important question on this issue thus: 'Was there a measurable improvement in the status of Roman women in the classical period, particularly in the last century B.C. and the first two centuries A.D., and if so, is this change best described as an "emancipation"?'[17]

J. A. Crook writing in 1967 suggested that it was not possible to evaluate in any satisfactory way the much-asserted (or implied) independence of Roman women. His reason for saying this was that the early age for the marriage of women would tell against any concept of emancipation.[18]

McGinn notes: 'As the sophistication of method of the new social history of antiquity has grown in the last two and a half decades, this idea of the Roman woman's emancipation has received a rather emphatic rejection.'[19] He

16. Susanne Dixon, "Re-readings: A Partial Survey of Scholarship," in *Reading Roman Women* (London: Duckworth, 2001), ch. 1, has provided a helpful thumbnail sketch of the history of interpretation.

17. T. A. J. McGinn, "Widows, Orphans and Social History," *Journal of Roman Archaeology* 12 (1999): 621.

18. J. A. Crook, *Law and Life of Rome, 90 B.C.–A.D. 212,* pp. 103-4.

19. McGinn, "Widows, Orphans and Social History," p. 621, cites examples in n. 15. R. P. Bond, "Anti-feminism in Juvenal and Cato," in C. Deroux, ed., *Studies in Latin Literature and Roman History* 1 (Brussels: 1979), p. 142; Averil Cameron, "Women in Ancient Culture and Society," *AU* 32.2 (1989): 17; and A. J. Marshall, "Roman Ladies on Trial: The Case of Maesia of Sentium," *Phoenix* 44 (1990): 49.

goes on to make an astute observation: 'This is not the essential point, however, at least in itself. If Roman women were not emancipated, that does not mean that they were enslaved. Krause does not state the matter quite so baldly, but it is clear that he views social status, sexual freedom, and the economic power of Roman women as fatally compromised in the absence of their "emancipation".[20] Without seeking in any way to be what McGinn calls 'ungenerous', he noted that Roman women have become the subject of renewed discussion by ancient historians in recent literature. He sees this happening at an important moment in the decades at the end of the last century with moves to redress blatant discrimination against women *per se* in academic and other circles that was rightly high on the agenda.[21] But for that sea change, the research for this book would have been extremely difficult, if not impossible. What has emerged in recent decades has been an enormous scholarly output of monographs and helpful collections of primary sources on women as the bibliography bears witness.

It is felt in the light of the dichotomy in which the discussion of enslavement *v.* emancipation was framed, these are not particularly helpful categories, though explicable. This book does not claim that the 'new women' were totally emancipated or that, by implication, all were psychologically enslaved in a way comparable to their household servants who were legally bound to their masters. The extant evidence, whether epigraphic or literary, indicates that, compared with their sisters in Classical Greek and Hellenistic times, some first-century women did enjoy an important measure of social interaction denied to Greek women in a previous era.[22]

VII. The Structure of This Book

Chapters 2-4 are essential prolegomena for any interpretation offered on ancient texts of which the New Testament corpus is but one in the first century. Extra-biblical sources are explored in their cultural setting hopefully to guard

---

20. McGinn, "Widows, Orphans and Social History," pp. 620-21. He is interacting with this view in the work on widows and orphans by J.-U. Krause, *Witwen und Waisen im Römischen Reich* (Stuttgart: F. Steiner, 1994-5), Vols. I-IV who raises the issue on eight occasions: I, ix, p. 137; II, p. 133, p. 203, p. 250, p. 253; III, p. 32; IV, p. 109.

21. McGinn, "Widows, Orphans and Social History," p. 621, n. 14.

22. See for example, J. F. Gardner, "Out of the *Familia*: The Practice of Emancipation," in *Women in Roman Law and Society* (Oxford: Clarendon Press, 1986), pp. 257-66; McGinn, "Widows, Orphans and Social History," p. 620; S. Dixon, *Reading Roman Women* (London: Duckworth, 2001), pp. 8-9 n. 34.

against a blanket eisegesis that unguardedly reads into New Testament texts one's own social contexts as the ancient setting.[23] These chapters should challenge the reconstruction of many New Testament commentators who often repeat the received views of their colleagues or cite outdated discussions by former generations of ancient historians on this topic. These preliminary chapters will seek to take due cognisance of the primary setting and recent secondary discussion. The book shows that the texts suffer acutely from the lack of a first-century social context and have become in some cases the proverbial pretexts for proof texts.

The steps that need to be taken in examining these texts are not dissimilar from those involved when a papyrus is discovered. First there is the prior knowledge of extant evidence in the field germane to the newly discovered document, e.g., court proceedings based on legal and literary evidence of the period and non-literary ancient official court transcripts found in papyri. Even at an early stage of translation the editor of the papyrus will be alert to other known non-literary and literary texts that might throw light on it. Matters such as similarity and distinctiveness will be probed in the hope that this new document might add to the body of knowledge or confirm what is already known either by the initial editor or from subsequent scholarly discussion.[24]

This book, therefore, is divided into three sections. Part I examines the 'new' Roman women and Roman imperial society in order to provide information that will enable the reader to begin to read particular New Testament texts through a first-century lens of literary, legal, philosophical sources. Chapter 2 gathers some of the evidence of the lifestyle of 'new' women from late Republic and early Imperial extant sources. Chapter 3 discusses the moves by Augustus to intrude into this private domain with legal measures aimed at curbing the licentious behaviour of certain married women and promoting marriage among men of the upper classes of society. Chapter 4 is

23. Regrettably, what is popularly designated as New Testament 'background' has been relegated to first-year courses in Christian or Religious Studies Departments in many colleges and religious institutions. It is seen as an optional extra and not critical for understanding texts such as these and others.

24. For an excellent example of this activity on published non-literary sources by ancient historians in their service to N.T. scholars, see *New Documents of New Testament Times*, Volumes 1-9 from the Ancient History Documentary Research Centre, Macquarie University, now published by Eerdmans. This is an invaluable, but neglected, source for those for whom it was primarily designed. The way evidence and secondary discussion on an issue are brought to bear in this series with its connection to a particular aspect of the N.T. world and its concerns is a paradigm for scholarly discussion of the ancient texts that comprise the *corpus* of the N.T. It is also a short cut for those wanting to benefit from important ancient texts seen to have relevance to N.T. studies and the specialist discussion by ancient historians.

devoted to the response of two philosophical schools to the phenomenon of the new liaisons of Roman woman and the demands teachers, both men and women, made on the married women and young unmarried men who adhered to their schools.

In Part II individual New Testament passages concerning women in the Pauline communities are discussed in the light of the material in Part I, including the responses to the same issues addressed in the philosophical schools. The latter provide a helpful comparison and contrast. The focus will not be on the solutions being proposed in the texts themselves but on the women being addressed or discussed through the important lens of the 'appearance', the signals it sent and how that was encapsulated in Roman law. The discussion begins with 1 Corinthians 11:2-16 and continues in a trajectory into the Pastoral Epistles.[25]

Chapter 5 examines the signal that the removal of the marriage veil sent to the outsiders as well as to the Christian insiders in Roman Corinth. Then follows chapter 6 on 1 Timothy 2 concerning the appearance of married women and the deciphering of their dress code. The young widows in 1 Timothy 5 are the next issue to be addressed in chapter 7. The unique privileges afforded married women on Crete for well over four hundred years constitute the subject matter of chapter 8 along with the appearance of the values of the 'new' women, and its effects which were reflected in attitudes toward their husbands, children and households.

Part III consists of one chapter which commences by presenting important evidence for the new roles for women in public life, especially the crucial epigraphic material. It will then examine the possible influence that those rules had on the opportunities for some Christian women in the Pauline mission. The ministries of such women have not been seen through that grid and, until recent times, were underestimated in the expansion of early Christianity. Their contribution was not necessarily replicated in the history of the churches in subsequent centuries in spite of confessional claims to be modelled on apostolic traditions.

The letters discussing Christian wives and widows also demanded an end to the culturally accepted promiscuous behaviour of both single and married men in the Pauline communities. This will be referred to for comparative purposes in Part II. The letters to the Pauline communities did not perpetuate the gross inequality that the secular society and Roman law condoned either explicitly or implicitly.

---

25. The dating of the latter is not critical to this discussion as the evidence for the 'new' woman is not restricted to the Julio-Claudian periods.

I have returned yet again to 1 Timothy 5:3-16 but for a very different reason. In 1988 I published an article on the role of the dowry and the care of widows in 1 Timothy 5:3-16 where the focus was on the dowry's importance and the binding legal obligations of 'the lord' of the dowry. These factors had not been incorporated into the discussion as to why Christians who failed to provide support were condemned as behaving not just like 'unbelievers' but as 'worse than unbelievers' — they had thrust their widowed mothers and older female relatives onto the charity of the church.[26] In 1994 'Widows and Legal and Christian Benefactions' was restricted to exploring the role of older widows in the church, and the appropriate response to them with the invoking of benefaction language which 'honoured' them for their deeds of service to others.[27] In neither work did I deal with the *Sitz im Leben* of the young widows. The requirement under Roman law that they remarry was only alluded to in the first essay, as was its possible connection with the intention of Augustus' law to curb the promiscuous behaviour of some of the young widows.[28] The issues young widows experienced were not discussed in any further detail in either essay. Their connection to the new woman is explored here in detail.

My reason in so soon revisiting 1 Corinthians 11:2-16 arises from important monographs that have been published in the past two years on dress codes of women and the official enforcement of them. They add further to the discussion and alter aspects of my former interpretation of the passage.[29]

My approach in research has been to seek to read the primary sources and only then have recourse to any secondary discussion by ancient historians. I owe this to the lifetime example of Emeritus Professor E. A. Judge who demonstrated the importance of the primary focus on sources.[30] In this book the ancient texts are separated in the main body to assist the reader to focus on the ancient material. I have departed from the usual convention of an opening chapter that rehearses the history of the discussion of this subject.

26. B. W. Winter, "*Providentia* for the Widows of 1 Timothy 5:3-16," *TynB* 39 (1988): 83-99.

27. B. W. Winter, "Widows and Legal and Christian Benefactions," in *Seek the Welfare of the City: Christians as Benefactors and Citizens* (Grand Rapids and Carlisle: Eerdmans and Paternoster, 1993), ch. 4.

28. Winter, "*Providentia* for the Widows of 1 Timothy 5:3-16," p. 85.

29. See chapter 5, n. 1. B. W. Winter, "Veiled Men and Wives and Christian Contentiousness (1 Cor. 11:2-16)," in *After Paul Left Corinth: The Influence of Secular Ethics and Social Change*, ch. 6.

30. He demonstrated once again the fruitfulness of being source-based when he gave the Tyndale Lectures in the Faculty of Divinity, University of Cambridge as the Senior Visiting Research Fellow at the Institute for Early Christianity in the Graeco-Roman World, Cambridge in Michaelmas Term, 2000.

The past treatment has already been documented in a number of monographs as well as the many New Testament commentaries produced on letters sent to the Pauline communities.[31] I have been keen to take an independent look at the issues involved, beginning with the primary sources.

There have been an enormous growth and specialisation in the disciplines of archaeology, epigraphy, and papyrology. The result has seen the fragmenting of ancient history as a single enterprise, in spite of the retrieval by electronic means of so much information from the ancient world, including both literary and non-literary sources. That ought to have resulted in harvesting this information more quickly. However, even those working in the various sub-disciplines of ancient history are not always able to integrate the information from across these specialised areas, given the degree of sophistication and the specialised technical language and documentation that have developed.[32]

The New Testament context should now be more easily investigated than in past generations with speedy access to existing databases. If at times ancient historians find themselves struggling with all the primary evidence, then it is little wonder that their New Testament cousins feel overwhelmed by the amount of material on the TLG and PHI CDRoms and access to an avalanche of secondary material.

Cambridge Greek and Latin Texts on the first or other centuries which are edited in the light of other extant material in endnotes, can help in the translation and illumination of particular aspects of the texts. They were produced in order to help the reader understand both the text and its *Sitz im Leben*. This monograph stands more in that tradition by drawing attention to relevant ancient sources not generally known by those who read the New Testament, and it parallels Hennie J. Marsman's *Women in Ugarit and Israel: Their Social and Religious Position in the Context of the Ancient Near East.*[33] The aim, then, has been to place before the reader new material, regarded as apposite to the texts, for the consideration of those in the academy as well as the church.

This book on women in the Pauline communities is something of a par-

---

31. See, for example, D. Doriani, "A History of the Interpretation of 1 Timothy 2," in A. J. Köstenberger, T. R. Schreiner, and H. S. Baldwin, eds., *Women in the Church* (Grand Rapids: Baker, 1995), appendix 1.

32. On the problem of this growing chasm, see R. Lawrence and J. Berry, eds., *Cultural Identity in the Roman Empire* (London: Routledge, 1981), p. 1.

33. (Leiden: E. J. Brill, 2003).

34. *Gospel Women: Studies in the Named Women in the Gospels* (Grand Rapids: Eerdmans, 2002).

allel treatment to Richard Bauckham's recent book, *Gospel Women*.[34] The first two sections go beyond the scope of his work which dealt with those women who are actually named in the gospels. It finds a parallel in the last chapter for he comments on Joanna whom he identifies with Junia in Romans 16:7. This book, however, is more limited in its focus because it argues that the setting of the texts on women in the Pauline communities was that of the 'new women'.

All authors hope that their readers will read the book from beginning to end before forming a judgement, and especially so where methodological considerations and important primary evidence that is germane to subsequent discussion are embedded in the opening chapters. Studies on the intersection between New Testament sources and others of the same period can be highly productive for ancient historians and biblical scholars alike. I leave it to the reader to assess how helpful this study has been in locating first-century horizons and whether it illuminates aspects of the texts addressed to the Pauline communities.

PART I

CHAPTER 2

The Appearance of New Wives

New Testament scholars have generally assumed that in the first century, there was a longstanding and broad societal consensus on the roles of women, wives and widows in public and in private. As a result, it is often concluded that female converts to Christianity would have needed to make little or no significant changes in their general lifestyle or relationships. Cultural mores were simply endorsed or, as the evidence is sometimes read, were actually re-enforced in the Pauline churches. Therefore Paul becomes at best a social realist or, at worst, a social conservative who encouraged realism or conservatism in his communities. It is perhaps because of this, that discussions have concentrated on Pauline traditions and not enough on the social context in which these first-century women lived.

I. Roman Women

Wives and the Legal Power of Husbands

The power of husbands over their wives can be paralleled with that of the father over his children. 'Of the various aspects of *patria potestas* . . . that of the notorious right of the father to put his children to death' is known. According to Harris, it was very rarely exercised in Republican times and not at all in the imperial period.[1] However, there certainly are recorded instances resulting in capital punishment where a wife was subjected to the judgement of her hus-

---

1. W. V. Harris, "The Roman Father's Power of Life and Death," in R. S. Bagnall and W. V. Harris, eds., *Studies in Roman Law in Memory of A. A. Schiller* (Leiden: Brill, 1986), pp. 81, 88.

band or his family for the murder of her spouse. In the Republican period, Pullicia, who poisoned her husband, the consul Postumius Albinus, and Licinia who did the same to her spouse were put to death by their late husband's relatives.

Sexual debauchery connected with cultic activities saw the Senate c. 155 B.C. commissioning the Consuls 'to investigate women who had made impure use of Bacchanalian rites. Many were found guilty by them and all were executed in their homes by their kinsfolk'.[2]

In the time of Claudius, Tacitus records the case of Pomponia Graecina, who, being

> a woman of high family, married to Aulus Plautius — whose ovation after the British campaign I recorded earlier — and now arraigned for alien superstition, was left to the jurisdiction of her husband. Following the ancient custom, he held the inquiry, which was to determine the fate and fame of his wife, before a family council, and announced her innocent.

'Her creed, as was often the case, gave rise to immorality, on which she was tried and acquitted by the family council.'[3] It has been suggested that the superstition referred to was Christianity.[4] In terms of life and religion in Republican times in the early Empire, heads of some households could hold total sway over their wives, making them subject to their husband's domination and their position vulnerable to exploitation.

Wives and the Portrayal of Affectionate Husbands

However, this is not the total picture. What is to be made of the affection reflected in an early-first-century A.D. statue from Rome in the British Museum? It represents the marriage of Lucius Aurelius Hermia and his wife, Aurelia Philematium. She is modestly attired with the traditional marriage veil over her head, wearing an ankle-length dress and kissing his hand; he is dressed in his toga affectionately looking at her.[5] This figure with the approving gaze of the husband and the modestly dressed and demure wife is a statue type from the late Republican period and the early Empire. He was a freed-

---

2. Valerius Maximus, *Memorable Doings and Sayings*, 13.3.8, 6.3.7.

3. Tacitus, *Annals*, 13.32.

4. The catacombs have inscriptions to Pomponius Bassus and Pomponius Graecinus; see J. Jackson, *Tacitus*, Loeb series (1956), pp. 52, n. 3; 53 (cf. 2.50).

5. No. 2274, British Museum.

man of Lucius and a butcher from the Viminal Hill in Rome. The epitaph on
the tombstone reads —

> My wife, who died before me, my only wife, chaste in body, a loving woman
> who possessed my heart, she lived faithful to a faithful husband; equally in
> her devotion, she never let avarice keep her from her duty.[6]

Affection on the part of first-century husbands in the marriage relationship does not normally spring to twenty-first-century minds, but it did exist,
and there was no reluctance to portray it in statues or inscriptions commem-
orating deceased spouses. What feelings lay behind the grave stone erected by
a plasterer in Rome who recorded his love for his wife who 'was 18 years, 9
months and 5 days when she died and had been married to him for 5 years, 6
months and 18 days'?[7] This, however, is by no means the complete picture.

Wives and Unfaithful Husbands

It is well known that the sexual propriety expected of a wife contrasted starkly
with the culturally acceptable unfaithfulness of her husband with household
slaves and female dinner companions. Chastity was expected of wives both in
Greek and Roman times.

Aulus Gellius recorded an attitude where some husbands in the Republican period boasted they were exonerated from any accountability. They were,
however, free to bring the ultimate penalty against their wives.

> It is also written, regarding the right to kill: 'If you catch your wife in adul-
> tery, you can kill her with impunity; she, however, cannot dare to lay a fin-
> ger on you if you commit adultery, *nor is it the law*'.[8]

The early-second-century A.D. writer, Plutarch, presents the rationalisation of
the husband's behaviour in a speech that was traditionally delivered in the
nuptial bedroom.[9] It demanded of the wife both her faithfulness to him and

---

6. *CIL*, I.1221 (*c*. 80 B.C.).

7. *CIL*, XIII.1983.

8. *Attic Nights*, 10:23. He 'copied Cato's words from a speech called *On the dowry*, in which it is
stated that husbands who caught wives in adultery could kill them. "The husband," he says, "who
divorces his wife is her judge, as though he were a censor". However, S. Treggiari, *Roman Marriage:
Iusti Coniuges from the Time of Cicero to the Time of Ulpian* (Oxford: Clarendon, 1991), p. 274, cautions against the uncritical acceptance of this report.

9. For a full discussion of this important discourse see S. B. Pomeroy, ed., "Part I, Interpre-

his gods, and the acceptance of his casual sexual liaisons. Plutarch justified the husband's activity on the grounds that extra-marital escapades were a means of gratifying his lust, for it would be entirely inappropriate for him to use his wife in this way.[10] The fact that Plutarch knew both young people as friends only highlights the widespread acceptance of a husband's adultery. In another illustration, when L. Aelius Caesar's wife criticised his adulterous behaviour he was said to have justified this by asking her to let him exercise his lust on other women because a wife was for *dignitas* and not sensuality.[11]

When it is remembered that many brides were married (in most cases in their mid-teens) to men who were some ten years older,[12] then such a speech could only re-enforce both his demand of faithfulness on her part and her expectations of his casual sexual dalliances. Treggiari in her *magnum opus* on Roman marriage explains this inequitable situation thus: 'Implicit in the advice to wives to ignore the philandering of their husbands is the idea that it meant little. We may picture a continuum that runs roughly from brief encounters with a man's own slaves or prostitutes and music-girls though other people's slaves (where negotiation or poaching was involved) to respectable but unmarried women of a lower social class, and then to wives and women of his own class and long-standing affairs.'[13]

Beryl Rawson writes of this period that there was 'some discrimination against women . . . they could be punished for affairs with slaves and low-class persons while men could not be. But the area of discrimination was much narrower than is sometimes suggested'.[14] In the time of Augustus adultery on the part of a wife was not, in most cases, a capital offence but rather a criminal one, as Chapter 3 will show. The husband could still operate with a mea-

---

tative Essays," in *Plutarch's Advice to the Bride and Groom and A Consolation to His Wife: English Translations, Commentary, Interpretative Essays and Bibliography* (Oxford: Oxford University Press, 1999).

10. Plutarch, "Advice to Bride and Groom," 140B, D.

11. Martial, *Epigrams*, 11.104. Treggiari, *Roman Marriage: Iusti Coniuges from the Time of Cicero to the Time of Ulpian*, p. 314.

12. P. Veyne, "The Roman Empire," in P. Veyne, ed., *Histoire de la vie privée*, ET, *A History of Private Life* (Cambridge, MA: Harvard University Press, 1987), p. 20, where he indicates that a girl was regarded as an adult at age fourteen, based on M. K. Hopkins, "The Age of Roman Girls at Marriage," *Population Studies* 18.3 (1965): 309-27. R. P. Saller, "Men's Age at Marriage and Its Consequences for the Roman Family," *Classical Philology* 82.1 (1987): 21-34, places the age higher and suggests that men were married *c.* 25 years old.

13. Treggiari, *Roman Marriage: Iusti Coniuges from the Time of Cicero to the Time of Ulpian*, p. 315.

14. B. Rawson, "The Roman Family," in B. Rawson, ed., *The Family in Ancient Rome: New Perspectives* (London: Croom Helm, 1986), p. 34.

sure of impunity in his sexual liaisons, and his behaviour was accepted on the grounds that women were less sensuous than men and had higher moral standards.[15]

II. 'New' Roman Women

We will now explore in detail some of the material of another group of first-century women from the late Republican period and the early Roman Empire whose existence has not generally been noted in New Testament studies. It provides a somewhat different picture to that normally associated with the stereotype of the domestic life of Roman women, and wives in particular. On the basis of this material Part II of this book will argue that it provides the critical *Sitz im Leben* for concerns expressed to the Pauline communities about certain patterns of behaviour judged to be inappropriate for Christian women, wives and widows.

Change

Ancient historians have observed that around 44 B.C. evidence of a 'new' type of woman emerged in certain circles in Rome.[16] Both in ostensibly factual texts and in imaginative writing a new kind of woman appears precisely at the time of Cicero and Caesar: a woman in high position, who nevertheless claims for herself the indulgence in sexuality of a woman of pleasure.[17]

What could have given rise to such a change in the traditional behaviour of married women? Wives still brought to marriage the all-important dowry but could now retain their own property. It was also possible for them to terminate the marriage, and receive back a portion of, or the whole dowry.[18] Along with this financial independence some also experienced a measure of

---

15. Treggiari, *Roman Marriage: Iusti Coniuges from the Time of Cicero to the Time of Ulpian*, p. 316.

16. See R. A. Bauman, *Women and Politics in Ancient Rome* (London: Routledge, 1992), pp. 78-90, on their so-called 'liberation' and the role of élite women in public life. See also E. D'Ambra, "Virgins and Adulterers," in *Private Lives, Imperial Virtues: The Frieze of the* Forum Transitorium *in Rome* (Princeton: Princeton University Press, 1993), ch. 3.

17. E. Fantham *et al.,* "The 'New Woman': Representation and Reality," in *Women in the Classical World* (Oxford: Oxford University Press, 1994), p. 280.

18. S. Treggiari, *Roman Marriage: Iusti Coniuges from the Time of Cicero to the Time of Ulpian*, ch. 10 and p. 446.

social freedom. Roman wives began to compete for men with those from whom they had been traditionally differentiated, *viz.*, foreign women and freedwomen. The latter two groups defended their activities thus:

> They [the wives] claim we always go with their men, they say we are their concubines, and try to squelch us. Because we are freedwomen, both your mother and I became prostitutes.[19]

They had been former slaves who plied their charms as *hetairai* during the banquets and provided sexual pleasures for their individual dinner companions in what were popularly called 'after dinners'.[20] Among their clients were, of course, the husbands of Roman wives. It is explicable that wives of social status should revolt against these totally inequitable moral standards made possible when financial security gave them power to act independently.

'To judge from our sources in the last years of the republic, the more independent women of good family were beginning to decide for themselves what kind of social occasion they enjoyed.'[21] The 'realistic prose reportage and the emerging genre of the personal love elegy offer glimpses of glamorous and assertive women, living a life of parties and self-gratification and choosing their own lovers.'[22] At least two of these women named by Cicero and Sallust have been identified from other evidence. Of the women celebrated in love poetry Catullus's beloved has been identified with the historical Clodia, wife of Metellus, and so has Sempronia.[23]

The literary evidence we possess of the new Roman woman is threefold and consists of (a) the views of contemporary writers covering the late Republic and the early second century A.D.; (b) those of the poets and the playwrights; (c) and the legal moves of Augustus where he specifically legislates against this new phenomenon in the late Republican period and the early Empire.

---

19. This citation is from the early 2nd century B.C. play from Rome by Plautus, *Cistellaria*, *ll.* 36-37; for the full discussion see *ll.* 22-41, which reveal the competition between wives and high class prostitutes in Rome, the latter being of freedwoman status.

20. On the use of the term 'so-called after dinners' (τὰς λεγομένας ἐπιδειπνίδας) see Philo, *Vit.* 54. λεγομένας indicates 'popularly' but for Philo it meant 'erroneously or misleadingly so designated'. Fantham *et al.*, "The 'New Woman,'" pp. 281, 285. Or as Cicero, *pro Caelio*, 2.68, said, 'those matters that come afterwards'. Aspects of this have been challenged. M. Wyke, *The Roman Mistress* (Oxford: Oxford University Press, 2002), and her "Mistress and Metaphor in Augustan Elegy," in I. McClure, *Sexuality and Gender in the Classical World: Readings and Sources* (Oxford: Blackwell, 2002), ch. 7.

21. Fantham *et al.*, "The 'New Woman,'" p. 280.

22. Fantham *et al.*, "The 'New Woman,'" pp. 281, 285.

23. Fantham *et al.*, "The 'New Woman,'" p. 281.

Contemporary Writers

Sallust (*c.* 86–*c.* 35 B.C.) in *Catiline* said of Sempronia who was a married woman with children that she was

> able to play the lyre and dance more skilfully than an honest woman should, and having many other accomplishments which minister to voluptuousness. But there was nothing which she held so cheap as *modesty* and *chastity*. Her desires were so ardent that she sought men more often than she was sought by them . . . she was a woman of no mean endowment; she could write verse, bandy jests and use language which was modest or tender or wanton.[24]

Sallust himself took a noble woman ten years his senior as his mistress. Of her Cicero wrote that she was

> the daughter of one of Rome's noblest families, claiming the sexual freedom of a woman of no social standing to lose, and making no effort to conceal her behaviour — 'a woman not just noble but notorious'.[25]

A subsequent lover, Caelius, was accused of 'passions, love making, adulteries, visits to Baiae, beach picnics, parties and revelling, songs, choruses and boat-trips'.[26]

In a letter written from Laodicea in March, 50 B.C. to his friend Atticus, Cicero also records the conduct of Vedius Pollio, a friend of Augustus and a wealthy and powerful son of freed persons. His baggage, mistakenly taken to be that of his host who had died suddenly, was opened for inventory purposes. In it were found five cameos of distinguished Roman women, who had given them to him as mementoes of their sexual liaisons. One of the high-class women was, he tells Atticus, 'the sister of your friend "the brute" and wife of that "charmer" who takes things like this so lightly'.[27] It was but one instance of a husband turning a blind eye to his wife's promiscuous conduct.

Tacitus recorded that in A.D. 19

> the senate passed severe provisions to repress women's dissoluteness and prohibited prostitution for granddaughters, daughters, and wives of Roman knights. For Vistilia, a woman of a praetorian family, had made pub-

24. Sallust, *Catiline*, 25.
25. Cicero, *pro Caelio*, 32.
26. Cicero, *pro Caelio*, 35.
27. Cicero, *ad Atticum*, 6.1.24-25.

lic, before the *aediles,* her practice of prostitution. This was done in keeping with a valid and venerable custom by which it is considered sufficient punishment for unchaste women to admit their shame publicly. The senate wanted to know why Titidius Labeo, Vistilia's husband, had not carried out the punishment provided by law for his patently guilty wife. He explained that the sixty days allowed for him to institute criminal proceedings had not yet elapsed, so the senate passed judgement only on Vistilia, who was relegated to the island of Seriphos.[28]

Plutarch also comments on the 'new' women. He refers to those who were 'bored by uncompromising and virtuous men [*sic*], and take more pleasure in consorting with those who, like dogs and he-goats, are a combination of licentiousness and sensuality'.[29] He warned husbands that 'those who are not cheerful in the company of their wives, nor join with them in sportiveness and laughter, are thus teaching them to seek their own pleasures apart from their husbands'.[30]

The Promotion of Promiscuity by Poets

In her introduction to *The Erotics of Domination* Greene also notes of poets that they all 'proclaim in their poems a radically unconventional philosophy of life with their apparently deliberate inversion of conventional sex roles — in which women are portrayed as dominant and men as subservient. . . . The conventional stance of the elegiast lover is one of enslavement to his emotions and servitude to his mistress'.[31] The poems recorded and promoted this behaviour on the part of the 'new' women.

---

28. Tacitus, *Annals,* 2.85. On the period of 60 days' grace for the husband to prosecute his wife in the courts, see p. 42.

29. Plutarch, "Advice to Bride and Groom," 7, *Moralia* 139B.

30. Plutarch, "Advice to Bride and Groom," 15, *Moralia* 140A.

31. Ovid, *Art of Love.* E. Greene, *The Erotics of Domination: Male Desire and the Mistress in Latin Love Poetry* (Baltimore: Johns Hopkins, 1998), p. xiii; M. Wyke, "Mistress and Metaphor in Augustan Elegy," in I. McClure, *Sexuality and Gender in the Classical World: Readings and Sources,* ch. 7, for this portrayal primarily in terms of a metaphor used by poets. She further explores her theme in *The Roman Mistress,* making comparisons with British television drama, nineteenth-century Italian anthropology, classical coinage and college websites as poetic metaphor, and the Hollywood star system.

Catullus (c. 84-54 B.C.)

On the emergence of new Roman women, Fantham *et al.* ask, 'Why had these noblewomen suddenly kicked over the traces? And why does a well-brought-up son like Catullus disdain the usual casual fooling around and become infatuated with a bored noblewoman and endow their relationship with all the highest values of Roman public and private life?' The reply is given: 'In Catullus the trigger may have been a unique conjunction of provincial innocence and metropolitan decadence, but the exaltation of extramarital love that is first found in this poetry becomes the dominant principle of a generation of love-poets — poets who found nothing similar in the Greek model of their formal genre.'[32]

Propertius (c. 48-16 B.C.)

'New' wives pursued wealthy young single men. At the very beginning of his love poems Propertius acknowledges that he has become the slave of his Roman mistress, Cynthia, who was later identified by Apuleius as Hostia.[33] Allen comments on his view of love *(miser):* 'love is a violent passion, a fault which destroys the reason and perverts the will, but a power which the lover is helpless to control and from which he can find no release'.[34] He was one of the equestrian order who was educated in Rome. There he formed a tempestuous relationship with an older 'free' married woman. He was so besotted with her that he neglected for a time the normal career path open to a member of the equestrian order. The poems reflect their stormy relationship with him declaring her 'my caring pain'.

> My fate is not to abandon her or love another:
> Cynthia my first, Cynthia shall be the end.[35]

His father had died when he was young, and his negative attitude towards Augustus' attempts at social control may well have been conditioned by the latter's confiscation of most of his family property in Umbria to provide land for returning soldiers — 'but the pitiless measuring rod took off your wealth

32. Fantham *et al.,* "The 'New Woman,'" p. 285.

33. Apuleius, *Apology,* 10.

34. Propertius, I.12. A. W. Allen, "Elegy and the Classical Attitude towards Love: Propertius, I,1," *YCR* 11 (1950): 264.

35. See H.-P. Stahl, "'Betrayed Love: Change of Identity' (1.11 and 1.12)" and "'Love's Torture: Prophetic Loneliness' (1.1)," in *Propertius: 'Love' and 'War'; Individual and State under Augustus* (Berkeley: University of California Press, 1985), chs. I and II.

of ploughed land'.[36] As we will see in the following chapter it was against such young men as Propertius that Augustus introduced penalties for not marrying and also provided a rapid career promotion into the Senatorial class for those fathering children.

The poems reflect the pain of a young man's enslavement to a relationship with a married woman whose own husband's infidelity to her was replicated in her affair with Propertius. His possessiveness demanded exclusive loyalty but she refused to give that. Some poems express love's torture and betrayal.

> Cynthia does not follow office or care for honours,
> she is always one who weighs her lovers' purses.[37]

By means of casual liaisons she, in effect, prostituted herself for gifts. He portrayed himself as being besotted with her, but not her with him. In retrospect he asks —

> Was I really fool enough, over so many years
> To put up, selfish woman, with you and yours?
> Have you ever thought of me as free, or will you always
> Hurl at my head your arrogant words?[38]

As Papanghelis comments, 'Tears of rage and grief over the loss of *puella* [his 'girl'] (1-6) give place to attempted consolation (7-10) and retrospective realisation of misplaced, poetic and otherwise, donations (11-12); this, in turn, releases a savage indictment of the tyranny imposed by her and endured by him.'[39] Griffin notes: 'In contrast to the Roman life of *prudentia*, disciplined action, Propertius claims to live *nullo consilio*; he renounces the Roman marriage.'[40] On a broader canvas he encapsulated in verse the sexual activities of a Roman wife who enjoyed this extra-marital affair with a younger man whose strong desires she satisfied, and yet sadly he testified 'in my case Venus [the goddess of love] inflicts the pain of bitter nights'.[41] He contrasts his own ex-

---

36. Propertius, IV.1.127-30.

37. Propertius, I.5.59-60, 67-68; II.16.11-12.

38. Propertius, II.8.13-16.

39. T. D. Papanghelis, *Propertius: A Hellenistic Poet on Love and Death* (Cambridge: Cambridge University Press, 1987), p. 115.

40. J. Griffin, "Propertius and Antony," *JRS* 67 (1977): 17-26, *cit.* 22. Propertius, II.6.41, cf. II.7.

41. Propertius, I.34. Allen, "Elegy and the Classical Attitude towards Love: Propertius I,1," 276.

perience with the wish that he has for happy lovers — that they will not experience the pain he had at the hands of Cynthia.

Ovid (43 B.C.–A.D. 17)

Ovid, after the publication of two books on the *Art of Love* in *c.* A.D. 1, added a third volume *c.* A.D. 8 giving advice to women also.[42] At the end of his second book he had indicated: 'Lo, the girls are asking my counsel. You will be my next concern.' Towards the end of Book 3 he said that he would deal with 'naked matters, which I blush to tell' but then proceeded to give totally uninhibited advice to women.[43] It is true that although he specified that his third book was for courtesans who were exempted from the Augustan laws on adultery, he was compelled to justify it. He sought to defend what he had written with *The Remedies of Love* and noted that 'Some people have recently criticised my works as shameless'.[44] He tried hard to defend his work from exile.

> [My *Art of Love*] does not contravene the laws, it does not teach the young married women of Rome. Four times have I declared that "I shall sing only of what accords with the laws, of permissible secret loves". But, you say, "the matron can use arts intended for others". Let the matron give up reading then, for every poem can teach her something wrong.[45]

In spite of his strong protestations, Ovid had scoffed at husbands who were so old-fashioned as to feel injured by their wife's infidelity — 'That man is so provincial who is hurt by an adulterous wife'. The implication is that he was so unsophisticated. He went on to argue that Rome was founded on adulterous practices for that husband 'does not recognise the character for which Rome is famous. Romulus and Remus, Ilia's Martian twins, were not born without guilt'.[46]

The second distich of the famous *triclinium graffito* from Pompeii tells the guests to keep their eyes off other men's wives.[47] Horace (65-8 B.C.) speaks of an older woman *(matura virgo)* wanting to have intercourse with 'junior adulterers' at her husband's feasts *(inter mariti vina),* nor 'is she nice to choose to whom she (hurriedly) grants her favours when the lamps are re-

---

42. Griffin, "Propertius and Antony," *JRS* 67 (1977): 23.
43. Ovid, *Art of Love,* 2.745-46, 3.747-808.
44. Ovid, *Remedies of Love,* 357-62.
45. Ovid, *Sorrows of an Exile,* 2.243-56.
46. Ovid, *Amator l.* 37, *ll.* 38-40.
47. *CIL* 4.7698.

moved'.[48] Green argues, 'By having the husband to "pimp" for their wives and justify it by alluding to a "heroic" tradition that sanctions brutality towards women, Ovid presents a view of Roman society which includes a persuasive acceptance of deception and exploitation as an inevitable part of amatory relations, including marriage. By constructing an argument in favour of adultery from the perspective of how it will benefit the husband, Ovid reveals a climate in which at least for some it was now easy to rationalise such practices.'[49]

Ovid's evidence is important for this discussion because of the connection between his highly active political role as a member of the equestrian order and his defiance of Augustus' legislation on adultery. Ovid himself attributed his unfortunate imperial exile to two errors on his part.

> Although two crimes, a poem and a blunder,
> Destroyed me, one unmentioned must remain.
> For who am I to renew your wounds, great Caesar?
> It's overmuch that I once caused you pain.
> The other's left, that a foul poem proves me
> A teacher of obscene adultery.[50]

The former was his *Ars Amatoria* and possibly its explication in the *Art of Love*. It was 'the ill-conceived invitation to the matrons of Rome to tread the primrose path with "the girls,"' for Ovid had incited married women to break the law against adultery.

Syme devotes a chapter, "The Error of Caesar Augustus,"[51] to a careful discussion of this issue — one that has provided some two hundred scholars with the opportunity to speculate and to weigh up the evidence.[52] He notes three important 'failures' on the part of Augustus in his relegation of Ovid. He had been unjust for he chose to incriminate him on the basis of a work of his youth written some twenty years previously. 'No law laid down the place of residence when an offender was banished by *relegatio*.' Since Augustus was a divinity 'he ought not to display anger since he is omnipotent'. As far as Ovid was concerned, 'Caesar Augustus is unjust: not a true "princeps", and no

---

48. Horace, *Odes*, 3.6.25-28. See also Pliny, *Natural History* 14.141; Juvenal, *Satires*, 1.55ff; Suetonius. *Augustus*, 69.1.

49. Greene, *The Erotics of Domination*, pp. 105-106.

50. *Sorrows of an Exile*, 2.206-11.

51. R. Syme, "The Error of Caesar Augustus," in *History in Ovid* (Oxford: Clarendon Press, 1978), ch. 12.

52. J. C. Thibault, *The Mystery of Ovid's Exile* (Berkeley: University of California Press, 1964).

gentleman.' It is Syme's view that 'The error of Augustus played into Ovid's hands. It gave him something to write about and a reason for waging defensive warfare over long years, although he abated one theme towards the end: the last book has only *princeps ira . . .* showing up illegality and rancour in the rule.'[53]

Bauman concludes, 'Thus the entire corpus of works critical of the puritanical-demographic policy so dear to Augustus belongs to the one decade'. Ovid's third book on the *Art of Love* was published in A.D. 8 at a time when criticisms of the emperor were at their height.[54] Ovid's pleas to secure his return to Rome from his lonely exile failed to move either Augustus or Tiberius. Ovid would not mention the reference to the actual 'blunder' for it would 'renew your wounds'. Bauman rejects the specific identification of the 'blunder' with the adultery of Augustus' granddaughter, Vipsania Julia.

In terms of the focus of Ovid's Book 3 there is a striking similarity between the sexual mores of 'new' Roman women which the poet promoted, even though he himself might argue ostensibly that his whole work was meant only for *hetairai*, and the misconduct of Julia, the daughter of Augustus and wife of Tiberius, and Vipsania Julia, his granddaughter. The former was publicly denounced for her adultery and divorced on the initiative of the emperor in 2 B.C.

The defence of Julia, the daughter of Augustus, reveals a well-educated woman with a taste for literature and 'a pungent, if bawdy wit'. Regarding her 'rowdy troop *(grex)* of young men' she boasted, 'I will soon make old men of them'; and thus inappropriate familiarity drew negative comments from her father. As the daughter of the divine Augustus she claimed, 'I am his true image, born of his heavenly blood', and asserted that whatever she was pleased to do was lawful *(quidquid liberet pro licito vindicans)*. Suetonius also noted, 'she did not neglect any act of extravagance or lust'.[55] While imperial politics and intrigues over succession were meshed in with her actions, it is clear that she and her circle operated on the extreme of new Roman woman in stark contrast to the modest Livia, Augustus' wife.[56] Seneca wrote, 'His failing years were alarmed by his daughter and the noble youths who were bound to her by adultery as if by a military oath. She headed a coterie that included adultery amongst its pursuits'.[57]

---

53. R. Syme, "The Error of Caesar Augustus," pp. 224-25.

54. Bauman, *Women and Politics in Ancient Rome*, p. 123.

55. Suetonius, *Augustus*, 65.

56. Bauman, "Julia's relations with her family," pp. 109-113; Macrobius, *Saturnalia*, 2.5.1-9; Lalleius Paterculus, 2.100.3; Suetonius, *Tiberius*, 10.

57. See pp. 51-52 for further discussion of Julia.

This is the background against which the relegation from Rome for adultery in A.D. 8 of Ovid and Julia's daughter, Vipsania Julia, should be considered. In her case her house in Rome was demolished and she was not buried in the mausoleum of Augustus, nor was her daughter permitted to marry Claudius for 'her parents had offended Augustus'.[58] At the same time Ovid was given the milder form of *relegatio*, being sent to Tomis in the Black Sea, although he retained his property and did not lose his equestrian status.[59]

While Bauman admits that aspects of these issues are insoluble,[60] it is no coincidence that Ovid opposed the legislation of Augustus on adultery. He also justified and promoted the patterns of conduct that it aimed to restrain, however much in retrospect he sought to be a revisionist of what he had written. For the purpose of our investigation it is clear that at the very heart of Rome's high society there was a pattern of sexual mores of women that openly defied the legislation on adultery and attendant issues.

Before concluding this section it is important to note that there was a significant nexus between extant literature on new Roman women and the reality of their social mores, and none the more so than with the Roman poets. J. Griffin in his important articles on this issue has argued that 'much recent scholarship has misjudged the Augustan poets in certain important respects, because it has been thought in principle possible to separate "literature" and "life", as if they were clearly distinguishable entities; in reality, the two affect each other in a ceaseless mutual interaction'.[61] The literary sources provide evidence of both, and Griffin's examination provides confirmation that poets played a significant role in helping both to promote moral mores and to confirm their legitimacy in the wider society. And the theatre was an important means of spreading them.

Playwrights and New Roman Comedy

The older woman with wealth and sexual prowess became an established character in Roman Comedy.[62] She could dominate the marriage because of

---

58. Seneca, *Brevitate Vitae*, 4.5; Bauman, *Women and Politics in Ancient Rome*, p. 114.

59. Bauman, *Women and Politics in Ancient Rome*, p. 119.

60. Bauman, *Women and Politics in Ancient Rome*, p. 121.

61. "Augustan Poetry and the Life of Luxury" and "Propertius and Antony," *JRS* 66 (1976): 87-105 and 67 (1977): 17-26, citation 16. He demonstrates this point further in his second essay with Propertius and Mark Antony.

62. E. Schuhmann, "Der Typ der *Uxor Dotata* in den Komödien des Plautus," *Philologus* 121 (1997): 45-65.

the size of her dowry.[63] Plautus refers to the arrogance of a wife who boasts about her sexual appetite both within and outside the boundaries of marriage, a theme not restricted to the young wives as his *Mostellaria* shows.[64]

From the perspective of a social historian, Crisafulli makes a critical observation on New Roman Comedy produced by playwrights such as Plautus and Terence. 'In essence, Comedy was a powerful discourse which shaped Roman society.'[65] The popularity of Comedy was a reflection of the concerns of society. It dealt with 'the conflicts, intrigues and relationships of private life . . . the depiction of women in Comedy had an enormous impact on other forms of literature that followed'. She further notes that 'we can see that a dynamic relationship developed between the theatre and its audience in Rome. New Comedy not only reinforced, but also influenced society's morals, modes of behaviour and understanding of relationships'.[66]

The reason for this impact was that, unlike some other cultures, men and women of all classes avidly attended the theatre. It remained popular in the time of Augustus and was a public occasion where his social manipulation of the class system was seen. The *equites Romani* were now permitted to sit in the front rows of the theatre and, in fact, in his *lex Julia theatricalis* he assigned seats according to social status, for all were to be well aware of their place within society. E. Rawson says, '. . . it is becoming more and more widely recognised that even in the imperial period the theatre was one of the central institutions of Roman culture; this is even more true of the Republican period'.[67]

Theatre-going was common among all classes in Rome and through New Comedy had a moulding influence on social mores.[68] Legislation such as *lex Julia theatricalis* not only heightened class consciousness in public contexts but was also counterproductive, for it was a powerful vehicle which promoted the new values against which Augustus would need to legislate.

63. Plautus, *Menaechmi*, ll. 766-67.

64. Plautus, *Mostellaria*, ll. 690-97.

65. T. Crisafulli, "Representations of the Feminine: The Prostitutes in Roman Comedy," in T. W. Hillard, R. A. Kearsley, C. E. V. Nixon, A. M. Nobbs, eds., *The Ancient Near East, Greece, and Rome*, Ancient History in a Modern University (Grand Rapids: Eerdmans, 1998), I, p. 223.

66. Crisafulli, "Representations of the Feminine: The Prostitutes in Roman Comedy," pp. 222-23.

67. E. Rawson, '*Discrimina ordinum*: the *lex Julia theatricalis*,' PBSR (1987): 83-114.

68. Crisafulli, "Representations of the Feminine: The Prostitutes in Roman Comedy," p. 223.

III. Roman Social Values in the East

Roman Culture

That there is evidence for the 'new' Roman wife is not in question, but what justification is there for projecting this perception of the 'new' woman beyond Rome itself to centres in the East where Christian communities had been formed in the first century? This is an important issue to pursue.

We know that there were Christian letters addressed to Philippi and Corinth, both of which were Roman colonies and centres of Roman culture,[69] with Corinth being the centre for the province of Achaia. What do we know of the cultural impact on the remainder of the centres which did not have this status? Did a cultural parochialism reign in the city of Ephesus and on the island of Crete where Christian communities were formed in the first century; were these centres isolated and immune from the influence of the dominant Roman power? This raises the issue of evidence for the penetration of Roman culture generally in the East.

There was something paradoxical about the Roman Empire. It was ruled with a minimum of Roman officials. The governor of a province brought with him a very small number of officials some of whom were legal advisers and friends. Because he exercised the Roman *imperium* in the province his essential role related to criminal jurisdiction in his capital and to his annual assize where he executed Rome's sword. There might or might not be a standing army depending on the reality of the *pax romana* but, by and large, the empire enjoyed peace and the emperors promoted themselves as the upholders of this blessing. Taxes for Rome were collected by tax farmers *(publicani)* and this meant that the revenue process was put out to tender and again did not need a provincial bureaucracy.[70] Local cities were, in effect, autonomous in that they were governed by annually elected magistrates and other office bearers who gave their services free of charge as the local élite. Their responsibilities related to civil law and the support of the infrastructure of the city, including the administration of the markets and the collection of indirect taxes. Rome ruled its vast Empire with none of the enormous bureaucracy normally associated with imperial forms of government.[71]

---

69. E. T. Salmon, *Roman Colonisation Under the Republic* (London: Thames and Hudson, 1969), p. 136; P. Cartledge and A. Spawforth, *Hellenistic and Roman Sparta: A Tale of Two Cities* (London: Routledge, 1989), p. 104.

70. J.-J. Aubert, "Direct Management and Public Administration: Four Case Studies," in *Business Managers in Ancient Rome: A Social and Economic Study of Institores, 200 B.C.–A.D. 250* (Leiden: E. J. Brill, 1994), ch. 5, esp. pp. 523-47.

71. R. Wallace and W. Williams, "Roman Rule in the Near East," in *The Three Worlds of Paul*

One would have thought that this structure might have lent itself to cultural isolationism in which there was the minimal impact of Romanization or none at all in cities outside Italy.[72] However, Rome skilfully engaged in the transformation of values by highly sophisticated forms of propaganda, and so succeeded that non-Romans embraced Roman values as part of first-century modernity. They achieved this at a provincial level as Ando has well demonstrated.[73] Even Athens, the highly influential custodian of Greek culture, absorbed aspects of Roman culture. Even though it resisted absorbing Rome's values fully there are clear indicators that it did not remain culturally isolated from them.[74] There a Roman forum was built distinct, but not far, from the Greek one which still functioned at that time, although the latter had curtailed powers following its Roman conquest by Sulla in 86 B.C. The placing and elevation of the Roman forum higher than the Greek agora sent a clear message to the Athenians of Rome's suzerainty. It was not only the imperial cult that found ready recognition in Athens which had a long tradition of 'welcoming' new imperial gods,[75] but other aspects pervaded the life of this traditional and proud custodian of Greek values.[76]

The penetration of Roman culture in the East meant that the transfer of the values of Roman women, both traditional and 'new', also occurred. How could this happen, given the isolation of first-century women from society generally assumed by New Testament scholars? C. Nepos writing in the first century B.C. draws attention to the significant differences between Greek and Roman conventions.

---

of Tarsus (London: Routledge, 1998), ch. 6. For a study of an individual province see S. Mitchell, ed., "The Administration of Roman Asia from 133 B.C. to A.D. 250," in *Lokale Autonomie und römische Ordnungsmacht*, ed. W. Eck (München: R. Oldenbourg, 1999), pp. 17-46.

72. E. Badian, *Publicans and Sinners: Private Enterprise in the Service of the Roman Republic* (Oxford: Blackwell, 1972); and D. Braund, ed., *The Administration of the Roman Empire, 241 BC–AD 193* (Exeter: Exeter University Press, 1988).

73. C. Ando, *Imperial Ideology and Provincial Loyalty in the Roman Empire* (Berkeley: University of California Press, 2000); R. Lawrence and J. Berry, eds., *Cultural Identity in the Roman Empire* (London: Routledge, 1998). For a detailed discussion of this in relation to Gaul see A. Woolf, *Becoming Roman: The Origins of Provincial Civilization in Gaul* (Cambridge: Cambridge University Press, 1998), and for Greece generally see S. E. Alcock, Graecia Capta: *The Landscapes of Roman Greece* (Cambridge: Cambridge University Press, 1993).

74. M. C. Hoff and S. I. Rotroff, *The Romanization of Athens: Proceedings of an International Conference*, Oxbow Monograph 94 (Oxford: Oxbow Books, 1997).

75. See inscriptions cited in my "On Introducing Gods to Athens: An Alternative Reading of Acts 17:18-20," *TynB* 47.1 (1996): 71-90.

76. See Hoff and Rotroff, *The Romanization of Athens*.

No Roman would hesitate to take his wife to a dinner party, or to allow the mother of his family to occupy the first rooms in his house and to walk about in public. The custom in Greece is completely different: a woman cannot appear at a party unless it is among her relatives; she can only sit in the interior of her house, which is called the women's quarters; this no male can enter unless he is a close relative.[77]

It is critical for this discussion to realise that Roman culture had borrowed substantially from aspects of Greek culture some two centuries before Augustus. 'The lifestyle [of the Roman élite] was formed by the Hellenisation of Roman society in the second century B.C., the results of which could be seen equally in the luxury and sophistication of their pleasures and in the respect . . . they paid to literary culture and the arts'.[78] So the planting of Roman values in the East in the Augustan era was not entirely in the foreign soil of the Hellenistic world.[79]

Roman Women

S. E. Wood begins her important book on *Imperial Women: A Study in Public Images, 40 B.C.–A.D. 69* with this observation: 'A woman living in any city or town in the Roman empire would have known the faces of most members of the ruling family, even if she had never seen them in person.' She goes on to comment that 'the married women of the imperial family would provide her with examples of appropriate ways for a wife to behave. Works of the visual arts would show her how they dressed and how they wore their hair'. They were 'models she should emulate, or *exempla,* to use the term that would come naturally to the mind of the Latin-speaking person'.[80] Juvenal asks, 'What woman will not follow when an empress leads the way?'[81]

'At the same time, our hypothetical observer of these statues and coins

---

77. C. Nepos, *Lives of Foreign Generals,* praef. 6.

78. T. P. Wiseman, *Catullus and His World: A Reappraisal* (Cambridge: Cambridge University Press, 1985), p. 3.

79. N. Petrochilos, *Roman Attitudes to the Greeks* (Athens: National and Capodistrian University of Athens, 1974); A. Wardman, *Rome's Debt to Greece* (New York: St. Martin's Press, 1977); J. Griffin, "Augustan Poetry and the Life of Luxury," pp. 87-105, and "Propertius and Antony," pp. 17-26; and R. O. A. M. Lyne, *The Latin Love Poets from Catullus to Horace* (Oxford: Clarendon Press, 1980), pp. 8-17 and 192-98.

80. S. E. Wood, *Imperial Women: A Study in Public Images, 40 B.C.–A.D. 69* (Leiden: E. J. Brill, 1999), p. 1.

81. Juvenal, *Satires,* VI.617.

might learn, either by word of mouth or some other means, in what sort of behaviour these women publicly engaged, and would understand that it was not inappropriate for a wife to present petitions to her husband about matters of public policy, to intercede with him on behalf of individuals, to lend money to people outside her own family, to make generous gifts of cash both to cities and individuals, to undertake building projects in her own name and at her own expense, and still to be presented in public as the embodiment of a wife's traditional virtues'.[82] There were, of course, also negative lessons to be learned with the sudden disappearance of an imperial statue, or its public defacing if she was guilty of a criminal offence or had fallen from grace with her husband. (See pp. 51-52.) Roman imperial marriage values had spread rapidly to the East. It is important to realise that, unlike the Republican period, statue types played an important role in the imperial propaganda 'war' against the trends of the new Roman wife. She was no straw woman that was being knocked down by such manipulation of the means of communication.

A good example of traditional values is found in the statue of Regilla, the wife of the famous sophist of Athens, Herodes Atticus, around whom Philostratus wrote his *Lives of the Sophists*.[83] The Council of Corinth had erected a statue in her honour, and the inscription which contained the resolution of the Council read —

> This is a statue of Regilla. An artist carved the figure which has translated 'all [her] prudent moderation' (πᾶσαν σωφροσύνην). It was given to the city by the great Herodes Atticus, 'pre-eminent above others, who has attained the peak of every kind of virtue, whom she took as her husband, Herodes famous among the Hellenes and furthermore a son (of Greece) greater than them all, the flower of Achaia. O Regilla, the City Council, as if hailing you Tyche (the goddess, Fortune) has set up this marble statue before Tyche's sanctuary.'[84]

There are a number of important statements enshrined in the inscription on the statue base. Her famous husband is described as possessing all the great civic virtues (παντοίης ἀρετῆς), while hers, on the other hand, are epitomised by the important term σωφροσύνη. Furthermore, the inscription boasts that the artist captured in stone all her prudent moderation. While the

---

82. Wood, *Imperial Women: A Study in Public Images, 40 B.C.–A.D. 69*, p. 2.

83. Her husband was a famous Athenian who was a Greek resident of Athens and also its leading orator and benefactor, *Lives of the Sophists*, 545-66.

84. J. H. Kent, *Corinth: The Inscriptions, 1926-1950* (Princeton: American School of Classical Studies, 1966), VIII.3, no. 128.

ruling Council of Corinth portrayed Regilla's features as divine, likening her to the goddess of Fortune, in her marriage relationship with her famous husband, she enshrines that virtue which epitomized a traditional Roman wife. It is of interest that her virtue had crossed the Greek and Roman divide, as indeed had many other characteristics, and became an 'empire' virtue.[85]

By contrast in the famous city of Epidaurus, south of Corinth, there was a 'new' woman called Pamphile who lived in the time of Nero. It is recorded that she wrote 'historical memoirs in thirty-three books, an epitome of Ctesias' history in three books, many epitomes of histories and other books about controversies'. *The Suda* also records that she wrote about 'sex and many other things'.[86] While her vast endeavours in the former genre would have commended her in literary circles, her latter output would certainly have indicated where she stood in terms of those seen as 'new' women. Her influence had spread to the provinces.

'We have the many testimonies to women in the eastern provinces going about veiled . . . others in mosaics without exception showing women with their faces and generally with their heads, too, quite uncovered — perhaps the better to display the modish arrangement of their hair. Here may be the clue that resolves the conflict in evidence: women who imitated the changes in style that went on in the imperial court, changes depicted in the provinces by portraits of the ladies of the imperial house, were the richer ones, the more open to the new ways and the more likely to belong to families on the rise. Women of humbler class were veiled, but these others behaved exactly like their counterparts in Italy, fully visible, indeed making their existence felt very fully in public.'[87]

In his Euboean oration Dio Chrysostom provides important evidence of the lifestyle of the 'new' woman at the end of the first century A.D. in the East. He noted —

> . . . men condone even the matter of adultery in a somewhat magnificent fashion and the practice of it finds great and most charitable consideration, where husbands in their simplicity do not notice most things and do not admit knowledge of some things but suffer the adulterers to be called guests and friends and kinsmen, at times even entertaining these themselves and inviting them to their table at festivals . . . and invite their bosom friends, and display but moderate anger at actions that are most glaring

85. Hoff and Rotroff, *The Romanization of Athens.*
86. *The Suda,* FHG 3.520ff. Diogenes Laertius and Aulus Gellius preserve fragments of her 33 books but nothing remains of her works on sexuality.
87. R. MacMullen, "Women in Public in the Roman Empire," *Historia* 29 (1980): 217-18.

and open — where, I say, these intrigues of the married women are carried on with an air of respectability. . . .[88]

D. A. Russell argues for an alternative translation for the last clause in this citation to that in the Loeb edition of the orations — 'where, I say, in houses where such generous hospitality is given in relation to the wives', which implies that instead of prostitutes being provided, some actually supplied their wives.[89] Hawley notes the sheer number of references that illustrate the problem and the concern of Dio on the issues of marriage fidelity and promiscuousness in the cities in the Roman East.[90]

The concern of the Roman authorities is reflected even in constitutions set up for Roman colonies. One framed in Rome in 44 B.C. for Urso in Spain prescribed —

> Respecting all persons, who are or shall be colonists of the *colonia Genetiva Julia,* the wives of all such persons, being within the colony in accordance with this law, shall obey the laws of the *colonia Genetiva Julia* and of their husbands.[91]

Given that the reference elsewhere in this particular constitution is to 'all the conditions and with all the rights in every colony', one is justified in drawing two conclusions. As Corinth was established in the same year that Urso's constitution was drawn up by Rome, that particular stipulation would be no different for Corinth. It is clear that by 44 B.C. there were concerns about appropriate conduct and possible misconduct on the part of Roman wives in the colonies; such concerns were not restricted to Rome.

IV. Conclusions

We have noted that first-century women, unlike their Greek sisters in Hellenistic and Classical Greek times, appeared in the public domain. The imperial

---

88. For an overall discussion see R. Hawley, "Marriage, Gender, and the Family in Dio," in S. Swain, ed., *Dio Chrysostom: Politics, Letters, and Philosophy* (Oxford: Oxford University Press, 2000), ch. 5, esp. pp. 133-34, where he notes that the sheer number of references illustrate the problem and the concern of Dio on the issues of marriage fidelity and promiscuousness.

89. Dio Chrysostom, *Or.* 7.141-42; D. A. Russell, *Dio Chrysostom, Orations VII, XII, XXXVI,* Cambridge Greek and Latin Classics (Cambridge: Cambridge University Press, 1992), p. 155.

90. R. Hawley, "Marriage, Gender, and the Family in Dio," p. 133. On this oration see also P. Desideri, "City and Country in Dio," and J. Ma, "Public Speech and the Community in the Euboicus," *Dio Chrysostom: Politics, Letters, and Philosophy,* ch. 3 and 4.

91. *Lex Coloniae Genetivae Juliae Ursonensis,* ch. CXXXIII, LXVI.

wives appear to have set a precedent for wives of senatorial rank and others in the social hierarchy. Chapter 9 will show that women of substantial means could have the title of magistrates and exercise political influence.

It has not been argued here that a stereotype of the 'traditional' republican wife no longer existed in the first century or, on the other hand, that the conduct of most (or all) wives was promiscuous. What has been shown is that 'new' women had emerged and they were supported by those who were themselves *avant-garde,* including some male literary figures of the early Roman Empire who were influential in promoting this lifestyle. These 'new' women had an unsettling influence on the *status quo.*

This chapter has not exhausted the extant evidence of the activities of first-century women or the 'new' Roman wife. Specific aspects relevant to individual texts relating to the Pauline communities will be discussed in Part 2. There we will locate texts relating to the Pauline communities in the cultural matrix of Romanization in the East as their *Sitz im Leben.*

We turn first to the legal responses to the 'new' Roman women. The following chapter will be devoted to seeing how the philosophical schools coped with this new phenomenon. This will be followed by a consideration of relevant New Testament texts and the possibility that this same phenomenon greatly influenced some of the first-century women in the Pauline communities.

CHAPTER 3

New Wives and New Legislation

'We shall never know to what extent women of an established family endorsed the life of pleasure described by the elegists, or the degree to which the poets' own actions matched their profession of enslavement to love.'[1] With this statement Fantham affirms for Roman society that which would be true for any ancient society where one wished to draw conclusions about aspects of the social life of all or a particular class of society.[2]

However, in the case of the conduct of women evidence exists from Augustus' legislative programme that he was seeking to curb the activities of those described in the last chapter as 'new' women. It prescribed moral conduct, financial disadvantages in remaining single, the procreation of children with resulting career advantages, and dress codes for wives; it proscribed marriage between certain classes, and punished inactivity on the part of husbands who ignored their wife's extramarital liaisons. Bauman has summarized the ramifications of this wide-ranging legislation: it 'regulated marriage, encouraged procreation by privileges and rewards, and penalized the unmarried and childless, in particular restricting their rights of inheritance'.[3] Among other things it was a negative move against 'new' Roman women that sought to curb their activity with their young sexual partners and to encourage bachelors to enter marriage and create a stable family by means of incentives. There are good reasons for concluding from the content of this legisla-

1. E. Fantham, *et al.,* "The 'New Woman': Representation and Reality," in *Women in the Classical World* (Oxford: Oxford University Press, 1994), p. 290.

2. In any case the former would be difficult to assess and the latter would be a matter of an investigation of the lifestyle of each poet, with the conclusions dependent on extant primary material.

3. R. A. Bauman, *Women and Politics in Ancient Rome* (London: Routledge, 1992), p. 105.

tion that it reflects the mindset both of a 'moral' reformer and a social engineer; this was not without precedence in Roman history. J. A. Crook cautions against concluding that this social intervention was revolutionary for the Romans and points out that there was a strong Republican tradition for interference in the behaviour of its citizens either through legislation, courts and, above all, censorship.[4]

The purpose of this chapter will be: (I) to examine Augustus' earlier legislation of 17 B.C. as it related to the activities of 'new' Roman women and the reasons for its introduction; (II) to explore the responses of contemporaries and near contemporaries to those laws; and (III) to investigate the extent of the amendments in A.D. 9 (inasmuch as they affected the new Roman wife) to his legislation brought forward in the name of others because of the necessary compromise they represented for Augustus.

I. Augustus' Marriage Legislation of 17 B.C.[5]

Suetonius records —

> He [Augustus] reformed the laws and completely overhauled some of them, such as the sumptuary law, that on adultery and chastity, that on bribery, and the encouragement of marriage in the Senatorial and Equestrian Orders.

He enacted *lex Julia de maritandis ordinibus* and the *lex Julia de adulteriis coercendis* between 18 and 16 and most probably in 17 B.C.[6]

The *lex Julia de maritandis ordinibus* dealt with the regulation of marriage, incentives for having children and penalties for refusing to do so.[7] The *lex Julia de adulteriis coercendis* legislated on promiscuity, making it a public crime which came within the jurisdiction of a specially created court with a permanent jury adjudicating.

4. J. A. Crook, "Augustus: Power, Authority, Achievement," in A. K. Bowman, E. Champlin, and A. Lintott, eds., *The Augustan Empire, 43 BC–AD 69*, 2nd edition (Cambridge: Cambridge University Press, 1996), vol. X, ch. 3, p. 131.

5. For a full discussion of the Augustan laws see S. Treggiari, *Roman Marriage: Iusti Coniuges from the Time of Cicero to the Time of Ulpian* (Oxford: Clarendon Press, 1991), pp. 60-80.

6. Horace makes reference to the law against adultery in the Centennial Hymn of 17 B.C., which is discussed on pp. 45, 49-50. See L. F. Raditsa, "Augustus' Legislation concerning Marriage, Procreation, Love Affairs and Adultery," *ANRW* II 13 (1980): 296-97.

7. Suetonius, *Augustus*, 34, 40.5.

According to Bauman, these reforms 'applied both to *adulterium*, illicit intercourse by and with a respectable married woman, and to *stuprum*, fornication with a widow or unmarried free woman who was not a prostitute'. The former could be committed only by wives and lovers.[8] Men and women could be charged with *stuprum* but only women could be charged with adultery, the latter relating to all women regardless of their social class.[9] Roman marriage not only had to operate within the laws of affinity[10] but it also had to take due cognizance of rank because of these new proscriptions.

Raditsa succinctly summarised the effects of the intrusion of the *lex Julia* into what had been primarily within the purview of the family and not the domain of the state. He wrote, 'the law on adultery threatened everyone . . . the laws on marriage interfered with the lives of everyone, both in what they forbade and in what they encouraged. Their sanction applied to traditional areas of freedom in private life, for instance to the *patria potestas*, to the freedom to make stipulations of a certain sort in wills, to inheritance and bequests when not within the sixth degree of relation in a family, to the *patronus'* relation to his freedmen and women. More importantly, they specified who could marry whom within the body of citizens'.[11]

Under the legislation of Augustus a wife's adultery was liable to 'public accusation' *(accusatio publica)* and was tried by a judge and jury. This represented a major change, for what were known as 'honour' killings had traditionally applied in Republican Roman society. Aulus Gellius said that he

> 'copied Cato's words from a speech called *On the dowry,* in which it is stated that husbands who caught wives in adultery could kill them. "The husband," he says, "who divorces his wife is her judge, as though he were a censor; he has power if she has done something perverse and awful . . . if she has done wrong with another man, she is condemned to death." It is also written, regarding the right to kill: "If you catch your wife in adultery, you can kill her with impunity; she, however, cannot dare to lay a finger on you if you commit adultery, nor is it the law".[12]

8. Bauman, *Women and Politics in Ancient Rome,* p. 105. For a full discussion see Raditsa, "Augustus' Legislation concerning Marriage, Procreation, Love Affairs and Adultery," pp. 278-339.

9. Raditsa, "Augustus' Legislation concerning Marriage, Procreation, Love Affairs and Adultery," p. 310.

10. W. W. Buckland, *A Text-book of Roman Law from the Time of Cicero to the Time of Ulpian* (Oxford: Clarendon Press, 1991), p. 115.

11. Raditsa, "Augustus' Legislation concerning Marriage, Procreation, Love Affairs and Adultery," p. 319.

12. Aullus Gellius, *Attic Nights,* 10:23. On the limited exercising of this power in Republican times see pp. 17-19.

The new law expressly forbade the husband to kill his wife if caught in the act but did permit him to kill the offender if he was an actor, a freedman, a member of the immediate family, a pimp, or anyone condemned by a public court. The alleged adulterer could be brought to trial, suffer the loss of half of his property and be relegated to an island.

Legal action on the charge of adultery could not commence until the accuser had actually divorced his wife which could be done on the witness of seven citizens.[13] Once divorced and found guilty of adultery by a court, the wife lost half of her dowry, one third of any other property she owned, and was relegated to an island. A women so convicted could not thereafter enter into a fully valid marriage.

While a husband could no longer act unilaterally against his wife, he was, however, required to initiate legal action against her within sixty days, otherwise he left himself open to the charge of 'pimping'. So this legislation not only made a woman's adultery a criminal offence once she was divorced but, for the first time, it also made 'the condoning of adultery by an "injured" husband an offence open to criminal prosecution and punishable by expulsion from society.'[14] The severe penalty of exile and loss of property for a husband unwilling to curb or punish his wife was meant to bring great pressure on him to take action against the profligate behaviour of a 'new' Roman wife. This legislation had teeth, for it would severely penalise him for failing to divorce and prosecute his wife for her sexual misconduct.

McGinn has drawn attention to another far-reaching effect of the legislative programme of Augustus, *viz.* the regulation of clothing which was originally designed to signal a woman's legal status and class.[15] 'Women [convicted of adultery] were also compelled to wear the *toga* as a symbol of their shame', and they were no longer eligible to wear the marriage veil. He also notes that 'Clothing's role as a status maker receives repeated recognition from the jurists'.[16] Augustus had taken upon himself to enact legislation for dress codes which would distinguish the modest wife from the adulteress and

13. *The Digest,* 48.5.25, Raditsa, "Augustus' Legislation concerning Marriage, Procreation, Love Affairs and Adultery," pp. 312-13.

14. Fantham, "The 'New Woman'," p. 290.

15. It is, in fact, an aspect of this legislation that has been overlooked. 'I know of no comprehensive treatment of this important subject,' i.e., 'Augustus's intervention in the field of clothing,' T. A. J. McGinn, *Prostitution, Sexuality, and the Law* (Oxford: Oxford University Press, 1998), p. 154, citing P. Zanker, *Power of Images in the Age of Augustus* (Ann Arbor: University of Michigan Press, 1988). See more recently A. T. Croom, "Women's Clothing," in *Roman Clothing and Fashion* (Stroud: Tempus Publishers, 2000), ch. 4.

16. McGinn, *Prostitution, Sexuality, and the Law,* p. 154.

the prostitute.[17] 'By law they [the latter two groups] were obliged to wear a kind of uniform — a short undergarment *(tunica)* without *instita* (the border, laid in several plaits) and a *toga* in a dark colour — by which they could be distinguished from respectable women, but quite often they cut a dashing figure by wearing a daring and often see-through dress.'[18]

Valerius Maximus, writing in the time of Tiberius, records 'the frightful marital severity of Sulpicius Gallus' *c.* 190 B.C. who divorced his wife because he learned 'she had gone about in public unveiled'. He justified his actions thus —

> To have your good looks approved, the law limits you to my eyes only. For them assemble the tools of beauty, for them look your best, trust to their closest familiarity. Any further sight of you, summoned by needless incitement, has to be mired in suspicion and crimination.[19]

He indicates that there were other examples from Republican times where a wife found 'in public talking tete-a-tete with a certain common freedwoman [a prostitute] was divorced for that reason'. P. Sempronius Sophus did the same to his spouse for watching the public Games without his knowledge. In citing these examples Valerius Maximus makes it clear that 'While women were thus checked in the old days, their minds stayed away from wrongdoings'.[20]

According to McGinn, 'The *lex Iulia* specified certain articles of clothing — such as the *stola* and *vittae* — as peculiar to *matronae* and forbade these to be worn by prostitutes: thus the *leges* in the passage drawn from the *De Cultu Feminarum* are simply the adultery statute itself. Matrons were not compelled by law to wear the *stola* and the other 'matronal' articles of clothing'.[21] The veil however was worn to signify the woman was married. (See pp. 78-81.)

It is interesting that Diodorus of Sicilia, who wrote *c.* 60-30 B.C., revived the legend that Zaleucus of Locri had enacted a law in the third century B.C. prescribing the behaviour of a married woman, where she was prohibited

---

17. McGinn, *Prostitution, Sexuality, and the Law*, p. 154.

18. E. Eyben, *Restless Youth in Ancient Rome* (London: Routledge, 1993), p. 232.

19. Valerius Maximus, *Memorable Doings and Sayings,* 6.3.10. See also Plutarch, *Moralia* 267C, where Calus in 166 B.C. divorced his wife because he saw her with her dress pulled over her head.

20. Valerius Maximus, *Memorable Doings and Sayings,* 6.3.10, 12.

21. McGinn, *Prostitution, Sexuality, and the Law*, p. 162. In a later period, Tertullian, *Pallio* 4.9, records that 'matrons had adopted the dress of prostitutes and *vice versa*', a situation that should have invited the unfriendly attention of public officials.

from wearing gold ornaments or clothes bordered with purple, unless she was a courtesan.[22]

Social engineering by Augustus, the aim of which was to give the senatorial class a higher profile in society, depended upon their wives living up to expected standards. Culham noted, 'Nor was it possible for Augustus to mark off a special élite and demand respect for them without including women of the senatorial class within the bounds. The public display of senatorial rank required that women who shared a family's status also behave in a way meriting respect. Augustan legislation also banned the daughters of senators from marrying freedmen, actors, or other disreputable people'.[23]

> It has been laid down in the Julian law: let no senator, senator's son, or grandson by a son, or great-grandson by a son and grandson knowingly and fraudulently have as betrothed or wife a freedwoman or a woman who herself or whose father or mother practices or has practised the stage profession. And let no daughter of a senator or granddaughter by a son or great-granddaughter by a son and grandson be knowingly and fraudulently betrothed or wife to a freedman or to a man who himself or whose father or mother practises or has practised the stage profession. And let not any of such people fraudulently and knowingly have such a woman as betrothed or wife.[24]

Syme pointed to the real effect of these measures — by including women in the strictures, Augustus effectively created a senatorial class.[25] He also noted that 'One of the consequences of this new legislative and political formalization of a senatorial status and rank hierarchy was that senators were kept from marrying freedwomen and thereby publicly compromising that special status Augustus wanted to claim for their group'.[26]

That Augustus attached a great importance to the intention of this legislation of 17 B.C. can be gauged from the evidence we have of the reinstatement of the Secular Games in the same year. They would henceforth commemorate the preservation of the State and, as Suetonius noted, it was Augustus who

22. Diodorus of Sicily, 12.21; cf. Athenaeus, *Deipnosophists*, 12.521B, who cites Phylarchus, *Histories*, 25, as his source.

23. P. Culham, "Did Roman Women Have an Empire?" in M. Golden and P. Toohey, eds., *Inventing Ancient Culture: Historicism, Periodization, and the Ancient World* (London: Routledge, 1997), p. 203.

24. *The Digest*, 23.3.44.

25. R. Syme, *The Augustan Aristocracy* (Oxford: Clarendon Press, 1986), p. 80. See also Treggiari, *Roman Marriage: Iusti Coniuges from the Time of Cicero to the Time of Ulpian*, p. 195.

26. Syme, *The Augustan Aristocracy*, p. 80.

commissioned Horace to write the 'Centennial Hymn' *(Carmen Saeculare)* for this extremely important occasion. It was sung on the third day of the festival by a choir of girls and boys in the temple of Apollo and at subsequent celebrations of the Games.[27] This hymn provided the opportunity to declare matters central to the welfare of the state. Not only was Augustus declared to be 'of Anchises' and Venus' pure blood' (hence Venus would be the mother of the imperial family and provide a warrant for the imperial cult, *l.* 49), but this composition also contained a clear reference to the intention of the *lex Julia.*

> Ilithyia, gently bring on birth
> at the proper time, whether you more approve
> the name Lucina or Genitalis, protect our mothers.
>
> Goddess, bring forth offspring, and prosper
> the Senate's edict on wedlock, that the new
> law on the marriage of women produce abundant children. . . .
>
> Gods! give proven morals to our ductile youth,
> Gods! give rest to our sober elders,
> give profit, progeny and every honour to Romulus' race. . . .
>
> Now Faith, and Peace, and Honour,
> and pristine Modesty, and Manhood neglected,
> dare to return, and blessèd Plenty appears, her horn laden.[28]

The first two verses belong to the second triad of the hymn with its theme on the outcome of the *lex Julia;* the third stanza is the final verse in the fourth triad on the divine activity that created Rome; and the last stanza cited above forms the third in the penultimate triad linking the return of modesty and manhood to its originator and his divine origins — Anchises and Venus.

Writing from his perspective, Williams comments, 'It is hard to see why a quarter of the space allotted to Augustus' achievements [four stanzas] should have been given to exaggerating the effects of this piece of coercive legislation, in such extravagant terms'.[29] Clearly, Horace saw it to be a matter of substantial significance for his generation, and behind this great Roman poet was the

---

27. Suetonius, *The Life of Horace.* For a helpful discussion of his role as a public voice in Augustan society see R. O. A. M. Lyne, "Horace in the First Augustan Period; The Adoption of the Role of Public, Moral Poet: Literary Strategies" and "The Resumption of the Role: 17-12 B.C.," in *Horace: Behind the Public Poetry* (New Haven: Yale University Press, 1995), chs. 4, 11.

28. Horace, *Carmen Saeculare, ll.* 13-20, 45-48, 57-60.

29. G. Williams, "Poetry in the Moral Climate of Augustan Rome," *JRS* 52 (1962): 35.

shadow of Augustus. Williams also notes, 'It is hard to sense any poetic qualities in these words, but Horace no doubt inserted them because of the moral
legislation of 18 B.C. [that] put the finishing touch to the new world'.[30] Given
these observations, the reference to the *lex Julia* is all the more poignant. Augustus had seen a nexus between his moral reform and the welfare of the Roman family and the state. It was therefore appropriate that he should be
lauded for 'the new law on the marriage of women' which was described for
public consumption as 'the Senate's edict on wedlock'. A specific petition,
'give proven morals to our ductile youth', was also made to the gods in the
hymn.[31]

Whatever clandestine or mixed motives are attributed to Augustus in initiating this legislation, the hymn provides an important insight into the stra-
tegic role which Augustus himself attached to the *lex Julia* and his vision that
there should be 'nothing greater than the city of Rome'.[32]

It is also important to note that as early as 28-27 B.C. Augustus revived the
cult of *Pudicitia* (Modesty) which had been established in 331 B.C. Only
women of patrician birth who had married only once, and that to a patrician
husband, had been allowed to participate in it.[33] This was a move that fore-
shadowed but one of the outcomes hoped for in the *lex Julia*.

In 28 B.C. Augustus had begun a programme of moral reform but the law
did not get on the statute books or, if it did, it was repealed. Propertius provides evidence.

> Cynthia rejoiced indeed when the law was lifted
> At the enactment of which we had both wept long
> In case it should divide us, though Jove himself
> Cannot separate two lovers against their will
> But Caesar is mighty.[34]

Propertius rejoiced in its failure, for it 'would have forced him to abandon
Cynthia and marry a wife to provide manpower for the state'.[35] Augustus saw
a critical nexus between the patricians and the moral conduct of wives a decade before his *lex Julia;* the latter was a long-projected piece of legislation.

---

30. Williams, "Poetry in the Moral Climate of Augustan Rome," 34.

31. Horace, *Carmen Saeculare, ll.* 18-19, 45.

32. Horace, *Carmen Saeculare, ll.* 11-12.

33. Bauman, *Women and Politics in Ancient Rome*, p. 15.

34. Propertius, II.7, *ll.* 1-5. F. Cairns, "Propertius on Augustus' Marriage Law," *Grazer
Beiträger* 8 (1979): 185-205.

35. Williams, "Poetry in the Moral Climate of Augustan Rome," 29.

Bauman acknowledges that there is no consensus among scholars as to the full intention behind the legislation, but he believes that some important conclusions can be drawn. He states 'in terms of the most viable theory the aim was to strengthen the traditional family unit, to stimulate the Italian birthrate [given 'the long years of anarchy and civil war'], and [he does not fail to add] to reinforce *pudicitia,* the strict moral standard expected of women'.[36]

II. Reactions to Augustus' Legislation

It was to be expected that legislation such as this, which moved into un-charted waters (or rather stormy seas), would not go unchallenged given that the lifestyle of men and women, not least the socially important interest groups, would be affected. Treggiari comments, 'The effect of the Augustan Law is attested by attempts made to evade it.' However she notes the effective-ness of the law on adultery in some cases and concedes that the results are im-possible statistically to know.[37] What remaining evidence do we have?

Women's Defiance

The 'defiance of the upper class women who tried to enrol themselves among the women exempt from persecution for *stuprum* and *adulterium* by publicly stating their loves' indicates 'how vividly the *lex Julia's* division of the society was perceived'.[38] As a response to this the Senate forbade women descended from, or married to, senators or knights from becoming high-class prostitutes *(hetairai).*

We know that the legislation on adultery committed by wives was imple-mented, because Dio Cassius records that 'Many women were accused but Augustus set a definite date as a limit'.[39] In A.D. 2 the five-year proscription (on the limitation of legal action) concerning such charges was introduced. Bauman argues that women alone would have pressed for such an amend-ment and speculates that they would have mounted a campaign for this relief.

36. Bauman, *Women and Politics in Ancient Rome,* p. 106.

37. Treggiari, *Roman Marriage:* Iusti Coniuges *from the Time of Cicero to the Time of Ulpian,* pp. 294-98.

38. Raditsa, "Augustus' Legislation concerning Marriage, Procreation, Love Affairs and Adultery," p. 318, citing Suetonius, *Tiberius,* 35; Tacitus, *Annals,* 2.85; Dio Cassius, 48.5.11, 20.

39. Dio Cassius, 55.10.16.

Ovid, having been trained in a progressive law school, gave the lobby his expert advice.[40]

Equestrians' Revolt

Certain men were unhappy with the implications of the legislation. Suetonius recorded that the knights 'persistently called for its repeal at a public gathering' but that did not influence Augustus, whose response was to display the children of Germanicus before the *Equites'* lobby as proof of the importance of the family. His action suggests that the dissatisfaction of the Equites at that particular time was with the penalties for those who had not married or who had not produced children.[41] It was meant to deprive young unmarried men who had received the *toga virilis* of their affairs with sexually experienced married women who were not prostitutes, and to penalise them for not marrying. The legislation affected 'bequests which played an important role in the social life of Rome, especially among the young and the aristocratic'.[42]

Others, according to Suetonius, who were bachelors were getting betrothed to little girls, which meant postponing the responsibility for fatherhood.[43] Married men were frequently changing their wives. Even making allowance for the exaggerated comments of Seneca, wives also engaged in changing partners. He hoped in the light of such intervention that no longer would 'illustrious and nobly born women count their age not by adding up consuls but by husbands, and go away [divorce] in order to marry and marry in order to divorce'.[44]

Members of the Equestrian Order sought to have the provision that discriminated against those of their class who were married, but had no children, rescinded.[45] This aspect of the legislation affected the laws of inheritance and touched primarily the wealthy, i.e., estates with over 100,000 sesterces and women with over 50,000 sesterces.

40. R. A. Bauman, *Lawyers and Politics in the Early Roman Empire: A Study of Relations Between the Roman Jurists and the Emperors from Augustus to Hadrian* (Munich: C. H. Beck, 1989), p. 51, n. 141.

41. Suetonius, *Augustus,* 34.2.

42. Horace, *Satires,* II.5. *ll.* 23-29; Raditsa, "Augustus' Legislation concerning Marriage, Procreation, Love Affairs and Adultery," p. 322.

43. Suetonius, *Augustus,* 34.

44. Seneca, *De beneficiis,* 3.16.2.

45. Dio Cassius, 56.1.2.

The social and legal pressure to have children was such that, if widows who were childless in their first marriage remarried and had a child by that marriage, they could enjoy the benefits from an inheritance. This aspect of the legislation is attributed to Augustus' concern about the falling birth rate in Rome compared with Republican times. This seems to have been a genuine concern given the census of 28 B.C.[46] As lines 18-20 in the *Centennial Hymn* record, the matter of children was a great concern of Augustus.[47]

Dio Cassius recorded 'he assessed heavier taxes on unmarried men and women without husbands, and by contrast offered awards for marriage and childbearing'.[48] By means of his 'social' legislation Augustus gave a further incentive to have children by giving preference to those who did so by moving them more rapidly through posts in the Senatorial class. Treggiari notes that 'Augustan marriage legislation slighted or rewarded men by enhancing or retarding (depending on their marital and reproductive choices) their ability to advance quickly within the new structure of clearly ranked jobs'.[49]

Horace on the lex Julia

Horace (65-8 B.C.) was an important commentator on the Augustan age and a poet of such significance in the early empire that his odes even became a school textbook. Juvenal noted his writings in the wake of their publication. Given the relationship Horace had with Augustus (Horace named him as his heir in his will), the former's assessment of Augustus' *lex Julia de adulteriis coercendis* is important — apart from what was sung at the state occasion in his Centennial Hymn.[50] (See pp. 45-46.)

> Augustus, your reign
> has brought rich harvests and fertile fields, and
> free from warfare preserves
> the Arcade of Janus closed, and by the bridle

---

46. P. A. Brunt, *Italian Manpower, 225 B.C.–A.D. 14* (Oxford: Oxford University Press, 1971), pp. 113ff. on the census.

47. See also Dionysius of Halicarnassus, *Roman Antiquities,* II.24-26.1, for an extended discussion on the traditional philosophical argument that the state depended on households and, of course, the children produced from marriages.

48. Dio Cassius, 54.16.1-2.

49. Treggiari, *Roman Marriage: Iusti Coniuges from the Time of Cicero to the Time of Ulpian,* p. 195.

50. Juvenal, *Satires* VII, *ll.* 266-67.

> drags back rank-breaking runaway licence
> to propriety, and cancels guilt.[51]

On its effects he commented —

> [N]o lewdness pollutes the chaste home;
> custom and law cast out spotted sin; mothers
> are praised for their children's family likeness;
> punishment presses close behind guilt.[52]

Elsewhere he addressed Augustus as one who carried 'many weighty affairs on your shoulders, strengthening Rome's defences, promoting decent behaviour, reforming our laws'.[53]

It is clear that unlike the majority of extant responses to the legislation, Horace not only acknowledges its reality but, even allowing for political pressure and poetic licence, reports with approval on its intention. (See p. 45 for his Centennial Hymn.) While there are discrepancies in the moral tone of Horace's public poems (with their praise of marital faithfulness) and his erotic ones, Raditsa feels that there is justification for the latter. He suggests, 'The erotic poems were acceptable, because they enjoyed the endorsement of a great tradition and did not directly address themselves to the present.'[54]

Legal Inequality

One of the ongoing criticisms of the original legislation was that it struck at the heart of a central pillar of Roman law, i.e., it created categories before the law and not equality before the law (aequa lex). Some objected to a law which prevented marriage between patricians and plebeians. Cicero (106-43 B.C.) recorded the resentment of any prohibitions that precluded them marrying those who were Roman citizens.[55]

As late as Tacitus, concern continued to be expressed about this breach of equality before the law, and the wedge he saw Augustus inserted in this legis-

---

51. Horace, *Odes*, IV.15, *ll.* 3, 9-12. The Arcade of Janus had two entrances which were kept open during wars and closed during a time of peace.

52. Horace, *Odes*, IV.5, *ll.* 21-24.

53. Suetonius, *Life of Horace*.

54. Raditsa, "Augustus' Legislation concerning Marriage, Procreation, Love Affairs and Adultery," p. 317.

55. Cicero, *de Republica*, 2, 37, 63.

lation between law and justice.[56] From the perspective of Roman jurisprudence 'these laws represented a considerable breach of that principle [of equality] and thereby testify to the fragmentation of society . . . equality before the law distinguished a body politic from a collection of persons (*multitudo*). If the Emperor was outside and above the law, others were being placed outside and below it'.[57]

Julia and lex Julia

However, the emperor's daughter, Julia, was not beyond the reach of this law.[58] She was tried at his instigation for her blatant, promiscuous adultery in 2 B.C. Sempronius Gracchus was named as the adulterer while Julia was married to Agrippa; they continued this relationship after she married Tiberius. She was prosecuted in a series of trials citing not only Gracchus but also other men. Antonius was sentenced to death but allowed to commit suicide while others, including Gracchus and a number of senators and knights, were banished from Rome.

Seneca reported that '[Augustus'] failing years were alarmed by his daughter and the noble youths who were bound to her by adultery as if by a military oath'.[59] He complained that 'she received lovers in droves . . . roamed the city in nocturnal revels. . . . Turning from adultery to prostitution . . . [she sought] gratification of every kind in the arms of casual lovers'.[60]

It was Augustus and not her husband, Tiberius, who intervened and made her scandalous behaviour public, punishing her lovers in varying degrees and permanently banishing his daughter from Rome. 'Julia and her friends publicized their activities. They made the forum and even the rostra from which Augustus had asked the people to vote his laws witness their making love. . . . Here and there are hints of something approaching an ideology justifying their promiscuity — as if some hoped the pursuit of licence could lead to freedom.'[61] She and her friends 'had something in common with the Bacchanals, whose *coniuratio* expressed by oaths what Seneca attributes only

56. Tacitus, *Annals*, 3.25-28.

57. Raditsa, "Augustus' Legislation concerning Marriage, Procreation, Love Affairs and Adultery," p. 322.

58. Raditsa, "Augustus' Legislation concerning Marriage, Procreation, Love Affairs and Adultery," pp. 290-94.

59. Seneca, *Brevitate Vitae*, 4.5.

60. Seneca, *De beneficiis*, 6.1-2.

61. Raditsa, "Augustus' Legislation concerning Marriage, Procreation, Love Affairs and Adultery," pp. 293-94. He cites Velleius, 2, 100, *quidquid liberet pro licito vindicans*.

notionally to the *grex Iuliae*. The two movements also shared nocturnal activities and the consumption of wine, those "infallible" proofs that women were up to no good'.[62] Her flagrant defiance of the law could not be allowed to continue. For Augustus she sadly epitomised the kind of new Roman woman with her flamboyant conduct, her circle of friends, and her blatant promiscuity against which he had legislated.

Her indiscreet behaviour in public could not have come at a more inopportune time for Augustus. As early as 29-27 B.C. he was seeking the title of 'father of his country' *(pater patriae)* which would be his last constitutional acquisition. 'It was seen as a transfer of the state into the power of Augustus, as if into the power of the head of a family.'[63] The nexus of a comparable title with promiscuity is reflected in Horace who wrote this ode in 28 B.C.

> If he [Augustus] aspire to be styled
> on monuments Father of Cities *(pater urbium)*,
> Oh, let him dare to bridle unbroken licence.[64]

It had taken a quarter of a century before the title of 'father of his country' was conferred on him in 2 B.C., and this prize, with the political power it conferred, occurred just before the trials of Julia.[65] The 'head' of 'The Family' had to act in the face of his daughter's flagrant flouting of his legislation.

III. The Subsequent Response of Augustus

Dio Cassius reports in a fulsome way the two addresses given by Augustus in response to the Equestrians' request for the repeal of what he cited as 'the law regarding the unmarried and the childless'. These were delivered in the Forum at the time of the triumphal games given by the consuls and provide evidence of his concerns about both Roman marriage and promiscuity.

Augustus, speaking first to the married men and beginning his address with the divine order of marriage, is somewhat effusive in his praise of them.

> Therefore, men, — for you alone may properly be called men, — and fathers, — for you are worthy to hold this title as I myself — I love you and praise you for this. . . .

62. Bauman, *Women and Politics in Ancient Rome*, p. 116.
63. Bauman, *Women and Politics in Ancient Rome*, p. 116.
64. Horace, *Odes*, III.24.27-29.
65. Dio Cassius, 55.10.10, 14.

He was unashamed that he had provided them with incentives as husbands and fathers.

> I not only bestow the prizes I have already offered but will distinguish you still further by other honours and offices, so that you may not only reap great benefits yourselves but may also leave them to your children undiminished.[66]

The promise of even further material and immaterial benefits suggests he was keen to secure their continuing support for his legislation and, as always, there were advantages for the State in terms of future generations of Roman citizens. Interestingly, he epitomised the estate of marriage in terms of having no better relationship than where 'a wife is of chaste conduct (σώφρων), domestic, mistress of the house, its good stewardess, a rearer of children; one . . . to restrain the mad passion of youth'.[67]

In a second address in another part of the forum he spoke to a much larger assembly of bachelors. He 'indicted' them on a number of accounts, explaining each 'charge' — committing murder, for not begetting descendants; sacrilege, in putting an end to the family names of their ancestors; impiety, in destroying the greatest gift of the gods, i.e., human life; destroying the State by defying its laws and finally betraying the country by 'rendering her barren and childless'.[68]

He warned them —

> I, now, have increased the penalties for the disobedient, in order that through fear of becoming liable to them you might be brought to your senses; and to the obedient I have offered more numerous and greater prizes than are given for any other display of excellence, in order that for this reason, if for no other, you might be persuaded to marry and have children.[69]

Augustus could not understand why they had not been moved by his incentives or driven by fear of the penalties.[70]

In citing their epitomising of the unmarried state in terms of being 'free and untrammelled' he unmasked what they really wanted as 'full liberty of wantonness and licentiousness'.[71] He cited the concessions of betrothal to

66. Dio Cassius, 56.3.6, 3.8.
67. Dio Cassius, 56.2.5, 3.3.
68. Dio Cassius, 56.5.2-3.
69. Dio Cassius, 56.6.5.
70. Dio Cassius, 56.6.6.
71. Dio Cassius, 56.6.6, 7.1.

very young girls as a means of deferring marriage until they were of age; these men should instead be classified as 'prospective bridegrooms' so that those who sought love and intimacy might secure this through lawful means, i.e., marriage. He commended his flexibility in not forcing them into marrying immediately and gave them three years leeway, later reducing it to two in order to accommodate them. Those not of senatorial rank were permitted to marry freedwomen. Yet this did not persuade the bachelors whom he addressed to marry.[72]

The freeing of slaves of Roman households and bestowing citizenship on them was another move calculated to increase the number of Roman citizens. Yet those born free had simply wanted to copulate and not populate Rome, to put it succinctly.[73] Dio concludes, 'Such were his words to the two groups at that time', and informs the reader that Augustus subsequently increased the rewards to those who had children and introduced a distinction between unmarried men and married men without children by imposing different penalties. He also gave a year's amnesty before bringing these penalties into force so that they could marry and those without children had time to qualify for the rewards. He also lifted the ceiling on the value of property which women could inherit to above 100,000 sesterces and granted the Vestal Virgins all the privileges enjoyed by women who had children. We know that the speech occurred before the *Lex Papia Poppaea* came into force because Dio specifically mentions that fact.[74]

IV. Amendments to the Legislation in A.D. 9

While the exact differences between the *lex Julia* and *lex Papia* are no longer clear given that the provisions were amalgamated in the Justinianic code, there are clues which help discern the thrust of the changes. Under the *lex Julia* no time limit had been specified for the period of engagement and, as a result, bachelors became engaged to very young children so as to prolong their freedom from marriage. The Papian law limited the period to two years, and forbade betrothal with girls under the age of ten, with the age of twelve being the time when they could marry.[75]

Rewards were used as a encouragement to freedman to produce children.

---

72. Dio Cassius, 56.7.2-4.
73. Dio Cassius, 56.7.6-8.1.
74. Dio Cassius, 56.10.1-3.
75. Suetonius, *Augustus*, 34; Dio Cassius, 54.16.7, indicates the limit was two years.

If he had three *liberi* (free-born children) he could exclude his patron from any claim on his estate. If he had only two, then the patron was entitled to one third of the estate, and one half if there was only one child. The law also 'extended the right of the female descendants of a patron . . . [if] the patron's daughter had three children. If a free-born patroness had three children she enjoyed the same privileges as a man, although this did not apply to a freed patroness'.[76]

The inheritance provisions were not abolished in the amended legislation of A.D. 9; the *lex Papia Poppaea* only modified the proportions of the inheritance for those without children. Nothing changed with respect to the issue of adultery and the legal responsibility on the part of the husband to act, or bear the possible consequences.

Augustus failed to assuage the public dissatisfaction and felt such pressure that he capitulated to some demands of the *lex Papia Poppaea*.[77] So committed was he to his beliefs on marriage that he himself would not bring forward amendments to the legislation but left it to two consuls to do so, neither of whom, ironically, was married. The concern for our investigation is both with what changed and what did not. The latter is critical, as was the unspoken acknowledgement on the part of Augustus. Political realist that he was, he had to yield in part to the pressure of the Equestrians.

The critical issues on which he would not negotiate are central to the concerns of this book. Tacitus illustrates the case in A.D. 19 of the Senate *v.* Vistilia, a married woman of a praetorian family.

> In the same year the Senate passed stringent decrees to repress women's immorality and prohibited prostitution for granddaughters, daughters, and wives of Roman Equestrians. For [Vistilia] . . . had made public, before the *aediles,* her practice of prostitution. This was done in keeping with a venerable custom of our ancestors by which it is considered sufficient punishment for unchaste women to admit their shame publicly. The senate also wanted to know why her husband [Titidius Labeo], had not carried out the punishment provided by law [the *lex* for his patently guilty wife]. But he explained that the sixty days allowed for him to make up his mind what to do had not yet elapsed, so the senate passed judgement only on Vistilia, who was relegated to the island of Seriphos.[78]

---

76. Treggiari, *Roman Marriage: Iusti Coniuges from the Time of Cicero to the Time of Ulpian,* pp. 74-75.

77. Raditsa, "Augustus' Legislation concerning Marriage, Procreation, Love Affairs and Adultery," p. 318.

78. Tacitus, *Annals,* 2.85.1.

Vistilia invoked an ancient tradition, wrongly anticipating that a public confession would result in no further penalties, for prostitutes operated with immunity in the legislation.[79] Her husband sheltered under the sixty-day rule
when faced with being found guilty for not instituting proceedings against
his delinquent wife.

It is clear that some high-class married women continued to operate like
prostitutes *(hetairai)*. In the time of Tiberius some of them registered themselves officially as prostitutes because the laws of Augustus covering adultery
did not apply to that class of society. This meant that this offence would no
longer be punishable by exile.[80] After the death of Augustus his laws did not
lapse, in spite of their unpopularity in certain quarters.

V. Conclusions

In the previous chapter we noted, among others, poets who actively endorsed,
justified and promoted the new set of rules on marriage infidelity for Roman
women. One consequence was that it encouraged new sexual mores for young
men of the Equestrian order and others who were the recipients of the sexual
favours of some of the 'new' wives. It was against these 'new' ground rules for
both female and male that Augustus legislated. The official image of the imperial wife portrayed in stone was that of the Roman matron discreetly
dressed in her fulsome *stola* and deliberately promoted by Augustus and his
successors. It was replicated in statue types of distinguished women throughout the Empire and, it is suggested, this was done in part to counter the new
Roman women operating with different dress codes endorsed by their 'new
rules'.

Krause had argued that the social status some women enjoyed and the
sexual freedom in which they indulged (as well as their economic power)
were compromised because they were not 'emancipated'.[81] McGinn responded to his conclusion: 'Was there a measurable improvement in the status of Roman women in the classical period, particularly in the last century
B.C. and the first two centuries A.D., and, if so, is this change best described as
an "emancipation"?'[82] He argued that while they did not secure this in the

79. McGinn, *Prostitution, Sexuality, and the Law*, p. 197.

80. Suetonius, *Tiberius*, 35; Tacitus, *Annals*, 2.85.

81. J.-U. Krause, *Witwen und Waisen im Römischen Reich I: Verwitwung und Wiederverheiratung*, HABES 16 (Stuttgart: F. Steiner, 1994), 137.

82. T. A. J. McGinn, "Widows, Orphans, and Social History," *Journal of Roman Archaeology*
12 (1999): 620.

twentieth-century understanding of women's emancipation, a negative answer would draw a wrong implication — that no changes occurred and that all remained enslaved in traditional roles. The ethics and activities of the 'new' Roman women (when compared with those of their Republican sisters) were different, especially given the measure of financial and social freedom they had gained.

What drove Augustus to legislate thus? Ancient historians have sought to provide answers. 'Augustus was trying to legislate shame into the upper class . . . [his] political stance and legislation intensified this concern for visible respectability. . . . Augustus' emphasis on élite male rank and on the regulation of sexual liaisons [was intended] to protect and mark a special senatorial status.'[83] He was an adept promoter of traditional Roman values, and his legislative answer was, in part, a response to the perceived threat to Rome's class system and its continuance with what he saw as the promiscuousness of wives. To us it may seem hypocritical that some seven years later, Augustus took Terentia, his mistress who was the wife of Maecenas, and left Rome. This led Dio Cassius to complain that he punished some, spared others, and broke the laws himself. Augustus was neither the first nor the last shrewd politician who operated with a dichotomy of public and private morality.[84]

Treggiari has asked, 'What difference did the Augustan legislation make? It may have persuaded upper-class men to marry earlier than they might otherwise have done. The incentives for the more prosperous freedmen should have had some impact. Women in both classes were given new reasons to want to be wives and prolific mothers. . . . What many Romans had henceforth to bear in mind was the effect of the law on disposal of property'.[85]

McGinn has concluded that 'The *lex Iulia et Papia* established a hierarchy of marriages based in turn on received notions — among the élite, at least — of the relationship between social position and moral worth. Like other rules the Romans developed in the field of sexuality and marriage, it sought to articulate a social order in terms of rank and gender and, at the same time, to assure the reproduction of this order over time. It helped ensure that Augustus' recasting of the social order (in large part of restating it) would not be

---

83. S. Treggiari, *Roman Marriage: Iusti Coniuges from the Time of Cicero to the Time of Ulpian*, pp. 195-97.

84. Dio Cassius, 54.19.2-3. On Augustus' private behaviour both as a youth and subsequently, Suetonius, *Augustus*, 69 had much to recount, although official presentations gave a very different picture. F. Jacoby, *Die Fragmente der griechischen Historiker* (Berlin: Weidmannsche Buchhandlung, 1926), II. 90.

85. S. Treggiari, *Roman Marriage: Iusti Coniuges from the Time of Cicero to the Time of Ulpian*, p. 80.

temporary in its effects but would, so to speak, be reproduced again and again in future, through the transmission of property and status to the next — deserving — generation'.[86] He has also argued that 'Concern with promoting marriage and the raising of children formed only part of Augustus' purpose — a crucial aim was to discourage the wrong kind of people from pursuing a path of social mobility . . . the law attempted to determine who was not to rise through marriage or testamentary windfall. The idea was to reconcile, through the instrument of law, actual social status with perceptions of what was appropriate. Law would now, more than ever before, define both status and mechanisms for advancement in society'.[87]

Phyllis Culham in her essay, "Did Roman Women Have an Empire?" has observed that the actual results of the legislation were more extensive and not necessarily all that were intended. 'Augustus' attempt to enforce public morality among the aristocratic élite, had the paradoxical effect of shoring up women's status: it caused them a flow-through of the public status enjoyed by their husbands.' This, Culham has argued, increased both their status and their personal freedom.[88] The following chapters will verify her observation.

However complex Augustus' motives were, no reconstruction can ignore the evidence which points to his desire to restrain through legal means the conduct of the new Roman wives and secure their commitment to chastity in marriage. It is only in response to changes in mores that the scope of parts of the legal reforms of Augustus in this area is explicable.

86. T. A. J. McGinn, "The Augustan Marriage Legislation and Social Practice: Elite Endogamy versus Male 'Marrying Down'," in J.-J. Aubert and B. Sirks, eds., Speculum Iuris: *Roman Law as a Reflection of Social and Economic Life in Antiquity* (Ann Arbor: University of Michigan Press, 2002), p. 83.

87. McGinn, "The Augustan Marriage Legislation and Social Practice: Elite Endogmy versus Male 'Marrying Down'," pp. 83-84.

88. Culham, "Did Roman Women Have an Empire?" Culham rightly does not use the term 'emancipation'. The citation summarizing Culham is found in the introduction to Part II ("Constructing the Past: The Practice of Periodization") in Golden and Tooley, eds., *Inventing Ancient Culture*, p. 95.

CHAPTER 4

New Wives and Philosophical Responses

There are significant philosophical sources that deal with issues relating to the 'new' women and provide an important comparison with the more succinctly expressed instructions to women in the Pauline communities. This is also true of the moral conduct of single and married men, striking the same balance in terms of equal ethical demands on men as well as married women required in the Christian communities. These philosophical discussions are invaluable as they show similar problems were created from the same source, the 'new' wives confronting their traditions, and complement the information derived from the Roman legal sources.

The purpose of this chapter is to examine the responses of the philosophical schools of the Stoics and the Neo-Pythagoreans. It discusses (I) the cardinal virtues and the mores of 'new' Roman wives that confronted married women like Seneca's mother; (II) the reasons why women studied philosophy; (III) the problem created by headstrong and arrogant wives who had used their education in an inappropriate way; (IV) the importance of educating daughters; and (V) the demand for sexual abstinence by young men with other women, including other men's wives, and for sexual fidelity by married men. The final section examines the instructions of older women to younger women in the Neo-Pythagorean school.[1]

To do this, the major portion of this chapter will focus on what Musonius Rufus (*c.* 30-100/101 A.D.), a Stoic philosopher teaching in the Flavian period, had to say on these issues. The teaching of the Pythagorean philosophical schools comes by way of letters from Melissa, an older woman, to Clearete, a

---

1. As many of the primary sources on the Stoics and Pythagoreans are not readily accessible, relevant sections have been cited at length.

young married woman, on being a wife and mother and manager of her household, and another from Theano to Euboule about raising children. These contrast with the values being promoted in the Julio-Claudian era by *avant-garde* women and those assumed to be the inalienable rights of men.

I. Cardinal Virtues and New Roman Wives

Unlike the great majority of women you never succumbed to immorality, the worst evil of our time; jewels and pearls have not moved you; you never thought of wealth as the greatest gift to the human race; you have not been perverted by the imitation of worse women who lead even the virtuous into pitfalls; you have never blushed for the number of children, as if it taunted you with your years; never have you, in the manner of other women whose only recommendation lies in their beauty, tried to conceal your pregnancy as though it were indecent; you have not crushed the hope of children that were being nurtured in your body; you have not defiled your face with paints and cosmetics; never have you fancied the kind of dress that exposed no greater nakedness by being removed. Your only ornament, the kind of beauty that time does not tarnish, is the great honour of modesty.[2]

So wrote Lucius Annaeus Seneca, the brother of Gallio and the governor of Achaia, to his mother in order to console her during his exile from Rome (A.D. 41-49) by the emperor, Claudius. Seneca the Younger (4 B.C.–A.D. 65), a Stoic, became a leading statesman during the Principate of Nero.

The importance of his letter for our purposes lies in the comments about his mother's modesty which starkly contrasted with that of other wives of her day. He describes the alternative lifestyle of the Julio-Claudian married women as lavish with jewellery and pearls and the over-use of cosmetics, vainly putting great store on physical beauty, immoral dressing immodestly after the fashion of the 'new' Roman woman, using contraceptives to avoid pregnancy (and, if not successful, aborting the child), pursuing wealth, and pressuring others to embrace the trendy way of life. He contrasts this with those who are the mothers of many children, dressing as befits the role of the married woman, and adorned with the greatest cardinal virtue of a wife, i.e., 'modesty' (*prudentia*, σωφροσύνη), which he sees as 'the lasting beauty of a woman'.[3] In Corinth, the sculptor of the statue of Regilla, the wife of the fa-

---

2. Seneca, *ad Helviam*, 16:3-4.

3. H. North, *Sophrosyne: Self-Knowledge and Self-Restraint in Greek Literature*, Cornell

mous orator Herodes Atticus, is said to have captured this same virtue epitomising the modest wife.[4] Although Seneca laments his mother receiving only a smattering of instruction in philosophy, he warmly commends her for she adhered to traditional values in the face of the new, alternative ones.[5] As a leading Stoic philosopher of the period, it was the teachings of that school which he had in mind in lamenting his mother's lack of formal instruction in its tenets.

Behind Seneca's ethical evaluations of his mother lay strong Stoic virtues. He wrote elsewhere that philosophy meant 'the study of virtue', that 'virtue was the object sought and philosophy the seeker', and that 'the two cannot be sundered'. He went on to argue —

> Philosophy cannot exist without virtue, or virtue without philosophy. Philosophy is the study of virtue, by means however of virtue itself; but neither can virtue exist without the study of itself, nor can the study of virtue exist without virtue itself.

For him 'philosophy and virtue cling close together'.[6]

What were these cardinal virtues which were to be embraced by young men and women, and what were the vices that conflicted with their beliefs and were to be avoided at all costs? The traditional virtues and opposing vices were

Virtue (ἀρετή)	Vice (κακία)
prudence (φρόνησις)[7]	folly (ἀφροσύνη)
self-control (σωφροσύνη)	intemperance (ἀκολασία)
courage (ἀνδρεία)	cowardice (δειλία)
righteousness (δικαιοσύνη)	injustice (ἀδικία)[8]

Studies in Classical Philology, 35 (Ithaca, N.Y.: Cornell University Press, 1966), p. 388, s.v. 'Feminine *arete*'.

4. For discussion of this Corinthian inscription, see pp. 35-36.

5. Seneca, *Ad Helviam*, 17:4. On the private instruction in philosophy of élite women, see E. A. Hemelrijk, Matrona Docta: *Educated Women in the Rome Elite from Cornelia to Julia Domna* (London: Routledge, 1999), pp. 37-41.

6. Seneca, *Moral Epistles*, 89.8.

7. It was Plato who used φρόνησις and σοφία interchangeably in a list of cardinal virtues in *The Republic*, 433b-d, and in *Phaedo* 69a-b he lists the former rather than the latter.

8. See Musonius IV. l. 15 for the traditional order. For the ordering and a discussion of these virtues see H. F. North, "Canons and Hierarchies of the Cardinal Virtues in Greek and Latin Literature," in L. Wallach, ed., *The Classical Tradition: Literary and Historical Studies in Honor of Harry Caplan* (New York: Cornell University Press, 1966), pp. 166-68.

Our particular interest is in the role of these civic virtues and vices in the discussion of the lifestyle of married women. They were also a challenge to the moral and social conduct of younger men who had received the *toga virilis,* some of whom constituted the illicit clientele of married women, and married men as well.

Yet it was the sophists among others who were their adversaries. They were accused of providing a philosophical basis for their lifestyle rooted in first-century Platonism where the body was no longer the prison house, but simply the house of the soul. The sophists of the day amalgamated this anthropology with the idea that the senses were the guardians and courtiers of the soul which nature meant to be indulged.[9] As the leading educators of the day the sophists did teach the cardinal civic virtues but argued for and promoted another lifestyle in terms of personal conduct.

Musonius Rufus discussed in detail how both men and women might live good lives according to his school's traditions. He had little time for the type of education being provided by the sophists to whom the young men flocked. This was contrary to previous eras where philosophers had dominated in the final level of education. It explains why he commenced his corpus with the treatise "That there is no need of giving many proofs for one problem."[10] After that, he explored the next proposition, "That man is born with an inclination toward virtue." This prepared the way for the important treatise that followed, "Should women study philosophy?" There he affirmed the need of both genders to pursue the cardinal virtues taught by the philosophers. He argued that daughters should be exposed to the same education as young sons because, like other Stoics, he believed in the equality of men and women. It was how that 'common' virtue was expressed in practical life that was important and particularly so for our inquiry in this chapter which primarily concerns women.[11]

9. Philo, *Det.* 34, and my discussion in *Philo and Paul among the Sophists: Alexandrian and Corinthian Responses to a Julio-Claudian Movement,* 2nd ed. (Grand Rapids: Eerdmans, 2002), pp. 102-5.

10. The text and translation of Musonius Rufus are those of Cora E. Lutz, "Musonius Rufus, 'The Roman Socrates,'" *Yale Classical Studies* 10 (1947): 3-147; and E. A. Judge, "A Woman's Behaviour," *New Documents Illustrating Early Christianity* 6 (1992): 20-21, both adapted.

11. C. E. Manning, "Seneca and Stoics on the Equality of the Sexes," *Mnemosyne* Ser. 4, 26 (1973): 170-77. That virtue is the same for men and women was held by Cleanthes (331-231 B.C.) and Diogenes Laertius 7.175. See also Seneca, *Ad Marciam,* 16.1, who believed that women were equal to men in their capacity for virtue.

II. Women Studying Philosophy

While Musonius indicated that the different abilities and roles of males and females must be recognised, his primary interest in this last treatise was how the study of Stoic philosophy influenced the lifestyle of wives. In his defence of women studying philosophy he related classical virtues to the patterns of their lives.

> Let us examine in detail each of the qualities that belong to a good wife, for it will become apparent that each of these qualities results from the practice of philosophy. For example it is necessary for a wife to be a good manager of a household, and capable of anticipating its needs (literally 'welfare') and able to direct the household slaves. In these activities I claim that philosophy is particularly helpful, since each of these activities is an aspect of life, and philosophy is nothing other than the science of living, and the philosopher, as Socrates says, continually contemplates this, 'what good or evil has been done in his house'.[12]

He then proceeded to explore how the traditional cardinal virtues of 'self-control' (σωφροσύνη), 'justice' (δίκη), and 'courage' (ἀνδρεία), affected the science of living for women.

Self-Control

But it is also necessary (ἀλλὰ δεῖ δὴ καί) for a woman to be self-controlled (σώφρονα). On the one hand she is free from lecherous recklessness (οἵαν καθαρεύειν μὲν ἀφροδισίων παρανόμων),[13] and on the other free concerning other pleasures (καθαρεύειν δὲ τῆς περὶ τὰς ἄλλας ἡδονὰς ἀκρασίας), not a slave of desire (μὴ δουλεύειν ἐπιθυμίαις), not contentious (μηδὲ φιλόνεικον εἶναι), not lavish in expense (μὴ πολυτελῆ), nor extravagant in dress (μὴ καλλωπίστριαν). These are the works of the self-controlled woman and to them[14] I would add these: to control her temper, not to be overcome by grief, and to be superior to uncontrolled emotion of every kind.[15] Now the philosopher transmits the instruction of these things.[16]

---

12. Lutz, p. 40, *ll.* 8-16.

13. Here the antecedent of οἵαν implies a class.

14. Lutz, p. 40, *ll.* 17-20. The plural neuter demonstrative pronoun 'these' (ταῦτα) refers to the immediately preceding section and all the works that are stated in the negative.

15. For the Stoic's teaching on good emotions see F. H. Sandbach, *The Stoics* (London: Chatto and Windus, 1975), pp. 67-68.

16. Lutz, p. 40, *ll.* 21-23.

According to Pomeroy, 'The term means "temperance" but also connotes chastity and self-restraint. It was the pre-eminent virtue of Greek women; it is mentioned more frequently than any other quality on women's tomb-stones.'[17] This was no less true in Roman society in the period with which we are dealing. The person, either male or female, who learns and practices these things becomes a well-ordered and seemly person. 'What then? So much for the one who has these things (ταῦτα)', i.e., the virtues, and avoids the cardinal vice of intemperance (ἀκολασία) — Musonius did not discuss this until the very end of the discourse.[18]

Justice

Musonius' explication of justice explores somewhat unexpected territory. 'As for justice (δίκη), would not a woman who studies philosophy be just?' He then raises further questions that relate to justice with respect to the conduct of a wife and mother.

> Would she not be a blameless life-partner, would she not be a sympathetic helpmate, would she not be an untiring defender of her children, and would she not be entirely free of greed and arrogance?[19]

He ends the discussion in a similar way to that of the first virtue, com-mending the role of philosophy in creating a disposition where the woman would 'look upon doing wrong as worse than suffering' and being 'defeated as much better than gaining an unjust advantage'. He concludes with the ques-tion, 'What woman would be more just than such a one?'[20]

Courage

An educated woman, i.e., in philosophy, will certainly be more courageous (ἀνδρειότεραν) than one not exposed to such teaching. She will be resolute in the face of submitting to anything shameful, and 'not be intimidated by anyone because he is of noble birth, or powerful or wealthy, no, not even if

---

17. S. B. Pomeroy, *Women in Hellenistic Egypt: From Alexander to Cleopatra* (Detroit: Wayne State University Press, 1990), p. 70.

18. Lutz, p. 42, *ll.* 5-8.

19. Lutz, p. 42, *ll.* 25-28.

20. Lutz, p. 42, *ll.* 28-32.

he be the tyrant of her city'. Musonius argues that, because she is high-minded, she will not shun hardship and 'never for a moment seek ease and indolence'.[21]

In the light of the teaching on this civic virtue he again draws implications for the sphere of the home. 'Such a woman is likely to be energetic, strong to endure pain, prepared to nourish her children at her own breast, and serve her husband with her own hands, and willing to do things that some would consider no better than slaves' work.' He concludes with the rhetorical question, 'Would not such a woman be a great help to the man who married her, an ornament to her relatives, and a good example for all who know her?'[22]

III. 'Headstrong and Arrogant' Women

The remainder of the treatise anticipates objections to the effect that philosophy might have on women educated in it. 'But, by Zeus, some people say that women who associate with philosophers are inevitably mainly headstrong (αὐθάδεις) and arrogant (θρασείας).' The detractors had argued that this happens 'if they give up their households and go about with men'.[23]

For a married woman to abandon, in effect, her household suggests impropriety in normal circumstances. Whether it is the case in this context is uncertain as the verb (ἀναστρέφω) implies more of a turning back to life as an unmarried woman. The following statement introduced by 'and' (καί) may well function epexegetically, for the critics indicate what these women are doing. They 'take an interest in orations' (μελετῶσι λόγους) and 'argue' (σοφίζωνται) and 'attack premises' (ἀναλύωσι συλλογισμούς) when 'they ought to be sitting at home spinning wool' according to the opponents of women's education in philosophy. This passage suggests that the philosophers were being blamed for the activities of the sophists of the first century.[24]

Valerius Maximus, who wrote his *Memorable Doings and Sayings* in the time of Tiberius (A.D. 14-37), recorded instances where educated women pleaded their causes before magistrates bringing various responses. Maesia of Sentinum presented her case 'going through all the forms and stages of a defence not only thoroughly but boldly'. There were also other wives who

---

21. Lutz, p. 42, *ll.* 33-35, 1-9.
22. Lutz, p. 42, *ll.* 5-8.
23. Lutz, p. 42, *ll.* 11-14.
24. Lutz, p. 42, *ll.* 14-15, and my *Philo and Paul among the Sophists*, pp. 81-87.

pleaded causes as effectively as men before a magistrate.[25] It is suggested that the reference in Musonius Rufus is to the wife who exposes herself to the results of an education at the hands of the sophists, which would have equipped her for *politeia*, for which training in oratory would have been an essential requirement.[26]

Musonius responded by arguing that if we look carefully at the contents and intentions of the philosophy that women ought to study, we will see that they were actually taught to avoid vices and embrace corresponding virtues that would benefit their home and families. Such philosophical instruction will have missed the mark for these women in four areas —

> if the study that shows the respect of the greatest good (μέγιστον ἀγαθόν) makes them bold (θρασεῖα), if the study that leads to the deportment makes them live more carelessly (ζῆν ἰταμώτερον), if the study that reveals that the worst evil is self-indulgence (ἀκολασία) does not teach self-control (σωφροσύνη), if the study that establishes household management as a virtue (ἀρετή) does not encourage them to manage their households.[27]

'The instruction of the philosophers encourages women to be content [or show affection] and to work with their own hands' are Musonius' final words as he concludes not only his *apologia* in the face of objections to women learning philosophy, but also this particular treatise.[28]

IV. Educating Daughters

The treatise that follows is not about married women receiving philosophical or secular 'education' (παιδεία) but the importance of educating daughters in the same way that sons were educated. What attracts our attention is that, in this treatise, Musonius Rufus referred to, and explicated, all the cardinal virtues and corresponding vices. Again his fundamental theses are that both men and women need this instruction and that there is a common set of virtues appropriate for both sexes.

---

25. *Memorable Doings and Sayings*, 8.3.1-3. For further discussion of this and further evidence see pp. 175-79. Unlike Musonius Rufus others had highly prejudicial and derogatory responses to the success of women in forensic oratory; see Hemelrijk, Matrona Docta: *Educated Women in the Rome Elite*, pp. 89-96.

26. See pp. 205-11 for epigraphic evidence of their public roles.

27. Lutz, p. 42, *ll.* 24-28.

28. Lutz, p. 42, *ll.* 28-29.

Both must (a) operate with 'understanding' (φρόνησις) — otherwise men and women act in a 'foolish' way (ἀφροσύνη); (b) exercise 'justice' (δικαιοσύνη) — otherwise the man cannot be a good citizen and the woman cannot manage her own household well (presumably the servants and others) and as a result they will be 'unjust' (ἀδικία). The same is also true of 'chastity' or 'self-control' (σωφροσύνη). Chastity applies to both, for she must be chaste in wedlock 'and so it is likewise for the man'. Musonius indicates that in the law, i.e., Roman law, there is no difference in terms of punishment 'for committing adultery as for being taken in adultery'.[29]

On the virtue of self-control he asserts —

Gluttony, drunkenness, and other related vices, which are vices of excess and bring disgrace upon those guilty of them, show that self-control is most necessary for every human being, male and female alike; for the only way to escape 'wantonness' (ἀκολασία) is through 'self-control' (σωφροσύνη); there is no other.[30]

He dismisses the idea that 'courage' (ἀνδρεία) is needed only for men, having argued in the previous treatise its importance for women so that they are not guilty of 'cowardice' (δειλία). These last two paragraphs cite all the cardinal virtues and their corresponding vices.

This section concludes by stating that all these virtues are necessary for both men and women, and hence are appropriate for the instruction of both sons and daughters. 'Shall we not teach them both alike the art by which a human being becomes good?' is answered with 'Yes, we certainly must do that and nothing else.'[31]

The arguments of his detractors have been again anticipated. Here Musonius draws conclusions which support his view of equal access in both education and work. In response to the above discussion he asks, 'Were the Stoic philosophers requiring men to learn spinning and women to undertake gymnastic exercises in the same way young men did at a particular stage of their education?' 'I should not demand that' is the response.[32] On the basis of a man's physical makeup he is better equipped to undertake heavy work, and indoor work is more appropriate for women, but Musonius adds —

occasionally, however, some men might more fittingly handle certain of the lighter tasks and what is generally considered women's work, and again,

29. Lutz, p. 44, *ll.* 9-15.
30. Lutz, p. 44, *ll.* 15-21.
31. Lutz, p. 46, *ll.* 10-13.
32. Lutz, p. 46, *ll.* 13-16.

women might do heavier tasks. . . . For all human tasks, I am inclined to believe, are a common obligation and are common for men and women, and none is necessarily appointed for either exclusively.[33]

There is no suggestion that gender demarcations were totally fixed, and this further supports his interesting view of the importance of education for both sons and daughters in order to equip them to act in their given responsibilities on the basis of the cardinal virtues. How people became good, whether male or female, was one of his fundamental concerns; the answer was found in being taught the cardinal virtues.

V. Single and Married Men and Sexual Indulgence

Another area covered by Musonius was the single men to whom (it was said) some married women gave their sexual favours, a matter that also concerned Augustus. The Stoic counter-cultural teaching *On Sexual Indulgence* for men must have shocked some, for fornication and adultery by men were seen as a given right in first-century society.

A century before, Cicero had poured scorn on the attitude of sexual abstinence by young single men on receiving the *toga virilis*.

> Is there anyone who thinks that youth should be forbidden affairs even with courtesans? He is doubtless eminently austere, but his view is contrary not only to the licence of this age, but also to the custom and concessions of our ancestors. For when was this not a common practice? When was it blamed? When was it forbidden? When, in fact, was it that what is allowed was not allowed?[34]

According to Cato, in Republican times '[a wife], however, cannot dare to lay a finger on you if you commit adultery, nor is it the law'.[35]

New ground is broken, for Musonius condemns fornication by young men as a severe failure in the virtue of self-control. His basic thesis on sexual excess is that it is a significant part of a life of luxury and self-indulgence and therefore unlawful. Sex is for procreation, not 'pleasure-seeking, even in marriage' is his opening, provocative statement. Adultery is unlawful and represents a lack of self-control on the part of married men.

---

33. Lutz, p. 46, *ll.* 23-29.
34. Cicero, *Pro Caelio*, 20.48.
35. Aulus Gellius, *Attic Nights*, 10:23, citing Cato, *On the dowry*. For the full quote see p. 19.

But of all sexual relations those involving adultery are most unlawful, and no more tolerable are those of men with men, because it is a monstrous thing and contrary to nature. But, furthermore, leaving out consideration of adultery, all intercourse with women which is without lawful character is shameful and is practised from 'lack of self-restraint' (ἀκολασία) — the vice whose antithesis is 'self-control'.[36]

He then proceeds to discuss the latter and its implications in terms of sexual partners. 'So no one with any self-control would think of having relations with a courtesan or a free woman apart from marriage, no, not even with his own maid-servant.'[37]

That illicit affairs are secretive shows that they are wrong, according to Musonius.

> The fact that those relationships are not lawful or seemly makes them a disgrace and a reproach to those seeking them; whence it is that no one dares to do any of these things openly, not even if he has all but lost the ability to blush, and those who are not completely degenerate dare to do these things only in hiding and in secret. And yet to attempt to cover up what one is doing is equivalent to a confession of guilt.[38]

As usual he anticipates possible objections.

> "That's all very well," you say, "but unlike the adulterer who wrongs the husband of the woman he corrupts, the man who has relations with a courtesan or a woman who has no husband wrongs no one for he does not destroy anyone's hope of children."[39]

He robustly responds on the basis that —

> everyone who sins and does wrong even if it affects none of the people about him, immediately reveals himself as a worse and less honourable person, for the wrong-doer by the very fact of doing wrong is worse and less honourable. Not to mention the injustice of the thing, there must be sheer wantonness in anyone yielding to the temptation of shameful pleasure and like swine rejoicing in his own vileness.[40]

---

36. Lutz, p. 86, *ll.* 10-12.
37. Lutz, p. 86, *ll.* 12-14.
38. Lutz, p. 86, *ll.* 15-19.
39. Lutz, p. 86, *ll.* 20-24.
40. Lutz, p. 86, *ll.* 24-29.

Musonius specifically denounces one culturally acceptable sexual liaison.

> In this category [of vileness] belongs the man who has relations with his own slave-maid, a thing which some people consider quite without blame, since every master is held to have it in his power to use his slave as he wishes.[41]

His response goes to the heart of the matter concerning equality between the sexes.

> In reply to this I have just one thing to say: if it seems neither shameful nor out of place for a master to have relations with his own slave, particularly if she happens not to be married, let him consider how he would like it if his wife had relations with a male slave. Would it not be completely intolerable not only if the woman who had a lawful husband had relations with a slave, but even if a woman without a husband should have one?[42]

It was not only Musonius who took this stance. Seneca did also and, as Rist has noted, 'As equals they should be given equal moral rights as well as responsibilities. If chastity should be expected of a wife, it should similarly be expected of a husband.'[43]

Musonius further pushes home his thesis by arguing —

> And yet surely one will not expect men to be less moral than women, nor less capable of disciplining their desires, thereby revealing the stronger in judgement inferior to the weaker, the rulers to the ruled. In fact, it behoves men to be much better if they expect to be superior to women, for surely if they appear to be less self-controlled they will also be baser characters. What need is there to say that it is an act of licentiousness and nothing else for a master to have relations with his slave? Everyone knows that.[44]

'Gluttony, drunkenness, and other related vices, which are vices of excess and bring disgrace upon those guilty of them, show that self-control is necessary for every human being, male and female alike, for the only way to escape from wantonness is through self-control.'[45]

41. Lutz, p. 86, *ll.* 29-30.

42. Lutz, p. 86, *ll.* 30-35.

43. J. M. Rist, "Seneca and Stoic Orthodoxy," *ANRW* 36.3 (1989): 2009, citing Seneca's *Ep.* 94.26. He speculates that this stance was probably traditional, and notes, 'Loss of evidence may prevent us from recognizing it as part of the teaching of Zeno and Chrysippus.'

44. Lutz, p. 86, *ll.* 36-40; p. 88, *ll.* 1-6.

45. Lutz, p. 44, *ll.* 18-22.

Musonius was neither the first nor the last person to observe this. Plutarch asked, 'Is there any difference for a man who employs aphrodisiacs to stir and excite licentiousness for the purpose of pleasure, or stimulates his taste by odours and sauces?' He had also commented that 'intemperate intercourse follows a lawless meal'.[46]

All this is important for both men and women, and it is for this reason that Musonius believes that women ought to receive the same education as men which he believes is important for women in respect to virtue. He also believes that husbands and wives 'should consider all their property to be common, and nothing private, not even their bodies'.

The complete picture of Musonius on marriage would not be presented if a segment was not cited from "What is the chief end of marriage?"[47]

But in marriage there must be above all perfect companionship and mutual love of husband and wife, both in health and sickness and under all conditions, since it was the desire for this as well as for having children that both entered upon marriage. Where, then, this love for each other is perfect and the two share it completely, each striving to outdo the other in devotion, the marriage is ideal and worthy of envy, for such a union is beautiful. But where each looks only to his own interests and neglects the other, or, what is worse, when one is so minded and lives in the same house but fixes his attention elsewhere and is not willing to pull together with his yokemate nor to agree, then the union is doomed to disaster, and even though they live together, yet their common interests fare badly; eventually they separate entirely, or they remain together and suffer what is worse than loneliness.[48]

Here, in the words of Shakespeare, 'the marriage of true minds' is described and also a very insightful, and almost timeless diagnosis of marriage breakdowns.

---

46. Plutarch, *Moralia* 126B, 997C. For further quotations and a discussion on gluttony, drunkenness and sexual indulgence by those who had received the *toga virilis* at dinners and what was politely called 'after dinners', see my *After Paul Left Corinth: The Influence of Secular Ethics and Social Change*, pp. 82-83.

47. Lutz, p. 88, *l.* 10.

48. Lutz, p. 88, *ll.* 17-29.

VI. Pythagorean Woman to Woman

The Stoics were not the only ones who discussed these matters. In a letter from the Pythagorean School of philosophy written by a woman, Melissa, to Clearete the issue of the modest wife was also the subject of discussion, while a letter from Theano to Euboule talks about raising children. Susan Pomeroy summarises the concerns of the Neo-Pythagoreans: 'Thus, adhering closely to Pythagorean doctrine, the Neo-Pythagorean treatises by women about women discuss the proper behaviour of women, recommending, for the most part, purity, control of one's appetites, and tolerance of a husband's vices. The authors are notably preoccupied with the temptations of adultery. Excessive use of makeup, fine clothing, and frequent bathing are viewed as preludes to seduction.'[49] While this school has its roots in Greek philosophical tradition, Treggiari has no doubts that it influenced first-century thinking, including that of the Romans.[50] The dating of the sources has long preoccupied ancient historians.[51] There are invaluable letters that preserve teaching concerning the modest wife. These are not the only treatises. As Judge points out, one from that philosophical school is written in Koine Greek and not in the Doric dialect as were more than forty from the Pythagorean corpus.[52] The latter was used by Greeks in the south of Italy in Roman times. Pomeroy has suggested that they were turned into Koine when brought to Alexandria.[53]

> Melissa to Clearete, Greetings.
>
> Of your own volition it appears to me that you have the characteristics of what is good. For you wish zealously to hear [teaching] about a wife's adornment. It gives a good indication that you intend to perfect yourself according to virtue. It is necessary then for the free and modest (ἐλεύθεραν καὶ σώφρονα) wife to live with her lawful husband adorned with quietness, white and clean in her dress, plain but not costly, simple but not elaborate or excessive. For she must reject [see Städele text] garments shot with purple or gold. For these are used by *hetairai* (call-girls) in soliciting men generally, but if she is to be attractive to one man, her own husband, the orna-

---

49. S. Pomeroy, *Women in Hellenistic Egypt: From Alexander to Cleopatra*, pp. 67-68.

50. S. Treggiari, *Roman Marriage: Iusti Coniuges from the Time of Cicero to the Time of Ulpian* (Oxford: Clarendon, 1991), p. 199.

51. Treggiari, *Roman Marriage: Iusti Coniuges*, p. 193.

52. *P.Haun.* II 13 is a third-century A.D. copy of a letter from a much earlier period. For a discussion of dating and the writing of a letter from one woman to another, see Pomeroy, *Women in Hellenistic Egypt: From Alexander to Cleopatra*, pp. 64-67.

53. Pomeroy, *Women in Hellenistic Egypt: From Alexander to Cleopatra*, p. 64.

ment of a wife is her manner and not her dress (στολή, *stola*). And a free and modest wife (ἐλευθέραν καὶ σώφρονα) must appear attractive to her own husband, but not to the man next door, having on her cheeks the blush of modesty (ὄψεως) rather than of rouge and powder, and a good and noble bearing and decency and modesty (καλοκαγαθίαν καὶ κοσμιότητα καὶ σωφροσύνην) rather than gold and emerald. For it is not in expenditure on clothing and looks that the modest woman (σώφρονα) should express her love of the good but in the management and maintenance of her household, and pleasing her own husband, given that he is a moderate man (σωφρονοῦντι), by fulfilling his wishes. For the husband's will ought to be engraved as law on a decent wife's mind and she must live by it. And she must consider that the dowry she has brought with her that is best and greatest of all is her good order and trust in both the beauty and wealth of the soul rather than in money and appearance. As for money and looks, time, hostility, illness and fortune take them away: rather the adornment of soul lasts till death with women who possess it.[54]

In another letter the issue of bringing up children is discussed.

Theano to Euboule, greetings. I hear you are bringing up (τρέφειν) the children indulgently. But a [good . . .] mother's interest is not [concern for the pleasure] of the children but their [training in moderation (τὸ σῶφρον ἀγωγή). Look] out lest you accomplish not the work of a loving mother, but that of a doting one. When pleasure and children are brought up together, it makes the children undisciplined. . . . Take care, my friend — conscious of the fact that children who live licentiously become slaves when they blossom into manhood — to deprive them of such pleasures. Make their nourishment austere rather than sumptuous.[55]

'In keeping with the musical metaphor, *sophrosynē* has been translated as "temperance", but it also connotes chastity and self-restraint. *Sophrosynē* was the pre-eminent virtue of Greek women; it is mentioned more frequently than any other quality on women's tombstones.'[56] A manual of female discretion *(sophrosyne)* attributed to another woman, Phintys, called it the greatest female virtue, since it enabled her to love and honour her husband.[57]

---

54. *P.Haun.* II 13, *ll.* 1-42.

55. For the text see A. J. Malherbe, *Moral Exhortation: A Greco-Roman Sourcebook* (Philadelphia: Westminster Press, 1986), pp. 35-36, with amendments in *ll.* 43-47 by Judge, "A Woman's Behaviour," pp. 20-21.

56. Pomeroy, *Women in Hellenistic Egypt: From Alexander to Cleopatra*, p. 70.

57. Treggiari, *Roman Marriage: Iusti Coniuges*, p. 196, citing Thesleff, *Texts*, 151.

Surely, by controlling her desire and passion, a woman becomes devout and harmonious, resulting in her not becoming a prey to impious love affairs. . . . For all those women who have a desire for extramarital relations [*lit.* "alien beds"] themselves become enemies of all the freedmen and domestics in the house. Such a woman contrives both falsehood and deceits for her husband and tells lies against everyone to him as well, so that she alone seems to excel in good will and in mastery over the household, though she revels in idleness.[58]

. . . a woman will neither cover herself with gold or the stone of India or of any other place, nor will she braid her hair with artful device; nor will she anoint herself with Arabian perfume; nor will she put white makeup on her face or rouge her cheeks or darken her brows and lashes or artfully dye her graying hair; nor will she bathe frequently. For by pursuing these things a woman seeks to make a spectacle of female incontinence. . . . A woman must bear all her husband bears, whether he be . . . drunk or sleep with other women. Rather it brings vengeance upon her. Therefore, a woman must preserve the law and not emulate men.[59]

Like the Stoics, the Neo-Pythagoreans did not restrict *sophrosyne* to women, but considered it especially appropriate for the married man.[60]

VII. Conclusion

The evidence assembled in this chapter on the philosophical schools provides further confirmation of the existence of the 'new' women. These sources are invaluable both in terms of what they reject and the alternative life style they present to men and women from their philosophical traditions. There has been a tendency to overlook the fact that in the early Empire, the Christian movement was not the only one that argued for a view of marriage and sexual morality where men and women operated with faithfulness and integrity against what had become a significant, alternative lifestyle for wives. This brings to a close Part I in which the evidence gives a common first-century *Sitz im Leben* for Roman wives and Roman widows. It is with this information that we now turn to Part II of this book.

58. Perictione, "On the Harmony of a Woman," cited by Pomeroy, *Women in Hellenistic Egypt: From Alexander to Cleopatra*, p. 68.

59. Perictione, "On the Harmony of a Woman," cited by Pomeroy, *Women in Hellenistic Egypt: From Alexander to Cleopatra*, p. 69.

60. Pomeroy, *Women in Hellenistic Egypt: From Alexander to Cleopatra*, p. 70.

PART II

CHAPTER 5

The Appearance of Unveiled Wives in 1 Corinthians 11:2-16

In the last three years significant new material has been published by ancient historians which throws important light on the issue of veiling in 1 Corinthians 11:2-16.[1] It supports the interpretation that the wives praying and prophesying with their heads uncovered in the Christian gathering were replicating the attitude and actions of 'new' wives. As Christians, they defied a traditional imperial and Corinthian norm for wives engaging in what their compatriots would have judged to be a religious activity.

This chapter will explore (I) the significance attached to the veil in marriage in the first century; (II) the symbolic importance attached to its removal in public; (III) the defining in Roman law of modesty and immodesty based on appearance; (IV) the official policing by specially appointed magistrates of the dress codes of those women participating in religious festivals; and

---

1. Since researching 1 Corinthians 11:2-16 in 2000, for my chapter in "Veiled Men and Wives and Christian Contentiousness," in *After Paul Left Corinth: The Influence of Secular Ethics and Social Change* (Grand Rapids: Eerdmans, 2001), ch. 6, three important monographs have been published. They add substantially to our knowledge of Roman dress (including the policing of it) and therefore to my original discussion. These are A. T. Croom, *Roman Clothing and Fashion* (Stroud: Tempus, 2000); L. Llewellyn-Jones, ed., *Women's Dress in the Ancient Greek World* (London and Swansea: Duckworth and University Press of Wales, 2002); and S. B. Pomeroy, *Spartan Women* (Oxford: Oxford University Press, 2002). An important review article by T. A. J. McGinn, "Widows, Orphans and Social History," also appeared in the *Journal of Roman Archaeology* 12 (1999): 617-32, in which he assessed Krause's *Witwen und Waisen im Römischen Reich*, Heidelberger althistorische Beiträge und epigraphischer Studien 16-19 (Stuttgart: F. Steiner, 1994-95), Vols. I-IV. An earlier work, *The World of Roman Costume*, ed. L. Bonfante and J. L. Sebesta (Madison: University of Wisconsin Press, 1994), also adds to the evidence and supplements the interpretation presented in my original chapter.

(V) the appearance of contentiousness on the part of those wives who removed the veil in the Christian community.

I. The Significance of the Veil in Marriage

The veil was the most symbolic feature of the bride's dress in Roman culture. Plutarch indicated that 'veiling the bride' (τὴν νύμφην κατακαλύψαντες) was, in effect, the marriage ceremony. Other writers in the early Empire confirm that the bride's veil was an essential part of her apparel.[2] The Romans evidently thought of her as one who was 'clouded over with a veil', because Felix, writing in the late fourth century A.D., speculated on the nexus of the Latin word for 'cloud' *(nubes)* with the verb 'to be married' *(nubere)*. 'Nuptials are so called because the head of the bride is wrapped around the bridal veil, which the ancients called "to cloud over" or "veil".'[3]

This philological nexus suggested in the fourth century has been recently challenged by La Follette.[4] She herself speculates on the origins of the veil: it 'apparently was a symbol of constancy and lifelong fidelity because of its ritual association with the faithful wife of the priest of Jupiter'.[5] The later tracing of possible philological links in order to uncover the origin of a custom is an inexact endeavour if there is no literary evidence of any discussion at the point at which it is alleged to have begun.

However, the symbolic significance of the veil can be verified from important extant evidence in the early Empire statue types. G. Davies in an essay, "Clothes as Sign: The Case of the Large and Small Herculaneum Women," draws attention to the two distinct statue types prevalent in the first century that were thought to have been borrowed from the early Hellenistic period.[6] In the larger Herculaneum statues depicting the modest married women, the female figure was sculptured wearing the veil thus representing the married woman. She was portrayed clothed in a long dress with a large mantle drawn around her which she used to cover the back of her head

---

2. Plutarch, "Advice to the Bride and Groom," 138D. See also Juvenal, *Satires,* 2.119ff.; 10.333ff.; and Tacitus, *The Annals,* 11.27.1; 15.37.9.

3. Felix, 174.20. Translation is by La Follette, see n. 4.

4. L. La Follette, "The Costume of the Roman Bride," in L. Bonfante and J. L. Sebesta, eds., *The World of Roman Costume,* p. 61, n. 10, where she states that 'recent linguistic work indicates that the roots are probably not the same'.

5. La Follette, "The Costume of the Roman Bride," pp. 55-56.

6. G. Davies, "Clothes as Sign: The Case of the Large and Small Herculaneum Women," in L. Llewellyn-Jones, ed., *Women's Dress in the Ancient Greek World,* p. 227.

to form the marriage veil. Her right arm was drawn across her body to hold her veil in place on her head so that the right breast was hidden from view. Davies observes that these statues were 'heavily draped, not much body showing, [posing] defensive gestures [with the right arm above their breasts], with their modesty often reinforced by a lowered gaze and [in all statues reproduced in this type] veiled.'[7]

The smaller statue type had two important distinguishing features. First, the right arm was bent at the elbow so that the hand touched the mantle at the top of the right shoulder. The left hand was not relaxed, as in the larger statue type, but rested protectively on her thigh and also revealing only the tips of her fingers instead of her whole hand. This represented the younger, unmarried woman who was expected to arrive at her marriage a virgin, hence the slightly more guarded body language compared with that of the married woman.[8] The second feature was the absence of any veil, with the mantle drawn over her shoulder and not her head.[9]

Davies also observes that the long dress falling down to her feet and in the case of the married woman the large mantle drawn over the head epitomised modesty. This was not peculiar to the Herculaneum statue type, but was shared by an earlier type called 'Pudicitia', so named because of the Latin term that conveyed the most important Roman virtue of married women, i.e., modesty.[10] The examples Davies uses in her essay were drawn from the famous Nymphaeum in Olympia given by the noted orator and benefactor of Athens and Corinth, Herodes Atticus. It is specifically stated in the inscription at the base of a statue of his wife in Corinth that the sculptor had captured her modesty. (See pp. 35-36.) Other extant examples have been located in numerous cities in the East of the Empire.

This representation was not restricted to statues in formal settings such as the forum and private homes or gardens. As La Follette observed, wives

7. Davies, "Clothes as Sign: The Case of the Large and Small Herculaneum Women," pp. 228, 237-38.

8. S. Blundell, "Clutching at Clothes," in *Women's Dress in the Ancient Greek World*, ch. 9, suggests that there were a number of reasons for a woman clutching her clothing in the classical Greek period, including disguising her face with a veil when about to engage in sexual intercourse. However, this does not apply in the Roman statue types under discussion.

9. Davies, "Clothes as Sign: The Case of the Large and Small Herculaneum Women," pp. 234-35, draws attention to the portrayal of Greek women where the veil is used in the small Herculaneum statue of a later period and it is removed in a large statue of a later period when the Roman stola was no longer in fashion and Roman society under Hadrian was captured by a revival Hellenism.

10. Davies, "Clothes as Sign: The Case of the Large and Small Herculaneum Women," p. 236.

'depicted on tombstones are most typically in the pose called *pudicitia* (modesty), in which they have the mantle (*palla*, i.e., the veil) up over their heads, holding part of it in front of their faces'.[11] Therefore, it can be confidently concluded that the veiled head was the symbol of the modesty and chastity expected of a married woman.

Some twenty years ago R. MacMullen sought to argue that, because of the influence of the imperial court in the early days of the Latin West, veiling was less common among women of the higher classes in the East. 'Women of humbler class went veiled, but these others behaved exactly like their counterparts observed in Italy, fully visible, indeed making their existence felt very fully in public.'[12] More recently, however, Sebesta refutes this thesis by drawing attention to statues showing an empress veiling her head with a *palla*, the rectangular mantle of a woman. It 'was used to veil her head when she went out in public'.[13] Davies' discussion re-enforces Sebesta's conclusion.

How did the dress of the immodest woman differ from that of the modest wife? Two bronze statues found in a house in Herculaneum are now located in the Museum of Classical Archaeology, University of Cambridge. They portray two dancing girls who wear no veils or mantles; one, in fact, is depicted undoing her dress *(chiton)* so as to expose her shoulder and part of her breast. These were clearly struck to convey the exact opposite of the modest wife.[14] In keeping with the double standards of Roman society, these women were dressed in different and not Roman attire to convey the idea of promiscuity by portraying them as foreign rather than Roman women.[15] The statues were meant to pander to the sexual propensities of their owner and the guests in his household even though the home was meant to convey domestic bliss between the husband, his wife and children.

In his essay "Levels of Concealment: The Dress of the *Hetairai* and *Pornai* in Greek Texts," Dalby also discusses at length the distinguishing features of the immodest woman, whether she is a high-class promiscuous person who 'entertained' at the dinners of the rich, or the prostitute who serviced clients

11. La Follette, "The Costume of the Roman Bride," p. 55.

12. R. MacMullen, "Women in Public in the Roman Empire," *Historia* 29 (1980): 208-18 *cit.* p. 218.

13. J. L. Sebesta, "Symbolism in the Costume of the Roman Woman," in L. Bonfante and J. L. Sebesta, eds., *The World of Roman Costume*, p. 48, and n. 41.

14. See www.romanchristianwomen.com for pictures of these and other statue types.

15. This was not untypical of Roman conventions and was also seen in the use of foreign words to indicate sexual activity of which they did not approve; see J. N. Adams, *The Latin Sexual Vocabulary* (London: Duckworth, 1982), p. 228.

from other classes.[16] He notes that the *hetairai* not only wore more clothes than other women, but also finer ones. If a woman wished to be considered respectable she did not dress ostentatiously. In comparison, a competitor for her husband's attention 'dressed better, more visibly, more expensively, more showily than other women'. He goes on to note, 'In such Greek views dress mattered to *hetairai:* they needed to catch the eye.'[17] The transparent material of which their dresses were made revealed as much as possible.

On the Roman side Seneca *c.* A.D. 41-49 wrote to his mother commending her choice of dress: 'Never have you fancied the kind of dress that exposed no greater nakedness by being removed', and elsewhere complained of young women 'in silk dresses, if dress is the word. Truly nothing shields their bodies, nothing guards their modesty: they are naked.'[18] The other feature that stood out and was linked to the dresses of *hetairai* was gold ornaments (ἱμάτια καὶ κρύσεα).[19] Dalby concludes that *hetairai*, compared with the ordinary prostitutes, did not need to advertise their 'wares' in public because they already had a distinguishing feature. They wore 'transparent veils' that were fastened at the shoulder with a brooch, unlike the marriage veil where a large mantle was drawn over the top of the head.[20]

II. The Significance of the Removal of the Veil in Public

What signals might be given by the actual removal of the veil? Sebesta argues, 'As the veil symbolised the husband's authority over his wife, the omission of the veil by a married woman was a sign of her "withdrawing" herself from the marriage.' She proceeds to illustrate this with an anecdote about Sulpicius Gallus, a consul in 166 B.C. Gallus divorced his wife because she had left the house unveiled, thus allowing all to see, as he said, what only he should see. When his wife removed her veil, she, in effect, excluded herself from the rank

16. A. Dalby, "Levels of Concealment: The Dress of the *Hetairai* and *Pornai* in Greek Texts," in L. Llewellyn-Jones, ed., *Women's Dress in the Ancient Greek World*, ch. 7.

17. Dalby, "Levels of Concealment: The Dress of the *Hetairai* and *Pornai* in Greek Texts," p. 114.

18. Seneca, *Ad Helviam*, 16.5, and *De Beneficiis*, 7.9.5. Pomeroy, *Spartan Women*, p. 25. γυμνός can mean lightly clad.

19. Dalby, "Levels of Concealment: The Dress of the *Hetairai* and *Pornai* in Greek Texts," p. 115, citing Plautus, *Pseudolus, l.* 182. See also A. M. Stout, "Jewelry as a Symbol of Status in the Roman Empire," in L. Bonfante and J. L. Sebesta, eds., *The World of Roman Costume*, ch. 5.

20. Antipater of Sidon, *Anthologia Palatina* 7.413. Dalby, "Levels of Concealment: The Dress of the *Hetairai* and *Pornai* in Greek Texts," pp. 119-20.

of matron. It was on the basis of her 'bare head' *(capite aperto)* that Gallus divorced her.[21] Valerius Maximus reported that Gallus had justified his actions thus —

> To have your good looks approved, the law limits you to my eyes only. For them assemble the tools of beauty, for them look your best, trust to their closest familiarity. Any further sight of you, summoned by needless incitement, has to be mired in suspicion and crimination.[22]

Valerius saw this as 'frightful marital severity' on the part of Sulpicius Gallus.[23]

Isidore argued that an adulteress wore an *amiculum* — the linen *pallium* dress of the prostitute.[24] 'We do know the dress of the adulteress. No longer a matron, the woman was not permitted to wear the *stola* or *vittae*. Instead, according to custom, the woman divorced for promiscuity wore a plain *toga*. The symbolism behind the assumption of the *toga* would seem not to be that the woman had assumed the sexual freedom allowed males, but that she had lost her status and role as a sexually mature woman in Roman society. If you were married you wore a *stola*; if you were not, you wore a *toga, praetexta* if you were still a child, plain if you were an adulteress.'[25] By implication she could no longer wear the traditional mantle to signify marriage and hence pull it over the top of her head in public.

1 Corinthians 11:5 itself provides an explanation of the significance of removing the marriage veil. 'It is one and the same thing' (ἓν γάρ ἐστιν καὶ τὸ αὐτό) as having your head shaved.[26] Dio Chrysostom records that 'Fortune' was sometimes blamed for emotional weaknesses and cites Medea in this regard because of her sexual passion for Jason. Dio noted: 'a woman guilty of adultery shall have her hair cut off according to the law and play the prostitute (καὶ τὴν κόμην ἀπεκείρατο κατὰ τὸν νόμον καὶ ἐπορνεύετο).' He also recorded that Medea's own daughter became an adulteress and had her hair cut off according to the law.[27] It is clear that part of the punish-

21. Sebesta, "Symbolism in the Costume of the Roman Woman," p. 48.

22. *Memorable Deeds and Sayings*, 6.3.10.

23. *Memorable Deeds and Sayings*, 6.3.10.

24. Isidore, *Origines*, 19.2.5.5, cited by Sebesta, "Symbolism in the Costume of the Roman Woman," p. 53, n. 50.

25. Sebesta, "Symbolism in the Costume of the Roman Woman," p. 50.

26. ὁ αὐτός operates as an associative instrumental; A. T. Robertson, *A Grammar of the Greek New Testament in the Light of Historical Research*, 2nd ed. (New York: Hodder and Stoughton, 1914), p. 687.

27. Dio Chrysostom, *Or.* 64.3. Cf. Tacitus, *Germania*, 19, which refers to German tribes.

ment for adultery was cutting off the offender's hair. In fact, 1 Corinthians 11:6 indicates that if a wife will not wear her marriage veil, then she should cut off or crop her hair. If it was a matter of shame to be shorn or shaven, then the only alternative for her was to wear the marriage veil as the text indicates.[28]

III. Modest and Immodest Appearances in Roman Law

In his book on *Law and Life of Rome*, J. Crook, who is an ancient historian specialising in Roman law, long ago argued that it is impossible to deal with Roman law and Roman society as if they were autonomous spheres. He has demonstrated that essential aspects of Roman society were consciously built on Roman law and operated on that basis; hence the title of his book.[29] It is therefore to be expected that the important social symbol of the veil and other distinguishing garments worn by married women would be underpinned by Roman law and be observed in the Roman colony of Corinth.[30] Whether they wished society to perceive them as a modest matron or the 'new' wife was a deliberate choice that they themselves made and conveyed to the public by the way they dressed.

Roman law encapsulated this in a number of ways. It specifically exempted from prosecution those men who acted on the basis of the sexual signal sent by what a married woman was wearing.

> If anyone accosts . . . women [who] are dressed like prostitutes, and not as mothers of families . . . if a woman is not dressed as a matron [veiled] and some one calls out to her or entices away her attendant, he will not be liable to action for injury.[31]

It takes little imagination to see how, after an illicit, consensual sexual encounter, it would be possible for the wife who had dressed like a prostitute to argue that she was an unwilling party. This legal provision closed that loop-

---

28. On the idea of shame (αἰσχρόν) in Roman society see the extended treatment by R. A. Kaster, "The Shame of the Romans," *TAPA* 127 (1997): 1-19.

29. J. A. Crook, *Law and Life of Rome, 90 B.C.–A.D. 212* (New York: Cornell University Press, 1967), and also pp. 7-8 for a discussion of the penchant of Roman citizens for a knowledge of legal matters for this very reason.

30. J.-J. Aubert and B. Sirks, Speculum Iuris: *Roman Law as a Reflection of Social and Economic Life in Antiquity* (Ann Arbor: University of Michigan Press, 2002), pp. vi-vii, recognise this contribution of J. A. Crook; see n. 29.

31. *The Digest*, 47.10.15.15.

hole.[32] A first-century married woman had to take personal responsibility for the way she dressed. Croom comments that protection from sexual predators and legal redress could be secured for the married women 'only if they looked *respectable*.'[33]

The dichotomy between the promiscuous wife and a modest one was also reflected in legislation on rape in Roman jurisprudence. *The Digest* states —

> The laws punish the detestable wickedness of [married] women who prostitute their chastity to the lusts of others, but do not hold those liable who are violated by force and against their will. And, moreover, it has very properly been decided that their reputations are not lost, and that their marriage with others should not be prohibited on this account.[34]

The woman who committed adultery was condemned, but a distinction was observed in law for the victim of a forced sexual assault. She was declared innocent, suffered no loss of respectability and was not thereby ineligible for marriage.

Roman law contained another important provision that seems to have been overlooked. Again, it was meant to send a clear signal to society concerning the status of the woman.[35] Augustus' legislation sought to distinguish between the modest wife, the adulteress and the prostitute.[36] 'Women [convicted of adultery] were also compelled to wear the *toga* as a symbol of their shame.'[37] 'The *lex Iulia* specified certain articles of clothing — such as the *stola* [suspended from the shoulder by straps and covering the feet] and *vittae* [a woollen band used in women's hairstyles] — as peculiar to *matronae* and forbade these to be worn by prostitutes.'[38] It is true that 'Matrons were not compelled by law to wear the *stola* and the other "matronal" articles of clothing',[39] but they did symbolise and advertise the wearer's chastity. It has been noted already that Roman law protected those who were accused of misread-

---

32. It was a legal requirement that the husband initiate criminal proceedings for adultery against her, otherwise he stood in danger of being prosecuted under Roman law for complicity in the affair. See p. 42.

33. A. T. Croom, *Roman Clothing and Fashion*, p. 75. Italics are hers.

34. *The Digest*, 9.9.20.

35. T. A. J. McGinn states, 'I know of no comprehensive treatment of this important subject', i.e., 'Augustus's intervention in the field of clothing'; *Prostitution, Sexuality, and the Law in Ancient Rome* (Oxford: Oxford University Press, 1998), p. 154.

36. McGinn, *Prostitution, Sexuality, and the Law*, p. 154.

37. McGinn, *Prostitution, Sexuality, and the Law*, p. 143.

38. McGinn, *Prostitution, Sexuality, and the Law*, p. 162.

39. McGinn, *Prostitution, Sexuality, and the Law*, p. 162.

ing the intentions of a matron because of her dress code.[40] So there were legal incentives to dress appropriately, and therefore McGinn's comment that 'you were what you wore' is highly apposite because it succinctly summarizes the principle underlying Roman law on this issue.[41]

IV. Official Policing of Dress Codes on Religious Occasions

Daniel Ogden has drawn attention to what he sees as a failure on the part of ancient historians to discuss the important civic role of the 'controllers of women' (γυναικονόμοι) in Roman times, a deficiency that he seeks to make good.[42] P. Cartledge and A. Spawforth had written earlier of the γυναικονόμοι, noting the office was not restricted to Roman Sparta. 'That the public deportment of free-born women was the object of civic surveillance is shown by the existence of a *gunaikonomos*, a type of magistrate widespread in the Greek world by the first century B.C.'[43] It was also prevalent in the following centuries.

Sarah Pomeroy, in a brief discussion of the role in Sparta, speaks of 'state surveillance' of women's activities. She speculates 'one imagines that some participants might have over-indulged in feasting, drinking, singing, and dancing in the guise of religious activity. . . . *Gynaikonomoi* in other *poleis* [cities] not only supervised women but imposed sumptuary restrictions'.[44]

A composite picture of the roles of *gynaikonomoi* emerges from the extant evidence. They were to enforce sumptuary laws, curb excessive spending by women on clothing for religious festivals, restrict the competitive display of wealth, promote female chastity for the sake of fathers and husbands and the gods, and standardise dress in processions. They were to maintain traditions in religious processions and ensure that the status difference was reflected in dress codes between (i) the initiated and newly initiated into the

40. Things were to change much later in the time of Tertullian; 'matrons had adopted the dress of prostitutes and *vice versa,* a situation that should have invited the unfriendly attention of public officials'; McGinn, *Prostitution, Sexuality, and the Law,* p. 162. Cf. the legal situation in Venice in the Middle Ages when only respectable women were permitted to wear jewellery but prostitutes were forbidden to do so.

41. McGinn, *Prostitution, Sexuality and the Law,* p. 162.

42. D. Ogden, "Controlling Women's Dress: *gynaikonomoi,*" in L. Llewellyn-Jones, ed., *Women's Dress in the Ancient Greek World,* ch. 11. Pomeroy, *Spartan Women,* pp. 127-28, briefly discusses them.

43. P. Cartledge and A. Spawforth, *Hellenistic and Roman Sparta: A Tale of Two Cities* (London: Routledge, 1989), pp. 200-201.

44. Pomeroy, *Spartan Women,* p. 127.

cult; (ii) wives and unmarried women; (iii) free women and slaves; (iv) respectable wives and adulteresses and prostitutes.[45]

To enforce these roles they had official powers to confiscate women's clothing, to impose certain fines and to restrict their conduct. They could tear or confiscate in public a dress that was considered offensive and dedicate it to the gods. This would be a public humiliation for the woman involved. They could also exclude women from public participation in festivals and sacrifices and downgrade women to a lower status on their festival lists.[46] Plutarch traced the origins of this office back to the Classical Greek period of Solon, whose laws 'prohibited wild and wilfully disorderly behaviour' on the part of women. He commented:

> Most of these practices [from ancient times] are also forbidden by our laws, but ours contain an additional *proviso* that such offenders shall be punished by the supervisors of women (ζημιοῦσθαι τοὺς τὰ τοιαῦτα ποιοῦντας ὑπὸ τῶν γυναικονόμων).[47]

Menander was known to have held this public office in Cornlia in Didyma in the second century A.D. and it also operated in Miletus. In the first century B.C. evidence comes from Crete and Ilion.[48] 'The survival of the liturgy [public office] throughout the Principate may well reflect the importance which the Roman city attached to the decorous celebration of its traditional festivals, in which wives and daughters of citizens played a prominent part, but strictly regulated as to dress and behaviour.'[49]

Ogden examines in some detail a long inscription from Andania dated 92-91 B.C. which is concerned primarily with instructions to the 'controllers of women' (γυναικονόμοι) for regulating the dress codes of women who participated in the religious processions connected with the cult of Demeter.[50] The dress of women was very closely defined by their class, i.e., matrons, girls and slaves, and also by their status within the cult. In addition, no female could wear 'gold jewellery, or rouge, or white lead, or a hair-band, nor plaited hair nor shoes, unless of felt or sacred leather.' The aim was to restrict elabo-

---

45. Ogden, "Controlling Women's Dress: *gynaikonomoi*," p. 210.

46. Ogden, "Controlling Women's Dress: *gynaikonomoi*," p. 210.

47. Plutarch, *Solon*, 21. The reason given for this additional punishment was that 'they indulge in unmanly and effeminate extravagances of sorrow when they mourn.'

48. Plutarch, *Solon*, 84, 361; *Milet.*, no. 264; *ICret.*, iv. 252; *Illion*, 10. For further evidence either earlier or later see Ogden, "Controlling Women's Dress: *gynaikonomoi*," pp. 216-19.

49. P. Cartledge and A. Spawforth, *Hellenistic and Roman Sparta: A Tale of Two Cities* (London: Routledge, 1989), pp. 200-1.

50. *IG* v.1 1390.

rate dress and placed a ceiling on how much money could be spent; this varied from 200 drachmas down to 50 in the case of slaves. Transparent clothing was specifically mentioned in the instructions and was banned from the procession; the 'controllers of women' had authority to tear any clothing that was worn contrary to the rules of the cult and to dedicate it to the deity.[51]

The office was clearly an onerous one as has already been noted and those elected to this honorary public liturgy discovered it was no sinecure. 'A person who dreams of being city warden, boy-warden or a γυναικονόμος" is beset with worries and anxieties concerning his state, his children or his women', a reference to the burden of responsibility of the separate offices.[52]

Evidence of this office has been found at Sparta in Achaia. The office operated 'according to the ancient traditions and the laws' (κατὰ τὰ ἀρχαῖα ἔθη καὶ τοὺς νόμους) of Sparta as an inscription in Trajan's reign records.[53] This Spartan magistrate had five others who carried the title of συνγυναικονόμος. The entry of *Liddell and Scott* on the latter group as 'fellow-γυναικονόμος' is not helpful. Cartledge suggests that 'At Sparta the post is attested from the Augustan until the late Severan age, its duties sufficiently weighty, it seems, to require the assistance of (usually) five junior colleagues (συνγυναικονόμοι).'[54] The need for assistance in policing dress codes was not because there was a greater degree of immorality among Roman Spartan women. 'Nor does the women's sphere at Roman Sparta display any of the licence for which it was notorious in Classical times. In honorific dedications for Spartan matrons from the second and third centuries the repetitive praise of their "moderation" *(sōphrosunē),* "husband-love" *(philandria),* "dignity" *(semnotēs)* and "decorum" *(kosmiotēs)* shows that the local society, at least in its upper reaches, valued the domestic virtues in women as those held up for praise by Plutarch of Chaeronea, in this period Greece's fullest surviving spokesman on the themes of love, women and marriage.'[55]

It has been suggested that 'the role of women in public life was largely

51. *IG* v.1 1390, *ll.* 16-26.

52. Artemidorus of Daldis, *Oneirocriticon,* 2.30 (second century A.D.).

53. K. Chrimes, *Ancient Sparta* (Manchester: Manchester University Press, 1949), p. 146. Chrimes links the office to girls as well as women and wrongly sees it as a parallel office to the one governing boys and men in athletics in the Roman period.

54. P. Cartledge and A. Spawforth, *Hellenistic and Roman Sparta: A Tale of Two Cities,* pp. 200-201. See *IG* v. 1.209 (1 B.C.), v. 1. 170 (ii A.D.), *SEG* xi. 626 (c. 110 A.D.), xi. 493 (c. 125-50 B.C.), 629 (138-61 A.D.), 498 (145-60 A.D.), 500 (160-80 A.D.) and 627 (161-80 A.D.).

55. P. Cartledge, "Spartan Wives: Liberation or Licence?" *CQ* n.s. 31 (1981): 84-109, republished in P. Cartledge and A. Spawforth, *Hellenistic and Roman Sparta: A Tale of Two Cities,* p. 200.

confined to religious cults'.[56] However in Menander Rhetor it is clear that the controller of women was also connected to the public sphere. 'Self-restraint (σωφροσύνη) is proven in two contexts, in the public community and in private houses. In the public community it is associated with the education of boys and girls, weddings and marriages, laws about offences of disorder (ἄκοσμος)'. Then immediately this observation was made, 'There are many cities that elect γυναικονόμοι'. On this evidence, this office clearly aimed to restrain women's conduct in public. Menander then refers to the private sphere with specific mention of adultery and 'other errors'.[57]

Was this liturgy also operational in Roman Corinth? There are two reasons for supposing so. We lack, to date, any extant evidence of inscriptions recording the office of the *gynaikonomos* in Corinth. This is not surprising given the destruction of the city by the Herulians in A.D. 267 and the violent sacking by the Goths in A.D. 395, but there is widespread epigraphic attestation for such a position in the East.[58] Sparta, estimated to have had some 100,000 inhabitants, was in the same province as Corinth. Cities elsewhere which had the cult of Demeter, would have possessed this office. There is firm evidence that Corinthian women were connected to the cult of Demeter which we know operated in Roman Corinth in Paul's day in the temple on the slopes of the Acrocorinth overlooking the city.[59] Curse inscriptions written by women have been discovered there.[60]

Do we have evidence that information concerning the conduct of married women while worshipping would have leaked out beyond the gathering of Christians in Corinth? 1 Corinthians 14:23 reveals the presence of outsiders and unbelievers at the gatherings with the implication that this was not unusual. The layout of the house was such that the main room, which would have been the place where they met, was immediately accessible from the entrance. While it is common to refer to the 'house' churches, the term consistently used in the New Testament is more specific. If one simply wished to indicate that the gathering was not in a hired hall but in the house (the physical building), then the term οἰκία would be the right designation. In all the refer-

---

56. P. Cartledge, 'Spartan Wives: Liberation or Licence?' *CQ* n.s. 31, pp. 84-109, republished in P. Cartledge and A. Spawforth, *Hellenistic and Roman Sparta: A Tale of Two Cities*, p. 200.

57. Menander Rhetor, 363-64.

58. H. J. Mason, *The Greek Terms for Roman Institutions — A Lexicon and Analysis*, ASP 13 (Toronto: Hakkert, 1974), fails to provide any entry for this office.

59. N. Bookidis and R. S. Stroud, *The Sanctuary of Demeter and Kore: Topography and Architecture* (Princeton: American School of Classical Studies in Athens, 1997), Part 3.

60. For a discussion of the evidence of yet unpublished curse inscriptions see my *After Paul Left Corinth*, pp. 168-69, kindly made available by R. Stroud.

ences to the locations in which Christians gathered in the Pauline communities οἶκος was used. This refers to 'a room' within the house (οἰκία) which would have been what we would now designate the sitting or lounge room.[61] Their meetings were readily accessible to anyone so that an outsider could readily come in.

In the passage under consideration a clue may rest in the fact that wives were under obligation to wear the veil because of the ἄγγελοι. While much attention has been given to the struggle to untie the Gordian knot when the Greek word is translated 'angels',[62] I have argued elsewhere that the term should be 'messengers'.[63] That word was used not only of those who brought information, but also of those who came to carry information away to others. Epictetus, writing in the early second century A.D., provides evidence of this. 'What messenger is so swift and so attentive as the eye?' he noted of one who could be sent 'as a scout' to report back. In discussing the role of the Cynic philosopher Epictetus observed that the present time could be compared to a war situation where the Cynic could not operate as he would normally do. If he did, he would destroy his role as 'the messenger, the scout, and the herald of the gods that he is'. Epictetus also reported that after Domitian banished the philosophers from Rome, a young man from Nicopolis was sent to Rome to spy out the land on their behalf. Philosophers had been banished from Rome from time to time by a number of emperors, hence the need for a messenger to report back to those exiled from the capital of the Empire on whether it was safe for them to return.[64] One reason why the term was always rendered as 'angels' is that it was presumed that the messengers only brought information. If this translation is used, as it is on other occasions in the New Testament, it is suggested that the impression given to the information-gatherer is Paul's concern (11:10) and is the reason for wearing the marriage veil while praying and prophesying.

What cultural precedents would have coloured the perception of the messengers? There are statue types of Livia, the wife of Augustus and mother of Tiberius, in the role of priestess with her marriage veil drawn over her

61. For a discussion of the use of these two terms to refer to a physical building or people in a household or the immediate family see my appendix "The Meaning of οἰκία and οἶκος," in *After Paul Left Corinth*, pp. 206-11.

62. See most recently J. T. Stuckenburch, "Why should women cover their heads because of the angels?" *Stone Campbell Journal*, 4.2 (2001): 205-34.

63. This evidence is also cited in *After Paul Left Corinth*, pp. 136-7. It was somewhat surprising that one reviewer of this book called my translation speculating when the term in Koine can be rendered messenger; evidence was provided justifying this possibility.

64. Epictetus, *Discourses*, II.23.4; III.22.23-24, 69-70; I.24.3-10.

head.[65] There is evidence of both the emperor's wife operating as a priestess and a provincial priestess of the imperial cult in honour of Livia not only in the East (see pp. 210-11) but also throughout the Empire.[66] 'What woman will not follow when an empress leads the way?' Juvenal asked.[67] Wives participating in pagan religious activities would have had the marriage veil drawn over the top of their heads. We know of at least one Corinthian woman who was a priestess whose inscription reads, 'To Polyaena, daughter of Marcus, priestess of Victory. The high priest [Publius] Priscus Juventianus [while still living (set up this monument)] with the official sanction of the city council to (this) excellent woman.'[68] It can be concluded, therefore, that those wives who undertook religious functions would have covered their heads with the marriage veil, given that all respectable married women would wear their veil outside the home, as Roman law and custom prescribed. This raises the possibility that those who sent messengers to spy out the activities of Christian gatherings could have reported to the men elected to officially supervise women's dress codes in Corinth that some Christian married women were inappropriately attired while engaging in a religious activity.

The other possibility is that messengers simply came to report back to a member of the élite of Corinth or any interested person who was curious but who did not feel free to attend in case it was a political gathering of an association. Augustus had legislated against the political activities of associations as soon as he had secured power, and all the emperors in the Julio-Claudian dynasty, apart from Gaius, remained highly suspicious of them.[69] Guilt by association had been established in the Principate of Tiberius in the famous trea-

---

65. Monumenti, Musei e Galeris Pontificie, Città del Vaticano, and another in Deutsches Archäologisches Institut, Rome, 67.1593. For photographic reproductions see A. A. Barrett, *Livia: First Lady of Imperial Rome* (New Haven: Yale University Press, 2002), p. 112.

66. For epigraphic evidence see D. Fishwick, *The Imperial Cult in the Latin West: Studies in the Ruler Cult of the Western Provinces of the Roman Empire*, vol. 3.2 (Leiden: E. J. Brill, 2002), pp. 96-98, 153-54, 185, 206, 209, 247, and 306-7.

67. Juvenal, *Satires*, VI.617.

68. Kent, *Corinth*, VIII, 3. 199. The date is uncertain but it was either late first century, i.e., after 73 A.D. or the middle of the following century. It was in Latin, the language of the first-century official inscription in Corinth. Greek was used in the second century.

69. W. Cotter, "The *Collegia* and the Roman Law: State Restrictions on Voluntary Associations, 64 BCE–200 CE," in J. S. Kloppenborg and S. G. Wilson, eds., *Voluntary Associations in the Graeco-Roman World* (London: Routledge, 1996), p. 78. In that very legislation where he restricted the meetings of associations to once a month he specifically exempted the Jews who were allowed to meet on a weekly basis to observe the sabbath. O. F. Robinson, *The Criminal Law of Ancient Rome* (London: Duckworth, 1995), p. 80.

son trial following the Sejanus conspiracy.[70] A client of a patron or a trusted household servant would have been a safe person to send to see that this meeting did not breach Roman law.

Whatever the motive in sending messengers, the report would have gone back telling of certain Christian women who were engaged in praying and prophesying, activities that would be interpreted in a religious context as connected to an important priestly office. Their deliberate removing of their veils while praying and prophesying would have sent a signal that they were identifying themselves in this religious gathering with the new women who behaved loosely at banquets which were often held in private homes. According to Acts 18:7, private homes were also the setting for Christian gatherings including the Lord's Supper (1 Cor. 11:17-34). As we will see, it was not unknown for married women to engage in inappropriate conduct in the 'after-dinners' in private homes. (See p. 153.)

V. What Was 'Proper' in Roman Corinth?

It should have been self-evident to the Corinthian Christians that the removal of their veil was totally inappropriate (1 Cor. 11:13). 'Judge among yourselves (ἐν ὑμῖν αὐτοῖς κρίνατε): is it proper (πρέπον ἐστιν) for a wife to pray to God with her head uncovered?' In the Roman world the expectation of conformity was at the heart of its cultural norms; such was the nature of Roman thinking and its impact throughout the Empire from recent social engineering on the part of Augustus.

The actual Greek sentence 'it is proper' (πρέπον ἐστιν) used in 11:13 appears elsewhere in contemporary and second-century literary sources to indicate this. Even noting the difference in character of those who attended the symposia of Epicurus and Plato — they were flatterers and snobs who jeered — Athenaeus recorded that the entirely inappropriate comment of Telemachus was 'neither proper (οὐ πρέπον ἐστιν) of a flatterer nor one who turns his nose up'.[71] The young men 'held their peace in the presence of Helen [of Troy], as is proper (πρέπον ἐστίν), struck completely dumb before her famous beauty'.[72] In 'The Precepts of Statecraft', Plutarch writes of what everyone would consider to be appropriate or inappropriate to ask for on the basis

---

70. B. Levick, "Tiberius and the Law: The Development of *maiestas*," in *Tiberius, the Politician* (London: Thames and Hudson, 1976), ch. 11.

71. Athenaeus, *Deipnosophists*, 186b-187a.

72. Athenaeus, *Deipnosophists*, 188c.

of their status: 'favours of this sort are proper for courtesans to receive, but not for generals (ἑταιριδίοις οὐ στρατηγοῖς πρέπον ἐστίν)'.[73]

Sextus Empiricus in discussing the rearing of a child argued that there were certain conventions which were considered to be appropriate for all children because of common characteristics.

> Having knowledge of a child, no less and no more of favourite than a non-favourite child, nor of female than a male; favourite or non-favourite, males or females, no different conduct, but the same things are proper and are proper to all alike (ἀλλὰ ταὐτὰ πρέπει τε καὶ πρέποντα ἐστίν).[74]

There were also certain things in first-century society that were considered to be improper or unseemly. Dionysius of Halicarnassus, who wrote a history of the Roman people in the Augustan period, condemned a custom concerning slaves, 'looking upon it as unseemly' (ὡς οὐ πρέπον). He refers to established procedures for consulting members of the magistracy of the consuls and tribunes for them to give their opinion in order of their seniority by beginning with the oldest and going to the youngest members as is 'customary' (πρέπον). He also wrote of an action disdainful for a father yet 'proper' (πρέπον) for a freedman of lofty spirit, and the bestowing of gifts that was 'proper' (πρέπον) for a ruler whose task it was to confer benefits upon good men.[75] Earlier Plato had contrasted 'propriety' (εὐπρέπεια) with 'impropriety' (ἀπρέπεια) with respect to writing, how that should not be done improperly (ἀπρεπῶς).[76] 'Impropriety' was also used of the conduct of men who were disreputable and indecent.[77] In Koine Greek πρέπον was the appropriate term to use for approved conduct, given that Roman society was clear as to what was proper and what was not, not least of all in terms of dress codes, because of the underlying protocol of Roman law. Therefore there was no need to use the prefix εὐ, as in Classical Greek, in the case of delineating 'propriety' (εὐπρέπεια) and its cognates.

The command 'You judge among yourselves' (ἐν ὑμῖν αὐτοῖς) includes the additional word αὐτός (11:13). The phrase 'among yourselves' (ἐν ὑμῖν αὐτοῖς) is used here emphatically both through its placement in the sentence and also by the addition of αὐτός, which in normal circumstances would be an unnecessary duplication. Its purpose is to give intensity to the

73. Plutarch, "Precepts of Statecraft," 808E.

74. Sextus Empiricus, "Outlines of Pyrrhonism," III.245.

75. Dionysius of Halicarnassus, *Roman Antiquities*, 4.24, 11.37, 14.2, 11.6.

76. Plato, *Phaedrus*, 274b.

77. Theocles, *Lyricus*, 5.40.

statement.[78] The implication is that, on reflection, it should be completely obvious to everyone why it is improper for the wife to do this. If 'you were what you wore' (or rather what you did not wear) while undertaking to pray and prophesy in public, then a clear signal was being sent and received by the messengers. Yes, they were married because they wore the mantle, the upper part of which was used as a veil. They were not dressed as prostitutes who wore the *toga*. However, they were flagrantly defying their status by deliberately removing the marriage veil from their head. They looked like the promiscuous married women, for the absence of the veil sent an unmistakable signal. It was not proper by first-century standards to do this.

Just as it was improper for a wife to pray unveiled, so too it was later said to be shameful for a woman to speak in the Christian meeting in the context of weighing up of prophecy, 'even as the law says' (14:34). While it has been argued that the law refers to the Mosaic Law, no specific injunction can be cited from it that forbids women speaking in the assembly. Women were not to intervene *(intercede)* in public settings or come between two parties, and an imperial ban had already existed from the time of Augustus on women intervening on behalf of their husbands in the context of legal argument. In the time of Claudius, according to Ulpian, the Velleian decree of the Senate *(senatus consultum Velleianum)* was passed by the Senate.[79] The disruption of Carfania from a previous era was still being held up as a negative example and was seen as the excuse for this prohibition. (See pp. 177-78.) Whether this was the law being referred to is uncertain, but it may provide an alternative explanation to the Mosaic law, where commentators refer to Genesis 3, which is not strictly the Torah, although the matter of subordination was established in that passage. The concern for the wrong impression being given to the outsider is also central to the issue of order in the service and particularly prophetic activity which is for unbelievers (14:22-25) and in which women also engage (11:5).

If propriety and shame were powerful arguments to invoke in Roman culture, so too was that of obligation, for it was a society ruled by the laws of obligation. The reason already given as to why the wife had to wear the marriage veil while praying and prophesying was that she was under an obligation to do so (11:10). Obligations were binding in Roman culture, and to lay something on the conscience of others as an obligation meant that there was

---

78. Robertson, *A Grammar of the Greek New Testament in the Light of Historical Research*, p. 687.

79. *The Digest*, 16.1.2 (Ulpian); see also 16.1.1 (Paulus) on the decree and the discussion in J. E. Grubbs, *Women in the Law in the Roman Empire: A Sourcebook on Marriage, Divorce and Widowhood* (London: Routledge, 2002), p. 55.

no alternative — in this case married women had to wear the marriage veil; otherwise their action would be misunderstood.[80]

VI. Appearing to Be Contentious

Before dealing with the motivation for removing their veil (11:16), it is important to examine the terminology used for veiling and unveiling in 1 Corinthians 11:2-16 because it is something of a puzzle and may throw light on what was happening. While Cairns in his short discussion on the meaning of veiling cautions against seeking to express the notion of status by the use of one Greek word,[81] the particular terminology used in 1 Corinthians 11:2-16 may provide clues as to what was actually happening during the Christian gathering. Neither the usual Greek term for a 'veil' (προκάλυμμα) was chosen, nor the verb 'I veil my head, I wrap up' (ἐγκαλύπτω), nor its antonym 'I unveil' (ἐκκαλύπτω). Elsewhere in the New Testament when veiling is mentioned the verb used is καλύπτω.[82] It is also used twice metaphorically in 2 Corinthians 4:3 to denote the gospel 'being veiled' from understanding (κεκαλυμμένον) in keeping with the idea of veiling the eyes, for which the second century A.D. writer, Athenaeus, provides an example.[83] However in 1 Corinthians 11:3-7 and 13 neither 'I unveil' (ἐκκαλύπτω), nor its antonym 'I veil my head, I wrap up' (ἐγκαλύπτω), was used but rather 'I veil' (κατακαλύπτω), its antonym 'I unveil' (ἀκατακαλύπτω) and the cognate 'unveiled' (ἀκατακάλυπτον). In 11:4 the clause κατὰ κεφαλῆς ἔχων which would be roughly synonymous for 'I veil' (ἐγκαλύπτω) is used. What is the significance of adding the prefix κατά to the stem of the verb?

The verb 'I veil' (κατακαλύπτω) was used in other ancient sources. In Diodorus Siculus it referred to the convention of covering the walls of the city in terms of tragedy and mourning.[84] It was used by Dio Cassius when Claudius ordered the statue of Augustus to be covered so that he would not witness the slaughter at the gladiatorial games, and by Strabo for the covering of the sacred tripods in the temple for ritual purposes.[85] At the Festival of Naked

---

80. For the wide-ranging issues covered by the term, see A. Watson, *The Law of Obligations in the Later Roman Republic* (Oxford: Clarendon, 1965); R. Zimmerman, *The Law of Obligations: Roman Foundations of the Civilian Tradition* (Cape Town: Juta, 1990).

81. F. Cairns, "The Meaning of the Veil in Ancient Greek Culture," in L. Llewellyn-Jones, ed., *Women's Dress in the Ancient Greek World*, p. 81.

82. Matt. 8:24, 10:26, Luke 8:16, 23:30, 1 Pet. 4:8 and James 5:20.

83. Athenaeus, *The Deipnosophists*, 564c, καταλύπτει τοὺς ὀφθαλμούς.

84. Diodorus Siculus, *History*, 19.106.4.

85. Dio Cassius, *Roman History*, 60.13.3; and Strabo, *Geography*, 9.2.4.

Youths in Sparta, Herodotus indicated that Demaratus covered his head and left the theatre, not because he was offended by the spectacle, for he had presided over it before, but because of the shame he felt having lost his position of power and being reminded of that fact in public.[86] In all these instances the action involved a cloth and an act of covering that was a considered response to a crisis situation or an offence.

However 11:16 states that they 'appear to be contentious'. This may throw some light on what these men and wives were doing. Plutarch drew attention to 'contentiousness and self-will that belong to vice', to the spirit of contentiousness and quarrelling over debatable questions, and to the fact that in learned discussions anger turns the love of learning into contentiousness.[87] The Stoics said that the 'new' Roman woman was contentiousness.

> But it is also necessary for a woman to be self-controlled (σώφρονα). On the one hand she is free from lecherous recklessness, and on the other free concerning other pleasures, not a slave of desire, not contentious (μηδὲ φιλόνεικον εἶναι), not lavish in expense (μὴ πολυτελῆ), nor extravagant in dress (μὴ καλλωπίστριαν).[88]

The exact same clause 'to be contentious' (φιλόνεικος εἶναι) is found in 1 Corinthians 11:16 with the implication that they deliberately did this.

The contentiousness of these women may well explain the use of the prefix κατά being added to the verb to describe the strength of the action — that it was a deliberate one (11:2-16) and hence a choice over alternatives. It seems to indicate that they deliberately did this in front of the congregation to signal something or to make a statement.[89]

This description of the wives differs from that of the men because of the clause 'having [the veil hanging] down from the head' (κατὰ κεφαλῆς ἔχων) (11:4). It was not over the head — if that had been the case then ὑπέρ with the genitive would have been used. Robinson cites examples in the New Testament where κατά means 'down from' and notes that in 11:4 the veil is hanging down from the head.[90] This confirms what we know from the statue type of the Roman priest — that the *toga* was drawn over the head and hung down the back.

---

86. Herodotus, *The Persian Wars*, 6.67.

87. Plutarch, "How to profit from one's enemies," 73C, 80B; and "The control of anger," 462B.

88. Musonius Rufus, "Self-control," *ll.* 17-25.

89. Liddell & Scott in their entry on κατά suggest that this is a reason for prefacing a main verb with it.

90. A. T. Robertson, *A Grammar of the Greek New Testament in the Light of Historical Research*, pp. 606-7.

The men were no less culpable than wives for they were drawing attention to the secular status by their action, copying a Roman convention of the emperor and the élite in a religious setting, as Gill has suggested.[91]

The married woman by deliberately removing her veil to pray and to prophesy was also making a statement. It did not mean that she was simply reacting against the actions of the Christian man who was imitating the custom of the imperial and élite in a religious context by pulling the *toga* over his head, so that by contrast she removed hers.

It was not that the Christian women had entered a home and were simply removing the veil because they were no longer in public. The term ἐκκλησία meant a formal gathering regardless of the setting.[92] This is reflected in the statement 'they gather together in one place (συνερχομένων . . . ἐπὶ τὸ αὐτό)' (1 Cor. 11:20), so this could not be construed simply as a social visit to a home of a fellow Christian.[93]

By deliberately removing her veil while playing a significant role of praying and prophesying in the activities of Christian worship, the Christian wife was knowingly flouting the Roman legal convention that epitomised marriage. It would have been self-evident to the Corinthians that in so doing she was sending a particular signal to those gathered (11:13). It is also clear from the comments that, if she wished to appear as an adulterous married woman, she should bear the full consequences of the shame associated with that, i.e., have her hair cropped or shaved off (11:6). From the text it appears that she was not only indifferent to looking disreputable by first-century standards but, by deliberately removing the marriage veil, she was being contentious — as were the men in the Christian gathering (11:4, 16). If, according to Roman law, 'she was what she wore' or in this case what she removed from her head, then this gesture made a statement in support of the mores of some of her secular sisters, the new wives, who sought to ridicule the much-prized virtue of modesty which epitomised the married woman.

91. D. Gill, "The Importance of Roman Portraiture for Head-coverings in 1 Corinthians 11:2-16," *TynB* 41.2 (1990): 260.

92. See my "The Problem with 'church' for the Early Church," in D. Peterson and J. Pryor, eds., *In the Fullness of Time: Biblical Studies in Honour of Archbishop Robinson* (Sydney: Lancer, 1992), ch. 13.

93. See my *After Paul Left Corinth*, p. 128.

CHAPTER 6

Deciphering the Married Woman's Appearance,
1 Timothy 2:9-15

An ancient historian could not but be arrested by the fact that in 1 Timothy 2:9-15 the virtues of the modest wife are contrasted with those of women who lead an alternative lifestyle. These lifestyles were distinguished by identifiable dress 'codes' in Roman law and society.

> Likewise also [I wish] wives to dress themselves in respectable apparel with modesty and propriety (ἐν καταστολῇ κοσμίῳ μετὰ αἰδοῦς καὶ σωφροσύνης κοσμεῖν ἑαυτάς), not with braided hair or gold or pearls or extravagant attire (μὴ ἐν πλέγμασιν καὶ χρυσίῳ ἢ μαργαρίταις ἢ ἱματισμῷ πολυτελεῖ) but that which is proper for a wife who professes godliness through good works (ἀλλ' ὃ πρέπει γυναιξὶν ἐπαγγελλομέναις θεοσέβειαν, δι' ἔργων ἀγαθῶν) (1 Tim. 2:9-10).

Traces of the mores of the 'new' woman in the city of Ephesus in the Roman period can be detected both in what this passage proscribes and what it prescribes. Ando's important observation about the cultural ethos of this major city in Asia Minor, 'Ephesian and Roman were no longer mutually exclusive categories,'[1] is significant for this study. There was no substantial distinction between a major city of Asia Minor, Roman Corinth and Rome itself; such was the ready embracing of Romanisation.[2]

---

1. C. Ando, "Images of Emperor and Empire," in *Imperial Ideology and Provincial Loyalty in the Roman Empire* (Berkeley: University of California Press, 2000), ch. 7, *cit.* p. 233.

2. See R. A. Kearsley and T. V. Evans, *Greeks and Romans in Imperial Asia: Mixed Language Inscriptions and Linguistic Evidence for Cultural Interaction until the End of* A.D. *III* (Bonn: Habelt, 2001), who record the Greek and Latin bilingualism of Asia Minor.

For such a short passage, 1 Timothy 2:9-15 has generated a disproportion-ate amount of literature among New Testament scholars in recent decades.[3] In spite of the vast amount written, aspects of the passage still remain some-thing of an enigma. This is due, in part, to the fact that there is no secure *Sitz im Leben* for these much traversed verses and that they still remain a text without any established social context.[4] The clue to understanding the setting of the passage lies largely in understanding the contrasting comments about feminine adornment. It is proposed to examine (I) the significance of the dress codes (2:9-11); (II) the option of contraception, abortion or childbear-ing (2:15); and (III) submissiveness and learning *v.* teaching and controlling (2:11-12). This will show that the issue within the Pauline community related to the possible influence of the adornment of the 'new' woman which had family and communal implications. (The Pythagorean letter of Melissa to Clearete also expressed a concern about the implications for the family. See pp. 72-73.)

I. Dress Codes in 1 Timothy 2:9-11

In a letter to his mother about the virtues that made her who she was in com-parison with others, Seneca wrote *c.* A.D. 41-49.

> Unchastity, the greatest evil of our time, has never classed you with the great majority of women. Jewels have not moved you, nor pearls . . . you have not been perverted by the imitation of worse kind of women that leads even the virtuous into pitfalls. . . . You have never blushed for the number of children, as if it mocked your age. . . . You never tried to conceal your pregnancy as though it was indecent, nor have you crushed the hope of children that were being nurtured in your body. You have never defiled your face with paints and cosmetics. Never have you fancied the kind of dress that exposed no greater nakedness by being removed. Your only or-nament, the kind of beauty that time does not tarnish, is the great honour of modesty.[5]

---

3. For an exhaustive survey see D. Doriani, "A History of the Interpretation of 1 Timothy 2," in A. Köstenberger, T. R. Schreiner and H. S. Baldwin, eds., *Women in the Church: A Fresh Analy-sis of 1 Timothy 2:9-15* (Grand Rapids: Baker, 1995), Appendix 1, pp. 213-67.

4. *Contra* S. M. Baugh, "A Foreign World: Ephesus in the First Century," in A. Köstenberger, T. R. Schreiner and H. S. Baldwin, eds., *Women in the Church*, pp. 13-52, who argues against attempts to establish a *Sitz im Leben* for the passage.

5. Seneca, *Ad Helviam*, 16.3-5.

Here Seneca compares the virtuous lifestyle of his mother with another set of competing female social mores prevalent not only in Rome in the late Republican period but also in the East by the time of the early Empire. This is confirmed by the extant evidence. His mother's virtues which he summarises so succinctly contrast sharply with the alternative lifestyle of the new Roman woman. He begins and ends with the dress codes epitomising the alternative lifestyles of married women. He also notes the social pressures on married women not to have children and, in particular, the pitfalls for the chaste wife because of the ease with which adultery had become a way of life.

In an era preoccupied with the beauty of the feminine form Seneca comments on the stigma felt by those who were pregnant. He graphically describes steps taken by others to prevent that happening. The excessive use of cosmetics also draws his censure as does the sexually provocative dress style of the 'new' Roman woman, which he contrasts with 'the great honour of modesty'. Some of the concerns reflected in 1 Timothy 2:9-10 and 15 are similar to those of Seneca; in fact, there are striking parallels. Seneca also bears witness to the great social pressure that these new mores exerted on his mother and other modest wives in the time of Claudius.

Respectable Apparel

First-century wives, both in statue types and literature, are recorded as having worn distinctive clothing requiring a considerable amount of fabric. It was intended to signal modesty that was the mark of the married woman. Zanker discusses what was understood by 'respectable apparel'. 'Married women also had a special form of dress that was meant to reflect the new spirit of morality in Rome. This was the *stola*, a large, sleeveless overgarment with narrow shoulders, which probably carried woven strips indicating the matron's social status, as on the *toga praetexta*. . . . In the context of social legislation the *stola* became a symbol of female virtue and modesty. For the dignified matron, wearing a *stola* was not only an honor but a "protection from unwanted attentions".'[6]

In his defence of his 'crime' committed in writing the poem, *Ars amatoria,* Ovid makes fun of the new spirit of morality represented by the *stola*. He refers to the garment 'on the shoulder', believing that 'that weight of the Roman name' (a possible reference to Augustus) would not divert 'divine

---

6. P. Zanker, *The Power of Images in the Age of Augustus* (Ann Arbor: University of Michigan Press, 1988), pp. 156-66, *cit.* 165.

attention to silly trifles'.[7] It has already been noted that wives wore the marriage veil in public thereby differentiating themselves from others.[8]

McGinn has documented the immodest dresses, outlandish hairstyles, and lavish jewellery including gold and pearls which distinguished the *hetairai* from the modest wives in first-century society.[9] Croom believes that 'There seems to be no evidence that prostitutes had to wear the toga, only that they were the only women who could.'[10] However, Martial comments that a toga would be a more appropriate gift for a notorious adulteress than expensive scarlet and violet clothes.[11] Horace contrasts the respectable matron with someone who wore the toga.[12]

Clothing which distinguished respectable married women from *hetairai* was not new in Roman society. Diodorus Siculus (*c.* 60-30 B.C.) repeated the legend that —

> Saleucus had enacted a law at Locri that a woman was not to leave the city at night, unless she was going to commit adultery, nor to wear gold or purple unless she was a courtesan.[13]

Epigraphic evidence witnesses to the traditional differences between the two.

> A courtesan describes her beauty, fine clothes and perfumes: her boast is 'For all desire me, for I pleased them all' (πάντες γὰρ μ' ἐπόθουν, ἤμην γὰρ πᾶσι προσηνής).[14]

By contrast a grave inscription reads, 'She did not admire fine clothes, nor gold, when she lived.'[15]

---

7. Ovid, *Tristia*, 2.212.

8. For the significance of the removal of the marriage veil as in 1 Cor. 11:2-16 see chapter 5, pp. 81-83.

9. T. A. J. McGinn, *Prostitution, Sexuality, and the Law in Ancient Rome* (Oxford: Oxford University Press, 1998), pp. 154-70.

10. A. T. Croom, *Roman Clothing and Fashion* (Stroud: Tempus, 2000), pp. 92-93.

11. Martial, *Epigrams*, 2.39.

12. Horace, *Satires*, 1.1.62-63.

13. Diodorus, XII.21.1.

14. *Epigrammata Graeca*, 610.

15. *Epigrammata Graeca*, 497a, *ll.* 7-8.

Modesty and Self-Control (2:9a, 15)

An inextricable link was made between dress codes and personal values with the term 'adornment' being used as a descriptor of the modest wife. Writing in the early second century A.D., Epictetus drew a contrast with the respectable woman in terms of adornment.

> As soon as they are fourteen, women are called 'ladies' by men. And so when they see that they have nothing else but only to be the bedfellows of men, they begin to beautify themselves, and put all their hopes in that. It is worth while for us to take pains, therefore, to make them understand that they are honoured for nothing else but appearing decent and modest (ἐπ' οὐδένι ἄλλῳ τιμῶνται ἢ τῷ κόσμιαι φαίνεσθαι καὶ αἰδήμονες).[16]

Elsewhere he speaks of a wife's 'modesty and a dignified deportment and gentleness' (αἰδῶ καὶ καταστολὴν καὶ ἡμερότητα).[17]

Plutarch corrected Herodotus' misunderstanding of the concept of modesty in a wife. He asserted —

> Herodotus was not right in saying that a woman lays aside her modesty with her undergarments. On the contrary, a virtuous woman puts on modesty (αἰδῶ) in its stead, and husband and wife bring into their mutual relations the greater modesty as a token of the greatest love.[18]

The term 'modesty' (αἰδώς) (2:9), with its Latin equivalent *pudor*, was used in relation to those parts of the female body that must be covered in respectable Roman society. The dresses of prostitutes (and 'new' Roman women who followed their lead) were at times so flimsy that Seneca observed in his letter to his mother that it was 'the kind of dress that exposed no greater nakedness by being removed'.[19] The call for modesty in this passage would have been well understood in the first century in the way it was expressed in terms of both 'respectable apparel' and an 'adornment' achieved by means of good deeds (2:10).[20]

1 Timothy 2:9 also requires the wife to adorn herself with that great Ro-

16. Epictetus, *The Encheiridion*, xl.
17. Epictetus, *Discourse*, 2.10.15.
18. Plutarch, "Advice to the Bride and Groom," 139C.
19. Seneca, *Ad Helviam*, 16.5.
20. The term was not restricted to women. Plutarch, "On Listening to Lectures," *Moralia*, 37D, cites with approval Herodotus, 1.8, who speaks of the loss of innocence that occurs when young men lay aside their modesty (αἰδεῖσθαι) on assuming the *toga virilis*.

man feminine virtue of 'chastity' or 'self-control' that is often translated as 'moderation' (σωφροσύνη), the Latin equivalent being *prudentia*. It was the cardinal virtue for women in the ancient world. Phintys, in a treatise "On Woman's Moderation", wrote, 'The virtue most appropriate to a woman is self-control (γυναικὸς δὲ μάλιστα ἀρετὴ σωφροσύνη)', because the author argued that it enabled her to love and honour her husband.[21] This was the virtue that epitomised the discreet matron and was lauded on the tombstones of women.[22] Attention has already been drawn to the fact that while the famous benefactor and orator, Herodes Atticus, possessed all the cardinal civic virtues, the sculptor of the statue erected to honour his wife in Corinth was said to have captured the cardinal female virtue.[23]

Marshall concludes that the two 'phrases ['modesty' and 'self-control'] thus express the discretion and decorum befitting the Christian woman which stands in contrast to the seductiveness and wealth displayed by the worldly woman'.[24] The above evidence enables us to be even more specific in identifying the latter. It referred not just to any married woman in secular society, however wealthy, but to those married women who flouted the acknowledged expressions of the cardinal virtue that was meant to epitomise her gender, her status and her conduct.[25]

1 Timothy 2:15 specifically highlights the cardinal virtue of 'self-control'. After the Christian virtues of 'faith and love' comes 'holiness' completing the trilogy. Then another phrase is specifically singled out — 'with self-control' (μετὰ σωφροσύνης) (2:15). 1 Timothy 2:9 began with an emphasis on the modest adornment and restraint reflected in the dress code of the respectable Roman wife; the passage concludes with an instruction to continue to live 'with self-control' (2:15) — the acknowledged virtue in first-century society in Rome and the East.

---

21. V. Lambropoulou, "Some Pythagorean Female Virtues," in R. Hawley and B. Levick, eds., *Women in Antiquity: New Assessments* (London: Routledge, 1995), p. 129. Phintys, "On Woman's Moderation," in Thesleff, *Texts*, 151ff. See also S. Treggiari, *Roman Marriage: Iusti Coniuges from the Time of Cicero to the Time of Ulpian* (Oxford: Clarendon, 1991), p. 196.

22. R. A. Kearsley, "Women in Public Life in the Roman East: Iunia Theodora, Claudia Metrodora and Phoebe, Benefactress of Paul," *TynB* 50.2 (1999), p. 197. See p. 35 for a discussion of this virtue on the statue of Regilla.

23. See p. 35.

24. I. H. Marshall, *The Pastoral Epistles* (Edinburgh: T&T Clark, 1999), pp. 448-49.

25. On the cardinal virtues see pp. 61-62.

Adornment

The excesses discussed in 2:9b related to the ancient Republican legislation known as sumptuary laws, *viz. lex Fannia* (161 B.C.) and *lex Licinia sumptuaria* (143 B.C.) which replaced the former. Valerius Maximus recorded the speech made at the beginning of the first century B.C. by Duronius who challenged this law. He wanted the Senate to —

> revoke the law passed to limit money spent on banquets. . . . 'A bridle has been laid upon you, citizens, quite intolerable. You have been bound and tied with a galling chain of slavery. A law has been passed commanding you to be frugal. Let us then revoke the regulation, overlaid as it is with the rust of rugged antiquity. For indeed, what use is liberty if we are not allowed to go to perdition with luxury as we want to?'[26]

Augustus also sought to curb excessive expenditure on banquets, clothes and jewellery with the revival of the sumptuary laws. They had to do, in part, with the avoidance of ostentation.[27] Plutarch warns the husband in the traditional speech at the marriage bed about possible confrontations with a wife over any excessive spending habits.

> When their husbands try forcibly to remove their luxury and extravagance they keep up a continual fight and are very cross; but if they are convinced with the help of reason, they peaceably put aside these things and practice moderation.[28]

Valerius Maximus, writing in the time of Tiberius, commented that while the ancient Romans forbade their wives to drink wine (see pp. 152-54) they had permitted them the indulgence of gold, purple and the dyeing of their hair. They permitted this so that the 'self-control' *(pudicitia)* of their wives should not look too austere.[29] However, by his day these indulgences had become the marks of excess, although he suggested that 'a woman's only joy and

---

26. Valerius Maximus, *Memorable Doings and Sayings,* II.9.5.

27. On consumption and indulgence and the laws seeking to restrain them see A. Dalby, *Empire of Pleasures: Luxury and Indulgence in the Roman World* (London: Routledge, 2000); and on the laws see D. Daube, *Roman Law: Linguistics, Social and Philosophical Aspects* (Edinburgh: University of Edinburgh Press, 1969), pp. 124-27; P. Wyetzner, "Sulla's Law on Prices and the Roman Definition of Luxury," in J.-J. Aubert and B. Sirks, eds., Speculum Iuris: *Roman Law as a Reflection of Social and Economic Life in Antiquity* (Ann Arbor: University of Michigan Press, 2002), pp. 15-33.

28. Plutarch, "Advice to Bride and Groom," 139 D-E.

29. *Memorable Doings and Sayings,* 2.1.5.

glory was in her dress and ornaments that were called *mundus muliebris*. This contrasted with men who could have insignias and public distinctions.'[30]

Hairstyles

Statue types displayed the simple hairstyles which epitomised the modest wife and were worn by members of the imperial family. These statues were replicated throughout the Empire and represented 'fashion icons' to be copied by modest married women.[31] Juvenal confirms this when he asks, 'What woman will not follow when an empress leads the way?'[32] It is for this reason that, in the statue found in a terraced house, Livia, the wife of Augustus, has her head uncovered so that her hairstyle could be seen and, presumably, copied.[33]

Susan Woods also noted, 'Works of the visual arts would show her [a married woman] how they [imperial wives] dressed and how they wore their hair.'[34] Their hairstyles were recorded on Roman coins in order to promote a standard image of the modest wife. It was also true that not everyone copied these simple hairstyles. Croom notes that, in contrast, 'Many of the hairstyles are very complex and would only have been for the rich and leisured classes.'[35] Juvenal comments on the incredibly lavish nature of some of the hairstyles — 'So important is the business of beautification; so numerous are the tiers and storeys piled one upon another on her head!'[36]

Gold

Juvenal identified the shameful woman by means of her jewellery.

> There is nothing that a woman will not permit herself to do, nothing that she deems shameful, when she encircles her neck with green emeralds, and fastens huge pearls to her elongated ears. . . .[37]

---

30. *Memorable Doings and Sayings*, 37.7.9.

31. See Croom, *Roman Clothing and Fashion*, p. 99, for a variety of simple first-century styles.

32. Juvenal, 6.617.

33. P. Scherrer, *Ephesus: The New Guide* (Turkey: Austrian Archaeological Institute, 2000), p. 199, fig. 2 of the statue in the Ephesus museum.

34. S. E. Wood, *Imperial Women: A Study in Public Images, 40 b.c.–a.d. 69* (Leiden: E. J. Brill, 1999), p. 1.

35. Croom, *Roman Clothing and Fashion*, p. 98.

36. Juvenal, *Satires*, 6.501-3.

37. Juvenal, *Satires*, 6.458-59.

Jewellery was made from a variety of metals but, because it was seen as the preferred and most expensive metal, gold was another indicator of extravagant adornment (1 Tim. 2:9).[38] Trimalchio pointed out to his assembled guests at a dinner the gold jewellery (and its weight) which his wife was wearing. He then proceeded to confirm his claim by weighing it in their presence. While his actions would have reflected badly on his sense of propriety, they do, however, indicate desirability in terms of female adornment.[39] Juvenal observed 'secrets bestow jewels' *(donant arcana cylindros)* where it is recorded that a husband paid his wife with jewellery to keep her quiet about his homosexual affair.[40]

Again the term 'jewellery' epitomised sumptuousness in Roman eyes and could be used by way of an analogy, for Valerius Maximus wrote —

A Campanian matron who was staying with Cornelia, mother of the Gracchi, was showing off her jewels, the most beautiful of that period. Cornelia managed to prolong the conversation until her children got home from school. Then she said, 'These are my jewels'.[41]

The law of Syracusans had stipulated that 'a woman should not wear gold (χρυσός) or a flowery dress (ἀνθινά) or have clothes with purple unless she accepted the name of a public *hetaira*'.[42] Dalby notes, 'This Greek phrase, "dresses and gold" is the standard statement of the two accoutrements of a *hetaira*.'[43]

Pearls

Pearls could be another epitome for sumptuousness. According to Suetonius, 'Caesar loved Servilia, the mother of Marcus Brutus, for whom in his first

38. Croom, *Roman Clothing and Fashion*, p. 115.

39. Petronius, *Satyricon*, 67. C. Edwards, *The Politics of Immorality in Ancient Rome* (Cambridge: Cambridge University Press, 1993), p. 203, notes, 'The freedman Trimalchio's dinner might be lavish but his refined guests still despised his ignorance of proper etiquette.'

40. Juvenal, *Satires*, 2.61; S. H. Braund, "A Woman's Voice — Laronia's Role in Juvenal Satire 2," in R. Hawley and B. Levick, eds., *Women in Antiquity: New Assessments* (London: Routledge, 1995), p. 211.

41. Valerius Maximus, *Memorable Deeds and Sayings*, 4.4.

42. Athenaeus, *Deipnosophists*, 521B.

43. A. Dalby, "Levels of Concealment: The Dress of the *Hetairai* and *Pornai* in Greek texts," in L. Llewellyn-Jones, ed., *Women's Dress in the Ancient Greek World* (London and Swansea: Duckworth and University Press of Wales, 2002), p. 115.

consularship he bought a pearl costing six million sesterces.'[44] Martial exaggerated to make his point when he wrote —

> Gellia does not swear by the mystic rites . . . but her pearls. These she embraces, these she covers with kisses, these she calls her brothers, these she calls her sisters, these she loves more than her two children. If the poor thing were to lose them, she says she would not live an hour.[45]

Pliny records that not only did 'women spend more money on their ears with pearl earrings, than on any other part of their person', but that the epitome of extravagance was sewing pearls on shoes and socks. He also notes that the most expensive pearls had brilliance, size, roundness, smoothness, and weight.[46] 'During the first century, authors frequently used pearls as a symbol of expensive jewellery, and wrote disapprovingly of their use.'[47]

How women came into possession of what were seen as extravagant accoutrements is not certain. Pliny the Younger wrote a moving letter to Aefulanus Marcellius concerning the grievous loss of the younger daughter of a mutual friend, Fundanus. She was just under fourteen years old, was educated by teachers, was studious, intelligent, well-read, and about to marry 'an excellent young man, the date was set and we were all invited'. Pliny notes the irony that 'the money that had been delegated to clothes, pearls and gems for the wedding was spent on incense, ointments and spices.'[48]

If the prospective husband gave the gifts, then Roman law allowed them to be received as such only before marriage, but not after the nuptials.[49] The reason for this legal proscription is not certain but may have arisen out of disputes in the cases of divorce concerning any division even though property assets in the first century were not integrated on marriage. Cherry has noted that, whatever the intention, the fact that the law underwent periodic modification indicates that 'the prohibition was laid down in response to claims that were both urgently felt and social in origin'.[50]

Plutarch commented on the discreet lifestyle of his own wife:

44. Suetonius, *Julius Caesar*, 50.2.

45. Martial, *Epigrams*, 8.81.

46. Pliny, *Nat. Hist.*, 11.50.136; see also 37.6.17, 9.56.114, 9.56.112.

47. Croom, *Roman Clothing and Fashion*, p. 116.

48. Pliny the Younger, *Letters*, 5.16 (A.D. 105/6).

49. J. E. Grubbs, *Women in the Law in the Roman Empire: A Sourcebook on Marriage, Divorce and Widowhood* (London: Routledge, 2002), pp. 98-100.

50. D. Cherry, "Gifts between Husband and Wife: The Social Origins of Roman Law," in Aubert and Sirks, *Speculum Iuris: Roman Law as a Reflection of Social and Economic Life in Antiquity*, pp. 34-45, *cit.* p. 44.

Your plainness of attire and sober style of living without exception amazed every philosopher who has shared our society and intimacy; neither is there any townsman of ours to whom you do not offer another spectacle — your own simplicity.[51]

He sees the virtues that adorn her as 'another spectacle' which can be taken as a pejorative comment on another spectacle, i.e., the showiness and brashness of the alternative lifestyle that also paraded itself in public in their city. The specific mention of gold, pearls and 'expensive attire' (ἱματισμῷ πολυτελεῖ) are indicators of the excesses of the 'new' wife (1 Tim. 2:9).

It also needs to be remembered that the same concerns raised in 2:9-10, 15 about clothing, jewellery and their relationship to modesty, are to be found in the letter from Melissa to Clearete on the Pythagorean and Neo-Pythagorean philosophy's stance on marriage. It stressed —

> a wife's adornment . . . with quietness, white and clean in her dress, plain but not costly, simple but not elaborate or excessive. For she must reject garments shot with purple or gold. For these are used by *hetairai* in soliciting men generally . . . the ornament of a wife is her manner and not her dress. And a free and modest wife must appear attractive to her own husband, but not to the man next door, having on her cheeks the blush of modesty rather than of rouge and powder, and a good and noble bearing and decency and modesty rather than gold and emerald. For it is not in expenditure on clothing and looks that the modest woman should express her love of the good but in the management and maintenance of her household.[52]

The wearing of modest clothing was both a concern for the philosophical schools and a social convention for respectable married women. It was not only secular authors who adopted 'adornment' terminology to describe behaviour rather than clothing. In the second century the Christian writer Clement of Alexandria wrote, 'I like old Sparta, which permitted only *hetairai* to wear flowery dresses and gold ornaments, thus forbidding finery to respectable women and allowing it only to those who plied their trade as prostitutes.'[53]

Judith Grubbs notes, 'Imperial legal sources frequently invoke the no-

---

51. Plutarch, "Consolation to His Wife," 609C.

52. *P.Haun.* 13, *ll.* 6-29, which is the Koine Greek rendering of the Städele edition of the Classical Greek text, III. For the full citation see pp. 72-73.

53. Clement of Alexandria, *Educator,* 2.10.105.

tions of female "modesty" *(pudor)* and "sexual chastity" *(pudicitia)*, and sometimes their "sense of shame" *(verecundia).*[54] Augustus had, in keeping with his underpinning of the social fabric by means of laws, also taken upon himself to legislate for distinctions in dress codes including that for the modest wife.[55] He proscribed in particular the wearing of the *stola* by the married woman who was convicted of adultery as well as the prostitute.[56] The concerns about physical adornment in 1 Timothy 2:9a can be understood in the light of this.

Godliness and Good Works

Mention was made not only of the adornment of virtues and modest dress (contrasted with braided hair, gold, pearls and extravagant apparel), 'but (ἀλλά) [of] that which is proper (πρέπει γυναιξίν) for a woman who professes godliness through good deeds' (2:10) — the nature of that godliness is explained with the addition of 'faith, love and holiness' (2:15). While the context in which these virtues were to be encouraged is not specified, it certainly would have included her own household, the neglect of which was the subject of concern in relation to the 'new' women.[57] Given the contrast between the lifestyle epitomised by extravagance and the strong adversative stressing godliness expressed by good deeds, there is, by implication, a reference to the inappropriate and antithetical actions of the new breed of women.

This section has discussed the significance of two dress codes (2:9-11). The first was apparel characterised by gold and pearls and extravagant clothing that signalled to others a sexually lax lifestyle. The second did not describe an actual dress code but rather used the concept of adornment as a metaphor for the virtues of a wife who was not only godly but also adorned her life with good works. She would have been represented visually by the modest dress of the first-century married woman that comprised a full-length garment with a discreet neckline. The way that wives dressed in public sent clear signals to men, thereby presenting themselves as either modest or promiscuous women. Just as philosophical schools were concerned about young wives entering marriage, so too a similar concern was expressed in the Pauline community about how Christian wives operated in marriage.

54. Grubbs, *Women in the Law the Roman Empire,* p. 48.
55. J. A. Crook, *Law and Life of Rome, 90 B.C.–A.D. 212* (New York: Cornell University Press, 1967), pp. 7-8.
56. McGinn, *Prostitution, Sexuality, and the Law,* p. 154.
57. See pp. 91-94.

Up to this point it has been assumed that the reference is to a married woman and not just a woman. Is that assumption justified, given that a single word in Koine Greek serves either status for a female on the basis that the context will readily determine the specific referent? It is not the indulged pre-puberty girls who wed at a very young age who are the subject of discussion in this passage, but the married women, whether young or old, and the way they dressed.[58] Furthermore, the reference to Christian wives giving birth to children (2:15), along with the introductory and concluding reference to modesty (2:9, 15b), gives secure grounds for arguing that the reference is to married women. It is in the light of the two ways in which a first-century married woman might live (2:9-10) that verses 11-12 need to be examined.

II. Abortion or Child-Bearing? (2:15a)

Does the enigmatic statement in 1 Timothy 2:15 — 'yet she shall be saved through the childbearing' (σωθήσεται δὲ διὰ τῆς τεκνογονίας) — reflect the aversion to having children by rich or progressive wives? The use of preventative measures often put them in physical danger, and sometimes led to death.

The term τεκνογονία (2:15) has been the subject of intense discussion.[59] Different words were used throughout the Greek *corpus* in connection with the role of childbearing/rearing. This is not untypical of the Greek language as *Liddell and Scott* record: 'I procreate children' (τεκνόω), 'the begetting of children' (τεκνοσπορία), 'the making of children' into adults (τεκνοποιΐα). The 'rearing of children' (τεκνοτροφία), the cognate of which (ἐτεκνοτρόφησεν) occurs in 1 Timothy 5:10, would rule out the possibility that the reference is to raising children.[60] Furthermore, in the late first century B.C. the Stoic Arius Didymus used this term when he wrote of the wise man's need to write down what would benefit his fellow men. This included 'having sexual intercourse both for marriage and for the bearing of children (καὶ τὸ συγκαταβαίνειν καὶ εἰς γάμον καὶ εἰς τεκνογονίαν), both for his own and his country's sake'.[61] The term refers to pregnancy.

---

58. See pp. 125 and 83.

59. For a detailed history of the term τεκνογονία and the interpretation of the text see A. Köstenberger, "Ascertaining Women's God-ordained Roles: An Interpretation of 1 Timothy 2:15," *BBR* 7 (1997): 107-144, reprinted in his *Studies in John and Gender: A Decade of Scholarship* (New York: Peter Lang, 2001), ch. 14.

60. *P.Haun.* 13, *l.* 44, 'bring up children' (τρέφειν).

61. *Epitome of Stoic Ethics*, 11b. The word συγκαταβαίνειν is a cognate of βαίνω that has sexual connotations; see J. N. Adams, *The Latin Sexual Vocabulary* (London: Duckworth, 1982),

What is the meaning of the phrase 'through the childbearing' (διὰ τῆς τεκνογονίας)? Köstenberger has provided philological analysis of 'saving through' and concludes that it 'should be understood as a reference to the woman's escape or preservation from a danger by means of childbearing'. He further argues that 'She (i.e., the woman) escapes (or is preserved; gnomic future) [from Satan] by way of procreation (i.e., having a family).'[62] The use of the article in 'the childbearing' together with the preposition διά with the genitive suggests that it is through the process of childbearing that she is preserved. The use of this construction indicates 'throughout' or 'through the course of' and is well attested in Classical and Koine Greek, and confirms that the phrase should be rendered 'through the childbearing, i.e., the pregnancy'.[63]

Avoiding Childbearing

The avoidance of pregnancy and the terminating of it by an abortion meant that however dangerous and life-threatening they were, it was possible to do so. The use of different forms of contraception in the first century is well documented. The use of abortion and contraceptives could be fatal.[64] Even Ovid speaks graphically against abortion — he may have lost a mistress through it.

> She who first began the practice of tearing out her tender progeny deserved to die in her own warfare. Can it be that, to be free of the flaws of stretchmarks, you have to scatter the tragic sands of carnage? Why will you subject your womb to the weapons of abortion and give dread poisons to the unborn? The tigress lurking in Armenia does no such thing, nor does the lioness dare destroy her young. Yet tender girls do so — though not with impunity; often she who kills what is in her womb dies herself.[65]

Abortion took many lives, in spite of the skills of doctors whom the rich could afford to employ.[66] The early-second-century gynaecologist from

---

p. 205, contra A. J. Pomeroy, *Arius Didymus: Epitome of Stoic Ethics,* Texts and Translations, Graeco-Roman Series 14 (Atlanta: Society of Biblical Literature, 1999), p. 121, where he suggests the term is pejorative and translates it as 'stoops to marriage', citing in support M. Schofield, *The Stoic Ideal of the City* (Cambridge: Cambridge University Press, 1991), p. 126, n. 14.

62. Köstenberger, *Studies in John and Gender,* esp. p. 307, *cit.* p. 320.

63. Liddell & Scott.

64. The use of contraception is well documented; see K. Hopkins, "Contraception in the Roman Empire," *Comparative Studies in Society and History* 8 (1965): 124-51.

65. Ovid, *Amores,* 2.14.5-9, 27-28, 35-38.

66. L. P. Wilkinson, "Population and Family Planning," in *Classical Attitudes to Modern Issues* (London: William Kimber, 1979), ch. 1.

Ephesus, Soranus, refused to undertake abortions, citing in support the *dictum* of Hippocrates, 'I will give no one an abortion.'[67]

It was Juvenal who observed —

> Childbirth hardly ever occurs in a gold-embroidered bed since abortionists have such skills and so many potions, and can bring about the death of children in the womb.[68]

The termination of a pregnancy also drew Seneca's censure as he reminded his mother, 'nor have you crushed the hope of children that were being nurtured in your body'.[69]

In spite of the idealising of the family in the first century, Seneca noted that some women in his day, his mother excepted, tried to hide their pregnancy, such were their disdain of pregnancy and the preoccupation with the shape of their body (and, it must be added, men felt the same about their body).

In some cases those who had children sought to avoid nursing them by employing a wet nurse. When Favorinus (*c.* A.D. 85-155) visited the home of a senatorial family to congratulate the father on the birth of a child, he challenged the attitude of the grandmother.

> 'I have no doubt that she will nurse the baby with her own milk.' But when the girl's mother said that her daughter should be spared this and nurses provided — so as not to add the burdensome and difficult task of nursing to the pains of childbirth. He said, 'I pray you, woman, let her be completely the mother of her own child. What sort of half-baked, unnatural kind of mother bears a child and then sends it away?' . . . they desert their newborn and send them away to be fed by others and thus cut or at least loosen the bond and that joining of mind and love by which nature links parents to their children. . . .'[70]

Such were the sentiments on childbearing and nursing which were harboured by some women in the first century that ostensibly motivated Augustus to legislate so intrusively on marriage and inheritance. (See pp. 52-54.)

These facts, together with the grammatical construction of 1 Timothy 2:15a, suggest that this text indicates that the Christian wife would be preserved by continuing in her pregnant condition (and thereby bearing a child) instead of terminating her pregnancy. This interpretation would also make sense of the

---

67. Soranus, *Gynaecology*, 1.19.60. See also Aulus Gellius, *Attic Nights*, 12.1.8, on abortion.
68. Juvenal, *Satires*, 6.593ff; cf. Tacitus, *Germania*, 19.5.
69. Seneca, *Ad Helviam*, 16.3-5.
70. Gellius, *Attic Nights*, 12.1.

conditional clause that follows — 'if she remains in faith, love and holiness' — together with the stress on self-control at the end of the discussion. The results of the decoding of the dress code (2:9-11) and the known reluctance and refusal of some married women to bear children (2:15) may be a further help towards understanding the *Sitz im Leben* of 1 Timothy 2:11-12 to be considered next.

III. Submissiveness and Learning, Teaching and Dominating (2:11-12)

It was possible for daughters who were from the ranks of the élite and the sub-élite to have an education in the first century. While sources are scarce, Hemelrijk, in her work on educated women, undertakes a chronological survey and notes the steep increase in evidence of this in the first and second centuries A.D.[71] Wives might also be exposed to some form of education from their husbands.

The Stoics argued that the education of daughters was essential because of the moral element in education related to the learning, and the embracing, of the cardinal virtues and the importance of avoiding the cardinal vices. This applied equally to daughters as to sons. In the case of the former, one of the virtues was modesty although they also learnt of the cardinal virtues for men as they were deemed appropriate for women in some instances. (See pp. 66-68.) The need for an education similar to that of sons was not related to a future public career but to the bringing up of children and the complex management of households.

The instruction of children was undertaken in the houses of the rich by tutors.[72] Lucian provides evidence of professional teachers selling their services to rich householders. While he mocks them and denounces their soft living, he was later forced to retract some of his comments when he himself entered the employ of a large household.[73] Teachers were also meant to provide intellectual stimulus to the family in the setting of dinners and appropriate and learned conversation at the *symposia*.[74] Daughters also participated in

71. E. A. Hemelrijk, Matrona Docta: *Educated Women in the Roman Elite from Correlia to Julia Domna* (London: Routledge, 1999), pp. 92-96. She conjectures that this may be related to there being more sources in this period compared with others, although compared with other centuries there are fewer. She does note a dropping away in the third century.

72. Winter, *Philo and Paul among the Sophists*, pp. 25-26.

73. Lucian, "On Salaried Posts in Great Houses" and his "Apology".

74. See the phenomenon and content of discussions in the fifteen books of the second-century Athenaeus, in his *The Deipnosophists*.

this form of home schooling in enlightened households. While Lucian lampooned those who taught men in the household, he also parodied that activity among wealthy women.

> After all, one could perhaps put up with the conduct of men. But the women! That is another thing women are keen about — to have educated men living in their households on a salary and following their litters. They count it an embellishment if they are said to be cultured, to have an interest in philosophy and to write songs that are hardly inferior to Sappho's. To that end they trail hired rhetoricians and grammarians and philosophers, and listen to their lectures — when? It is ludicrous! — either while their toilet is being made and their hair dressed, or at dinner; at other times they are too busy! And often while the philosopher is delivering a discourse, the maid comes in and hands her a note from her lover, so that the lecture on chastity is kept waiting while she writes a reply to her lover; she then hurries back to hear it.[75]

Hemelrijk comments on the basis of this extract: 'Lucian's mockery would make no sense if it did not reflect to some degree the actual practice among the upper-class women of his time.'[76]

Submissiveness or Teaching

Treggiari, in summarising concepts of marriage, concludes with a comment on the submission of a wife to her husband in the early period of the Empire over against the Republican period. 'Rome's particular (though not entirely original) contribution to the ideology of marriage was the ideal of the wife's faithfulness to one man, the eternity of the bond, and the partnership of the couple. Subordination of the wife, I would argue, was not essential or important by the time of Cicero [106-43 B.C.].' This is a surprising conclusion. We are dealing with the demise of the image of the subordination of wives by the end of the Roman Republic.[77]

In any case, 1 Timothy 2:11-12 refers not to a wife's submissiveness to her husband but rather to how the godly wife should respond to Christian in-

---

75. Lucian, "On Salaried Posts in Great Houses," 36.

76. Hemelrijk, Matrona Docta: *Educated Women*, p. 37.

77. S. Treggiari, *Roman Marriage:* Iusti Coniuges *from the Time of Cicero to the Time of Ulpian* (Oxford: Clarendon, 1991), p. 261. Her conclusion challenges the assumption of New Testament scholars that submission was the cultural norm in the period.

struction. This is conveyed by means of both negative and positive injunctions. The sentence reads literally, 'the wife in silence must learn in all subordination' (γυνὴ ἐν ἡσυχίᾳ μανθανέτω ἐν πάσῃ ὑποταγῇ). Had it meant to indicate that she was in a 'subordinate position' then the Greek would have been ἐν ὑποταγῇ, as, for example, in a third-century-A.D. papyrus.[78] The repeating of 'in' (ἐν) without any use of 'and' (καί) indicates that the silence was to be exercised during instruction. After the statement 'and (δέ) to teach I do not permit nor to αὐθεντεῖν over a man' comes the strong adversative clause again with the emphasis on quietness, 'but [she is] to be in silence' (ἀλλ᾽ εἶναι ἐν ἡσυχίᾳ) (2:12b).

Musonius Rufus argued that philosophical instruction would be misplaced for a wife 'if the study that shows the respect of the greatest good (μέγιστον ἀγαθόν) makes them bold (θρασεῖα)'.[79] For all his defending the education of daughters, his comment reveals his concerns about 'new' wives abandoning their households for philosophical *symposia* and the competitive nature of conversations with sophists and others at the banquet.

> Women who associate with philosophers are bound to be arrogant for the most part and presumptuous, in that abandoning their own households and turning to the company of men they practice speeches, talk like sophists, and analyze syllogisms, when they ought to be sitting at home spinning.[80]

According to Juvenal, who was threatened by the 'new' woman, she would be no less a threat at dinner as a dominant conversationalist.

> Let the wife, who reclines with you at dinner, not possess a rhetorical style of her own, let her not hurl at you in whirling speech the well-rounded syllogism. Let her not know all history. Let there be some things in her reading which she does not understand. I hate the woman who is always consulting and poring over the grammatical treatise of Palaemon, who observes all the rules and laws of correct speech, who with antiquarian zeal quotes verses that I never heard of and corrects her ignorant female friend for slips of speech that no man need trouble about: let her husband at least be allowed to make his solecisms [slips in syntax] in peace.[81]

---

78. *BGU*, 96, *l.* 7.
79. Lutz, p. 42, *ll.* 24-25. For full citation see p. 66.
80. Musonius Rufus, in Lutz, p. 42, *ll.* 54-58.
81. Juvenal, *Satires*, 6.448-56.

Hemelrijk notes the social tension between the politically prominent educated woman and the modest and submissive Roman *matrona;* also noted are the satire and invective against this shift in values.[82]

The *symposia* and the dinner parties were held in homes. This was the setting of the meetings of the early church. The concern that, at the Lord's Supper or in other forms of worship, women might behave in a similar way can be understood, for they aped secular customs.[83] Certainly the Corinthian experience of abuse at the former and disorder in the latter would provide a precedent to be avoided (1 Cor. 11:17-31; chs. 12-14).

Speaking and Teaching

The first century saw the rise of the Second Sophistic in which rhetorical education replaced to some extent that which had traditionally been provided by the philosophers. Its aim was to provide education for sons so that they could pursue a career as an orator in the public domain, a lawyer or a teacher *cum* sophist. All these demanded a tertiary education in rhetoric so that they could be public speakers. According to Hemelrijk educated daughters of the élite and the sub-élite lacked the career path of a public speaker although it had been the parental objective in educating their brothers.[84]

Is there evidence of wives actively engaging in speaking in a public gathering? Valerius Maximus asks this question and responds curtly: 'What business has a woman with a public meeting? If ancestral custom be observed, none.' However, he goes on to note that when the household is disturbed, the ancient convention is overridden. He indicates this in the present tense — 'But when domestic quiet is stirred by the waves of sedition, the authority of the ancient usage is subverted.' He then adds an enigmatic comment, 'and compulsion of violence has greater force than persuasion and precept of restraint'.[85] It is not clear what incident occurred at that time or what follows from it he is referring to; he may be regretting that women engaged in speaking in *politeia,* i.e., the courts and, in one instance, the forum. The rise of women advocates can be traced and those named were highly effective as lawyers. (See pp. 176-79 for this public role of women.)

Did women in the ancient world teach? We know that they were taught

---

82. Hemelrijk, Matrona Docta: *Educated Women,* p. 88.
83. See my *After Paul Left Corinth,* pp. 153-57.
84. Hemelrijk, Matrona Docta: *Educated Women,* p. 28.
85. Valerius Maximus, *Memorable Doings and Sayings,* III.8.6.

by their mothers or by male instructors, but there is no record of women undertaking the task of a teacher in a professional sense either in salaried posts in great houses or in running schools as sophists.[86] Hemelrijk, in her extremely thorough work on the education of women, provides no evidence of women who were professional teachers at any level of schooling outside the home.[87]

However, this does not mean that women had no educative role in their domestic domain. It was expected that upper-class women would take their sons in hand to help educate them and, above all, to exercise discipline.[88] Tacitus records the ideal mother who taught by word and example and cites his mother-in-law who educated her son in an exemplary fashion.[89] Hemelrijk rejects doubts that have been expressed that women needed to be well-educated in order to supervise their children's education. She cites Cicero and Quintilian who acknowledged their own mother's critical contribution to their education and careers as orators; Vitruvius and Martial also acknowledged both parents in this regard.[90] Furthermore, with the death of the husband, the full supervision of education was passed on to the mother. There is no lack of evidence of well-educated mothers, and this holds true for their devotion to the daughter's education as well as to their son's.[91]

To Have Authority or Dominate?

While the term 'to teach' has not attracted significant discussion, the infinitive that follows certainly has. This section will seek to explore what the term αὐθεντέω was meant to signify. Did it reflect a concern that Christian women wanted to have authority in Christian gatherings (which included men) or to dominate in the same way that some 'new' women were accused of doing in the civil courts and the forum?

Danker and Bauer concluded that the term αὐθεντέω means 'to assume a stance of independent authority, give orders to, dictate to'. They follow the

---

86. Philostratus, *The Lives of the Sophists.*

87. In the conclusion of her chapter "The Education of Upper-Class Women: Opportunities," Hemelrijk rightly draws attention to the scattered nature of her sources and the fact that they were written by men; Matrona Docta: *Educated Women,* ch. 2, pp. 57-58.

88. S. Dixon, *The Roman Mother,* 2nd ed. (London: Routledge, 1990), pp. 1-7.

89. Tacitus, *Dialogue,* 28, and *Agriculture,* 4.2-3.

90. Cicero, *Brutus,* 210; Quintilian, 1.1.4-5, Vitruvius, *Architecture,* 6, Preface 4; and Martial, *Epigrams,* 9.73.7.

91. Hemelrijk, Matrona Docta: *Educated Women,* pp. 68-71.

Liddell and Scott rendering 'to have full power or authority over [someone]'. In later editions they themselves have cited 1 Timothy 2:12 as an example, with the cognate αὐθεντία referring to absolute sway or authority.[92] One is grateful for the exhaustive studies that have been conducted on this verb.[93] However, citing the extensive examples of this term even before the *TLG* came on a CDRom and after does not necessarily clarify this issue. Are there any philological insights peculiar to the history of the Greek language that have been missed? Is giving equal weight to all examples appropriate with much of the later discussion from Christian sources? Has sufficient weight been given to the semantic domains?

Much of the information supplied by Hesychius of Alexandria from the fifth century A.D. can be important, although the significance of his evidence is often overlooked in Greek philology in general, and in the New Testament in particular.[94] His *Alphabetical Collection of All Words* has a list of Greek words whose meanings were no longer well known in his day. He supplied a synonym or synonyms for the benefit of his contemporaries, using examples of earlier readings of literary texts for which later correctors provided the word in vogue in later periods.[95]

Hesychius indicates that αὐθεντέω is a synonym for ἐξουσιάζειν, 'to have authority', and also records that the cognate αὐθέντης refers to the person who executes authority (ἐξουσιαστής), or who does things with his own hands (αὐτόχειρ), or who murders (φονεύς).[96] The fact that he also notes that αὐτοδικεῖ (he has 'jurisdiction over' or 'power over another') is a synonym for αὐθεντεῖ has been overlooked. In the case of the latter he adds the comment 'when he himself gives orders' (ὅταν αὐτὸς λέγῃ).[97] In the case of αὐθέντης as

92. F. W. Danker and W. Bauer, *A Greek-English Lexicon of the New Testament and Other Early Christian Literature*, 3rd ed. (Chicago: University of Chicago Press, 2000), p. 150. *Liddell & Scott*, 9th ed. (1996), p. 275.

93. G. W. Knight III, "ΑΥΘΕΝΤΕΩ in Reference to Women in 1 Timothy 2.12," *NTS* 30.1 (1984): 143-57; and L. Wilshire, "The TLG computer and further references to ΑΥΘΕΝΤΕΩ in 1 Timothy 2:12," *NTS* 34 (1988): 120-34; and a further discussion by H. S. Baldwin, "αὐθεντέω in Ancient Greek Literature," in A. Köstenberger, T. R. Schreiner and H. S. Baldwin, eds., *Women in the Church: A Fresh Analysis of 1 Timothy 2:9-15* (Grand Rapids: Baker, 1995), pp. 269-305.

94. For example, he provides καταργᾶν as a synonym for the not widely attested ὑπερακμάζειν and notes its importance for understanding the latter's use in 1 Cor. 7:36; see my *After Paul Left Corinth: The Influence of Secular Ethics and Social Change*, p. 248.

95. Wilshire, "The TLG computer and further references to ΑΥΘΕΝΤΕΩ in 1 Timothy 2:12," p. 125, may have misunderstood the importance of Hesychius, for he comments, 'He gives no reason for his listing although it may reflect his perception of the common usage of his day.'

96. Hesychius, *Lex.* 63, 64.

97. A good example of the use of αὐτοδικεῖ can be found in Thucydides, 5.18.2, on the

with other Greek words, the particular semantic field should secure the apposite rendering. Clearly neither rendering of the term in 2:12 as 'teaching and doing things with her own hands' or 'murdering' makes any sense, but 'having authority' in relation to teaching is an appropriate meaning.

Other evidence from a much later example with the equivalent Latin rendering may be of help. 'The women from the Agilians exercise authority over [have in their power] men and they do evil as they desire, not being jealous of men, but achieving in agriculture and in construction, and in all manly things' (παρ' Ἀγιλαίοις αἱ γυναῖκες αὐθεντοῦσι τῶν ἀνδρῶν, *Apud Agilaeos feminae sua viros in potestate habent*), καὶ πορνεύουσιν ὡς βούλονται, μὴ ζηλοτυπούμεναι παρὰ τῶν ἀνδρῶν αὐτῶν, γεωργίαν δὲ καὶ οἰκοδομίαν καὶ πάντα τὰ ἀνδρῶα πράττουσιν.) αὐθεντοῦσι is rendered in Latin as *potestate habent* and means to 'have in their power'.[98]

Also of importance in the midst of the large amount of extant material is the comment of Phrynichus in the late second-century A.D. on the usage of a cognate. He argues that one should never use the cognate αὐθέντης to refer to a 'master' (δεσπότης) as the legal rhetoricians do, but of the one who murders by his own hand (μηδέποτε χρήσῃ ἐπὶ δεσπότου, ὡς οἱ περὶ τὰ δικαστήρια ῥήτορες, ἀλλ' ἐπὶ τοῦ αὐτόχειρος φονέως).[99] However much Phrynichus may object, as he himself observes, this cognate was used to refer to those who controlled others.

Is this same sentiment expressed using another synonym? Plutarch comments on Fulvia who was an exceedingly powerful wife who marshalled troops. We are told —

> She was a woman who gave no thought to spinning or housekeeping, nor did she consider it worthwhile to dominate a man not in public life (οὐδὲ ἀνδρὸς ἰδιώτου κρατεῖν ἀξιοῦν). She wished to rule (ἄρχειν) a ruler and command (στρατηγεῖν) a commander.[100]

Diodorus of Sicily also comments on an unusual custom of the Egyptians that was enshrined in their law and contrary to that of other nations. He reports that 'the wife should enjoy authority over her husband, the husbands agreeing in the marriage contract that they will be obedient in all things to

---

treaty between the Athenians and the Lacedaemonians where it was agreed that the people of Delphi would not only have an independent tax system but also their own courts of justice (αὐτοδίκους).

98. *Corpus Scriptorium Historiae Byzantinae*, ed. I. Bekker (Bonn, 1836), p. 270.

99. Phrynichus, *Ecloga*, 96.

100. Plutarch, *Antonius*, 10.3.

their wives' (κυριεύειν τὴν γυναῖκα τἀνδρός). The term used in this instance is κυριεύειν that has clear legal as well as social and domestic implications.[101]

Given the antithetical comments that preceded (2:11) and followed (2:12b) and without at this stage foreclosing on the nature of the way in which authority was being exercised, it seems that here the term carries not only the connotation of authority but also an inappropriate misuse of it.

The significance to be given to this term needs to be assessed in the light of the preceding background discussion relating to 1 Timothy 2:9-11 and 15, the dress codes being proscribed there and the desire on the part of some first-century women not to have children. This would confirm Marshall's view of the meaning of αὐθεντέω. 'Ideas such as autocratic or domineering abuses of power and authority appear to be more naturally linked with the verb in view of the meanings of the cognate nouns αὐθέντης and αὐθεντία . . . '.[102]

Just as we have the erotics of domination (to use Greene's title to her work on the sexual domain),[103] so, too, certain married women had a parallel or similar desire to dominate in the Forum and the courts. Was there a concern that a comparable attitude might creep into the Christian community with the desire to use power to control, this time in the context of public instruction (1 Tim. 2:12)?

The immediate context of these verses is that of learning and teaching. The deciphering of the dress codes and its coded use in the previous section have gone a substantial way in locating the social *Sitz im Leben*. This latter section shows the public role of some women engaged in the public place and some form of social or intellectual control on the part of some. The cumulative evidence on the new women helps in the choice of the meaning of the term αὐθεντέω (2:11-12).

IV. Conclusions

A later Christian writer, Clement of Alexandria was addressing the same issues *c.* A.D. 200 in 'Against the embellishing of the body'. He refers to

> those women who wear gold, who occupy themselves in curling their tresses, and engage in anointing their cheeks, and painting their eyes, and

101. Diodorus Siculus, 1.27.2.

102. Marshall, *The Pastoral Epistles*, p. 457.

103. E. Greene, *The Erotics of Domination: Male Desire and the Mistress in Latin Love Poetry* (Baltimore: Johns Hopkins, 1998).

dyeing their hair, and practising the other pernicious acts of luxury, be-
decking the outer covering of the flesh — in true Egyptian fashion — to attract their idolatrous lovers . . . for love of finery is not for a wife but a
courtesan; such women think little of keeping house beside their husbands;
but, loosing their husbands' purse-strings, they expend its resources on
their pleasures, that they may have many witnesses to their seeming beauty,
and the whole day they spend with their slaves, devouring their attention
to beauty treatments.[104]

The external pressures on women in the philosophical schools and the community reflected in 1 Timothy 2:9-15 seem not to have diminished. The latter
passage does not indicate that this was an existing difficulty in that community at that time. It contrasts with the situation of widows dealt with in the
same letter where the problem clearly existed within the Christian community (5:15). So the aim appears to have been preventative and not remedial; the
reason for the concern was the possible influence on that community of the
norms of the 'new woman'.

It should be noted that the discussion of Christian wives does not conclude in 1 Timothy 2:9-15. In 3:11, in the midst of a discussion on roles of deacons (3:8-13), there are stipulations concerning wives — 'women [or wives]
must likewise be serious, not slanderers, but temperate, faithful in all things.'
If that refers to women deacons or the wives of deacons, then it would also
have a bearing on what it meant to be a godly one. Furthermore, the require-
ments of married women in the light of 2:9-15 need to be understood in the
context of the discussion of the young widows remarrying, raising children
and running their own households in 5:14, and *vice versa*. (See pp. 137-40.)

The evidence presented above may help resolve the concerns of commentators. For example, Marshall wrote: 'It may seem puzzling that ostentation
and seduction would be a concern when the heresy insisted on asceticism and
celibacy (4:3), but the presence of wealthy women and motives of greed (6:3-
10) and the concern for the perceptions of outsiders who would not appreciate fine points of doctrine are probably sufficient to make sense of the inclu-
sion of traditional *paraenesis*.'[105] When cognisance is taken of the immediate
social context, it is no longer necessary to posit a dichotomy of the rich men
and women, the poor and some connection to heresy. Furthermore, it is not
accurate to suggest from this passage that 'the author employs a disparaging

104. Clement, *Paidagogos* 3.2.4.2–5.4.
105. In that passage there is no specific reference to rich women but in 6:9 to 'the men'. It is
suggested that this passage is directed towards Christian workers and the temptation to become
financially acquisitive, for 6:17-19 provides instructions to the rich Christians.

caricature of wealthy women'.[106] However, Marshall rightly concludes 'that the main point is that true adornment will be internal, expressing itself outwardly in Christian character, whereas an emphasis on the external suggests a desire to attract attention to oneself, perhaps to seduce.'[107] The evidence does show that a woman so dressed certainly sent signals to all who saw her.

Judge concludes his examination of the important Neo-Pythagorean text with this observation: 'Although there are close similarities of detail between the letter of Melissa and the NT letters on the restraint of women's dress (*ll.* 1-15, 24-26, compared with 1 Tim. 2:9, 1 Pet. 3:3), the justification for it is different. Melissa is concerned about the sexual implications of display, and with the need to be attractive to her husband (*ll.* 20-22), whose will is the good woman's law.' He goes on to suggest that in 1 Timothy 2:10 the 'restraint on women's dress is desired because it goes with devotion to God'.[108] Our investigation seems to suggest that it was not her spirituality that was the concern but rather her modesty in the home, the Christian gathering and possibly in the public place.

McGinn put the matter succinctly: 'Clothing's role as a status maker receives repeated recognition from the jurists' and as a yardstick for morality among women.[109] In Roman law there was no culpability if a woman sent the wrong signals by the way she dressed, for 'matrons had more protection in law . . . only if they looked *respectable*.'[110] The focus of 1 Timothy 2:9-15 was not with the limited culpability of someone who made sexual advances towards a woman whose intentions were misread because of what she wore. Rather the Christian matron's modesty was set against the antithetical behaviour of the promiscuous wife in the public place. (See ch. 5.)

The public perception of Christian wives was a critical matter in the community; they would play into the hands of the enemy of the early Christian movement in Ephesus if they dressed like high-class prostitutes. The dress code was proscribed in 2:9b because it sent signals of a lack of moral respectability and sexual availability to those at banquets, other social gatherings or in the public spaces which women frequented, including theatres. 1 Timothy 2:9a seeks an adornment of the female virtues of modesty and self-control coupled with good deeds rather than the wrong attire.

106. *Contra* Marshall, *The Pastoral Epistles*, p. 449.

107. Marshall, *The Pastoral Epistles*, pp. 450-51.

108. E. A. Judge, "A Woman's Behaviour," *New Documents Illustrating Early Christianity* 6 (1992): 19.

109. McGinn, *Prostitution, Sexuality, and the Law*, p. 154.

110. A. T. Croom, *Roman Clothing and Fashion*, p. 75. Italics are hers. *The Digest* 47.10.15.15. For the citation see p. 83.

Outsiders read the activities of any association by Roman authorities from the time of Augustus onwards, including 'religious' ones. The problems of associations in the East in subsequent decades would easily explain the concerns about the dress codes of Christian wives in 1 Timothy 2:9-15.[111] Jewish communities were judged to be associations under Roman law,[112] but Christian communities in Rome and other places were not thought of as legal associations — ratification by the Emperor and then the Senate in Rome and the provincial governor elsewhere was required. They would be open to private prosecution by their enemies in a criminal action if they could be shown to be seditious or promiscuous.[113]

The issue of appearance in 1 Timothy 2:9-15 was not unlike that in 1 Corinthians 11:2-16 or that to be discussed in the following chapters, i.e., the perceptions of young Christian widows (1 Tim. 5:11-15) or young Cretan Christian wives (Titus 2:3-5). Furthermore, the concerns about giving the enemy no occasion to revile the Christian community (5:15) would have applied equally to married Christian women who had elaborate hair styles, decked themselves with jewellery of gold and pearls and wore expensive clothing (2:9-15). Such a dress code would have played into the hands of the opponents of Ephesian Christians by sending a wrong signal to all who saw Christian wives in public places. They could have concluded that they belonged to a promiscuous cult that endorsed *avant-garde* behaviour.[114] Because in Roman law you were what you wore, the concerns in this new community of Christians were that the values of the 'new woman' could intrude into the gatherings in Christian homes, and hence the concern for preventative measures in 1 Timothy 2:9-15.

111. O. F. Robinson, *The Criminal Law of Ancient Rome* (London: Duckworth, 1995), p. 80; and O. M. Van Nijf, *The Civic World of Professional Associations in the Roman East* (Amsterdam: J. C. Gieben, 1997).

112. P. Richardson, "Early Synagogues as *collegia* in the Diaspora and Palestine," in J. S. Kloppenborg and S. G. Wilson, eds., *Voluntary Associations in the Graeco-Roman World* (London: Routledge, 1996), ch. 6, argued that case.

113. See the evidence cited in my "Roman Law and Society in Romans 12–15," in P. Oakes, ed., *Rome in the Bible and the Early Church* (Carlisle and Grand Rapids: Paternoster and Baker, 2002), pp. 69-75.

114. A similar concern was expressed in Titus 2:5 'that the Word of God be not discredited'.

CHAPTER 7

The Appearance of Young Widows,
1 Timothy 5:11-15

At least three issues concerning the widows in 1 Timothy 5:3-16 resonate immediately with wider societal conventions and concerns about this group in the first-century world. McGinn observes in "Widows, Orphans, and Social History" — his review article of the monumental four volumes by Krause on this subject in the *Journal of Roman Archaeology* — that in the same way that 'Roman law wished to distinguish the good widows from the bad . . . the author of 1 Timothy sets himself . . . the same task, in the sense that he wished to define deserving widows apart from the rest'.[1] The 'real' Christian widow had an age qualification and was known for her faithfulness in marriage. She distinguished herself in her service as a Christian; she was 'well attested for her good deeds, as one who has brought up children, shown hospitality, washed the feet of the saints, relieved the afflicted, and devoted herself to doing good in every way'. She had no immediate family or relatives to support her financially. This was how the 'real' Christian widows were defined in the Pauline community in Ephesus (1 Timothy 5:4, 9, 10, 16).

Secular literature, including that from legal sources, described widows in the same way as did Paul in 1 Timothy 5:11-15.[2] It described their lifestyle as

1. T. A. J. McGinn, "Widows, Orphans, and Social History," *Journal of Roman Archaeology* 12 (1999): 617-632, cit. 632. J.-U. Krause *Witwen und Waisen im Römischen Reich:* I. *Verwitwung und Wiederverheiratung;* II. *Witschaftliche und die Gesellschaftlicher Stellung von Witwen;* III. *Rechtlicher und Soziale Stellung von Waisen;* IV. *Witwen und Waisen im frühen Christentum,* Habes 16-19 (Stuttgart: F. Steiner, 1994-95).

2. See P. Walcot, "On Widows and Their Reputation in Antiquity," *Symbolae Osloenses* lxvi (1991): 5-26, for a very broad ranging discussion of the fear of the sexually experienced and the sexually voracious widow. See also the primary evidence in this chapter.

'behaving promiscuously' (καταστρηνιάσωσιν) (5:11), i.e., they were guilty of *stuprum*. Roman law used this term to describe the sexual indiscretions of single women, widows and divorcees, rather than *adulterium*, which was the term reserved for the indiscretions of married women.[3]

'That it was the custom for a high-status widow to remarry seems borne out by the number who actually did so . . . the decision was essentially hers . . . as the standard for the young upper-class widow'.[4] McGinn does not discuss the requirement for the flighty young widows in 1 Timothy 5:11 to remarry — 'They are wishing to marry' (γαμεῖν θέλουσιν). Furthermore, in the midst of all the commands reflected by imperatives in 1 Timothy 5:3, 4, 7, 9, 11, 16 that aimed to resolve the problem of the church's support of 'real' widows, the matter of the remarriage of young widows was stated differently — 'I therefore wish widows to marry' (βούλομαι οὖν νεωτέρας γαμεῖν) (5:14). Given the use of the verb elsewhere in 1 Timothy, remarriage was not stated as an option.[5] These three observations provide an added stimulus to search for the cultural *Sitz im Leben* of the young Christian widows set, as it relates to the wider discussion of widows *per se* in the Ephesian church, the stated destination of the letter (1:3).

I. The Widows and the Christian Community

That both young and old widows should be present in such numbers and pose financial problems for the Christian community comes as no surprise. It has been estimated that forty per cent of women between the ages of forty and fifty were widows and that, as a group, they comprised some thirty per cent of women in the ancient world.[6] Admittedly such figures are at best only estimates.[7] However, Hopkins has provided significant statistical information

---

3. "*Stuprum* was committed by a woman who had never married or a widow; the Greeks called it corruption (φθορά), seduction," Papian, *The Digest*, 48.5.6.1. The term *adulterium* was reserved only for married women in Roman law; see T. A. J. McGinn, *Prostitution, Sexuality and the Law in Ancient Rome* (Oxford: Oxford University Press, 1998), p. 151.

4. McGinn, "Widows, Orphans, and Social History," p. 622.

5. Cf. 4:3 where there is a reference to those who forbid marriage. The two words function as synonyms: 'those wishing' to be teachers of the law, 1:7; 'God wishes' the salvation of all, 2:4; cf. βούλομαι: 'I wish' that men should pray everywhere, 2:8; 'those who wish' to be rich, 6:9. Cf. βούλομαι and ἐθέλω in *Liddell & Scott* where a significant distinction cannot be maintained.

6. Krause, *Witwen und Waisen im Römischen Reich*, I, p. 73.

7. McGinn, "Widows, Orphans, and Social History," p. 618, argues that Krause fails to take into account the differences between the privileged classes and others, but agrees that there were a large number of widows.

based on previous studies of epigraphic data and his own review of the major collection of Latin inscriptions in Rome. It records the chances of women being widowed in different age groups.[8]

Age Group	Percentage Widowed
15-19	1
20-24	5
25-29	9
30-34	19
35-39	18

While the age qualification for older widows warranting the support of the Christian community was specified at sixty years, no age parameters defined the 'young' widow in 1 Timothy 5:3-16. The term 'young', however, could be understood to apply to those who had not reached menopause and were therefore capable of bearing children; this was one of the stated purposes for remarriage (5:14). According to Soranus, an early-second-century A.D. Ephesian doctor, who wrote an extended treatise on gynaecology, menopause occurred after the age of forty and not later than fifty.[9] The *lex Julia* penalised unmarried women as well as those who were divorced or widowed between the ages of twenty and fifty years who failed to marry or remarry.[10] So the secular definition of 'young' can be fixed between twenty and menopause or, if Roman law was followed, an upper age of fifty years.[11] While there were young married women under twenty, in the case of widowhood that was the minimum age fixed by law that would attract a penalty for failure to remarry. The widow whom the Christian community was to support was to be no less than sixty years old (5:9).

Women came to marriage with a dowry that was accepted by the husband as his guarantee of her support.[12] The only legal obligation that the groom had

8. K. Hopkins, "The Age of Roman Girls at Marriage," *Population Studies* 18.3 (1965): 305-27, and the table on 325. His statistics, which are built on two previous studies, incorporate data from *CIL* IV, 1-30,000, which are Latin inscriptions in Rome.

9. Soranus, *Gynaecology*, 1.20. See D. W. Amunsen and C. J. Diers, "The Age of Menopause in Classical Greece and Rome," *Human Biology* 42 (1970): 79-88; A. Wallace-Hadrill, "Family and Inheritance in the Augustan Marriage Laws," *Proceedings of the Cambridge Philological Society* n.s. 27 (1981): 59; and J. F. Gardner, *Women in Roman Law and Society* (London: Croom Helm, 1986), pp. 178-79.

10. S. Dixon, *The Roman Mother* (London: Croom Helm, 1988), pp. 71-73, 84-103, for the complex legal situation that applied.

11. The actual consummation of a marriage before puberty was discouraged by ancient doctors. See Soranus, *Gynaecology*, 1.33.

12. S. Treggiari, *Roman Marriage: Iusti Coniuges from the Time of Cicero to the Time of*

toward the wife upon receipt of the dowry was her maintenance.[13] In the event of her husband's death, the laws governing that dowry were clearly defined.[14] The Graeco-Roman world sought to make sure that a widow had security by giving her shelter with her dowry in the household (οἶκος) of her eldest son, her other sons or her father. Someone in that social unit became 'the lord of the dowry' (κύριος or *tutor mulierum*) and accepted responsibility for her financial support. What Schnaps says of the classical Greek and Hellenistic period was also true of the Roman Empire: 'Legally, then, a woman was never as thoroughly protected as she was in her old age.'[15] Only in exceptional cases would a lord of the dowry have escaped legal and even social pressure if he reneged on this legal obligation.[16] In Athens there was not only a moral but also a legal obligation placed upon children to care for both parents, and failure to do so rendered them liable to prosecution in which 'the prosecutor ran no risk of punishment'.[17] The Roman woman had similar security. S. Dixon describes it as 'a dowager's life interest in her husband's holdings' based on the understanding that she would, at death, pass it on to children from that issue.[18] The Jewish position allowed the wife to hold her own property during marriage, and when made a widow to retain part of her dowry.[19]

Ulpian (Oxford: Clarendon, 1991), ch. 10; S. Dixon, *Reading Roman Women* (London: Duckworth, 2001), pp. 85-86.

13. Treggiari, *Roman Marriage: Iusti Coniuges from the Time of Cicero to the Time of Ulpian*, p. 338.

14. See R. Taubenschlag, *The Law of Greco-Roman Egypt in the Light of the Papyri, 332 B.C.–640 A.D.* (Warsaw: Panstwowe Wydawnictwo Naukowe, 1955), pp. 120-27 for non-literary evidence in the Roman period. For examples of legal extant marriage contracts all of which refer specifically to the contents or value of the dowry and its importance, see *PRyl* 154 (A.D. 66): 'received from him as a dowry on his daughter'; also *PTebt* 104 (92 B.C.); *BGU* 1052 (13 B.C.). J. P. V. D. Balsdon, *Roman Women: Their History and Habits* (London: Bodley Head, 1974), pp. 186-89, argues that the recovery of a dowry in part or whole was for its future use, *i.e.*, remarriage.

15. D. M. Schnaps, *Economic Rights of Women in Ancient Greece* (Edinburgh: Edinburgh University Press, 1979), p. 84.

16. B. W. Winter, "Widows and Legal and Christian Benefactions," in *Seek the Welfare of the City: Christians as Benefactors and Citizens* (Grand Rapids and Carlisle: Eerdmans and Paternoster, 1993), pp. 69-70. All who aspired to public office in the Greek cities were asked, 'Do you treat your parents well?'; W. K. Lacey, *The Family in Classical Greece* (London: Thames and Hudson, 1968), pp. 116-18.

17. W. K. Lacey, *The Family in Classical Greece* (London: Thames and Hudson, 1968), pp. 116-18.

18. Dixon, *The Roman Mother*, p. 47.

19. Z. W. Falk, *Introduction to Jewish Laws of the Second Commonwealth* (Leiden: E. J. Brill, 1978), p. 290.

That a Christian as 'the lord of the dowry' was not fulfilling this financial commitment underpinned by law is the reason why he was described not simply as 'an unbeliever' (ἄπιστος), but as behaving in a way that was 'worse than an unbeliever' (5:8). On the other hand, children expressed true Christian piety towards their parents and, in this particular discussion, to the mother or grandmother to whom some return was due, given their support of the children from childhood until adulthood (5:4).

Why was there a need for the church to support any Christian widow when a family member had undertaken to do so? We can rightly assume that most, if not all the widows, were being supported in the Christian community without any means test — either legal, financial or spiritual (5:3-16). The origin of this Ephesian Christian custom is uncertain. In Rome the corn dole that was given to the official *plebs* was not means-tested in terms of need, nor was the endowment system (which was for the élite) for children reaching adulthood.[20] Benefits and exemptions from taxes and liturgies were exploited and abused in the first century.[21] However, that widows should be supported by an institution was unprecedented in the Roman world, except for those who were Jewish.

Almost from its inception the Jerusalem church appears to have followed the procedures of the synagogues in charitable distributions to Jewish widows.[22] In the synagogues weekly distributions from the money chest were made every Friday to the poor, and among the recipients were the widows.[23] The Jerusalem church made a daily distribution (Acts 6:1). The reason for this adjustment may have been connected with its daily corporate activity described in Acts 2:46, which contrasted with the weekly synagogue gatherings

20. G. Rickman, *The Corn Supply of Ancient Rome* (Oxford: Clarendon Press, 1980), pp. 184-85. There was also the provision of child allowances, *alimenta*, which appear to have operated in some places in the empire from at least the time of Nero onwards, although Augustus appears to have created something of a precedent by including *minores pueri* among his *congiaria*, resources for which were raised from public benefactors and were private schemes in the first century A.D. See A. R. Hands, *Charities and Social Aid in Greece and Rome* (London: Thames and Hudson, 1968), pp. 71-73.

21. On the exemption from levies by Vespasian on 27th December, A.D. 75 see M. McCrum and A. G. Woodhead, *Select Documents of the Principates of the Flavian Emperors* (Cambridge: Cambridge University Press, 1961), no. 458, and discussion in my *Philo and Paul among the Sophists: Alexandrian and Corinthian Responses to a Julio-Claudian Movement*, 2nd ed. (Grand Rapids: Eerdmans, 2002), pp. 23-24.

22. E. Schürer, *The History of the Jewish People in the Age of Jesus Christ*, II (Edinburgh: T&T Clark 1979), p. 437 n. 45, notes that the 'officers charged by the primitive church with the care of the poor (διακονεῖν τραπέζαις)' in Acts 6:1-5 are fulfilling an identical role.

23. K. F. Nickle, *The Collection: A Study in Paul's Strategy*, SBT 48 (London: SCM, 1966), pp. 93-94.

and distributions. The latter's tried and tested method of collection and distribution was an appropriate one for the Christian community.

Ephesian converts to Christianity were of Jewish as well as Gentile origin; the former would have expected to be supported by a community that had its origins in Judaism. Had the church's administrative procedures for the distribution of aid to widows in Jerusalem simply been taken over by the Ephesian congregation and hence problems arose because all the widows qualified for the distribution? If so, then it would not be possible to discriminate against Gentile widows.[24] The Ephesians appear to have made no local adjustments to the Jerusalem church's distribution system.[25]

The intention, however, of the injunctions in 1 Timothy 5:3-16 was to change radically an existing procedure. While it is not possible to determine the number of Christian widows who were being supported, it is clear that some adjustments in the distribution were urgently needed. The church simply did not have adequate financial resources to support them all, nor should it be expected to do so according to the arguments put forward in this passage. The church would adequately honour with financial support those who were 'real' Christian widows, i.e., those who had somehow fallen through the established legal system and who also met new criteria. It was in the midst of these wider issues of the age qualification, appropriate conduct and a proven track record of the ministry of the widows that made them eligible for the support of the Christian community, that the discussion of young Christian widows takes place (5:11-15). The particular focus in this chapter is on the younger widows who were being supported by the church.

II. Inappropriate Behaviour by Young Widows

There were some in the church whose conduct was considered entirely inappropriate; they apparently wished to reverse the decision they themselves had made not to marry again. A clue as to why this was happening lies in the charge that those who had changed their minds were behaving promiscuously. Their 'passions draw them away from Christ' and, as a result, they had

24. Cf. Acts 6:1 where 'Hellenistic' Jewish widows complained of exclusion.

25. The N.T. gives no further indications that the mechanism for distribution to the poor in Jerusalem needed subsequent adjustments. It does, however, reveal that the problem continued to be a lack of resources from within the Jerusalem church. Only collections from the Diaspora Jewish and Gentile Christians saved them from destitution especially in a time of famine; see Acts 11:27-30; Acts 24:17 and 1 Cor. 16:1f.; 2 Cor. 8–9 and Rom. 15:25-27 (although in these instances there is no indication of the famine situation referred to in Acts 11:27-30).

already 'strayed after Satan' (5:11, 15). Earlier the spiritual state of the widow, whether young or old, is described as 'she who is self-indulgent is dead even while she lives' (ἡ δὲ σπαταλῶσα ζῶσα τέθνηκεν) (5:6). Polybius also wrote of the self-indulgent and pleasure-loving — in that instance, men of Greece from an earlier period.

> Men had fallen into such a state of pretentiousness, avarice, and indolence that they did not wish to marry, or if they married to rear children born to them, or at most as a rule but one or two of them, so as to leave these children in affluence and bring them up to be self-indulgent (σπαταλῶντας).[26]

The short passage (5:11-15) contains descriptive as well as evaluative and prescriptive elements. An examination of them in the light of appropriate external evidence helps reconstruct the Ephesian *Sitz im Leben* of the young widows.

Cicero wrote of the 'widow casting off restraints, a wanton living promiscuously, a rich woman living extravagantly and an amorous widow living a loose life'.[27] Her legal position allowed her to throw caution to the wind on being released from the constraints of her marriage; this was a huge concern in the Empire.[28]

Petronius, a courtier of Nero *c*. A.D. 65, discussed the promiscuousness of the young widow. He wrote about Eumolpus, who at a dinner party

> began to joke about the fickleness of women: how easily they fall in love, how quickly they forget even their own children. Now a woman was so chaste, he stated, that she would not under the right circumstances become insanely infatuated with a total stranger. He did not need the old tragic dramas or mythology as proof. There was something that had happened within his lifetime.[29]

Eumolpus then recounts a story about a widow in Ephesus who was renowned for her chastity. He records that when her husband died she was so restrained that she did not walk in the funeral procession with dishevelled hair or beat her breast, because every widow did that. She showed her true character by sitting by her husband in the underground tomb for five days with her servant girl, refusing to eat, in spite of the pleas of her parents, relatives and even the city officials who came in a delegation for the same purpose.

26. Polybius, xxxvi.17.7.
27. Cicero, *pro Caelio*, 38.
28. Walcot, "On Widows and Their Reputation in Antiquity."
29. Petronius, *The Ship of Lichas*, 110.

On the fifth night a soldier guarding two crucified bandits near the grave of the widow heard her wailing and finding this beautiful young widow guessed that she was 'a victim of unbearable grief'. He brought his own rations to share with her, and her maid finally persuaded her mistress to eat and drink. The soldier not only convinced the young widow to abandon suicide but then they 'slept together not only that night — their wedding night, so to speak — but the next night and the next'. The widow affirmed her love for the soldier who realized that he would be charged with the dereliction of duty — in this instance a capital offence — because relatives had come and taken away a bandit's body while the soldier was absent on his nocturnal escapades. She cried:

> The gods forbid that within so short a time I see the deaths of the two men dearest to me in all the world. I would rather hang the dead man [her deceased husband] up on the cross than be responsible for the death of my living lover.[30]

The alleged incident of this young Ephesian widow was meant to substantiate Eumolpus' claim of the sexual fickleness of ostensibly the most pure matron, who could be seduced even in such acute circumstances as grief. The retelling of this incident was meant to stimulate the expectations of the sexual availability of the most seemingly discreet woman, including one so recently bereaved.

Pliny records a dinner setting where 'their heavy glances betray it to her husband [the desire to seduce the wife]; then it is that the secrets of the heart are published abroad . . .'.[31] The husband had not only turned a blind eye but also had, in effect, acquiesced to the sexual indiscretions of his wife during the traditional drinking session that followed the meal.[32] Horace likewise records dinners where there were opportunities for the seduction of a young wife who learns

> Ionic dances, she studies the Arts, and all of her to her tender fingertips dreams of forbidden love. Soon, at her husband's drinking parties, that girl will be ready for younger men. Not that she will be choosing a secret lover, while the lights are out, to share her stolen pleasures; she will be called for openly, and off she will go upstairs, under her husband's eyes . . . prosperity [of the seducer] buys her disgrace.[33]

30. Petronius, *The Ship of Lichas*, 111.
31. Pliny, *Natural History*, 14.28.140-41.
32. See p. 153 for discussion.
33. Horace, *Odes*, 3.6.21-32.

Petronius writes of an old Roman matron, Philomela, who was apparently a widow. He describes her ironically as

> more respectable than most, who by the employment of her youthful charms had squeezed inheritances thick and fast out of susceptible persons. Now she was a crone,[34] with her youthful bloom perished, but she managed to teach her trade to the next generation by shoving her son and daughter at old men without heirs.[35]

We understand that she pushed her daughter at Eumolpus to secure what she saw as the only inheritance she could give her children. She did so on the tacit understanding that this wealthy man would sexually exploit her daughter and she, in exchange, would gain access to his inheritance.[36]

Society at large endorsed the expectation that men would be promiscuous in their youth and not sexually monogamous in their marriage. What justification was there for the fear that, after the conventional period of mourning, the young widow may replicate the conduct of single and married males? From the evidence in the opening chapters of this book, the explanation in some cases might be the influence of the life-style of the 'new' woman who, though still married, copied the sexual patterns of young men, including brothers and husbands. The custom of young women marrying at an early age, in many cases soon after puberty, was meant to ensure that they would almost certainly come to marriage as virgins.

The differential in the age of marriage for women and men, which has been estimated at seven to eight years, may account, in part, for these percentages.[37] Saller has argued that men of senatorial status married in their early twenties and the lower ranks in their late twenties and early thirties.[38] Aristocratic women tended to marry in their mid-teens and others in the Roman West in their later teens.[39] As McGinn points out, these figures are based on the senatorial class. Again they are only estimates but it is interesting that the medical text on Gynaecology by Soranus of Ephesus warns against the nuptial bed being consummated before puberty but recognises that with the on-

34. On the sexual repulsiveness of sensual old women, see Lucilius, 279-81.

35. Petronius, *Croton*, 140.

36. A. Richlin, *The Garden of Priapus: Sexuality and Aggression in Roman Humor*, 2nd ed. (Oxford: Oxford University Press, 1992), pp. 194-95.

37. Krause, *Witwen und Waisen im Römischen Reich* I, p. 73.

38. R. P. Saller, "Men's Age at Marriage and Its Consequences for the Roman Family," *CP* 82 (1987): 29-30.

39. B. D. Shaw, "The Age of Roman Girls at Marriage: Some Considerations," *JRS* 77 (1987): 43-44.

set of puberty young girls could marry.[40] The age gap accounted, in part, for the number of young widows in the Roman Empire.

Roman law did not specifically deal with the sexual abstinence of young widows; this meant that their sexual experience in marriage and the paradigm of the new woman could result in a promiscuousness of the sort so dramatically emphasised by Cicero. He commented on the wanton conduct of the widow, Clodia, whom he described in the trial of Caelius in 56 B.C. as 'not only of noble birth, but also of notoriety'.

> If a woman without a husband [a widow] opens her house to all men's desires, and publicly leads the life of a courtesan; if she is in the habit of attending dinner-parties with men who are perfect strangers; if she does this in the city, in her park, amid all those crowds at Baiae; if, in fact, she so behaves that not only her bearing but her dress and her companions, not only the ardour of her looks and the licentiousness of her gossip but also her embraces and caresses, her beach-parties, her water parties, her dinner-parties, proclaim her to be not only a courtesan, but also a shameless and wanton courtesan.[41]

Treggiari concludes that 'Clodia, as a widow who has adopted an openly immoral way of life, has put herself on the same level [as a prostitute]'.[42]

1 Timothy 5:11 notes that the young widows were 'behaving wantonly' (καταστρηνιάσωσιν) against Christ, because they desired to marry and so incur condemnation for having abandoned their former faith. To date, no instances have come to light from literary or non-literary sources of the use of the verb καταστρηνιάω; this is strange that no compound verb nor cognate form has been found on the TLG database or in non-literary sources. One would have expected these sources to throw up at least one or two examples in secular literature or papyri. It is usually assumed that the use of κατά only serves to re-enforce the action of wantonness (στρηνιάω).[43] In the most recent edition of Bauer and Danker the clause has been translated as, 'When they feel sensual impulses that alienate them from Christ.'[44] There is no basis

---

40. Sexual activity with females before menstruation was strongly discouraged by Soranus, the late-first-century gynaecologist from Ephesus, *Gynaecology*, 1:33.

41. Cicero, *pro Caelio*, 31, 49.

42. S. Treggiari, *Roman Marriage: Iusti Coniuges from the Time of Cicero to the Time of Ulpian*, p. 300, sees her being caricatured by Cicero at the trial.

43. καταστρηνιάω does not occur elsewhere in Greek but the meaning of στρηνιάω is clear, 'to run riot', 'become wanton'. Antiphon, 82, Sophilus, 6, Diphilus, 132, *P.Meyer* 20.23 (3rd century A.D.), Rev. 18:7, 9.

44. *BAGD*, p. 528.

for this rendering of the verb in terms of feelings rather than actions. It is not the case of a one-off sexual indiscretion but rather a promiscuous lifestyle that is under discussion.

On the use of the genitive with the compound verb, Robertson notes that 'there are occasions when the preposition in the composition gives a distinct change in idea to the verb'. He cites other instances where the genitive is used of the noun in the predicate because of κατά in the compound verb.[45] To be wanton (στρηνιάω) with someone has μετά, as is the case in Revelation 18:9 where the kings fornicated and were wanton with the prostitute. The idea in 1 Timothy 5:11 is that the widows were promiscuous and thereby adopted a lifestyle that was against Christ, i.e., in rebellion to his purposes. The use of ὅταν with the aorist subjunctive for indefinite future time suggests that when they became wanton against Christ, there was the inevitable desire to re-marry.[46] It is clear from 5:15 that some 'have already strayed after Satan'. In their rejection of a chaste life as a widow in favour of wantonness, they will incur judgement because they have 'set aside' their first faith.[47] It is suggested that it was not the vow or decision to remain unmarried that was the point at issue — it has been shown that it was their personal choice (p. 124) — but it was the rejection of Christ because of their promiscuousness, and hence their abandoning of their first faith. The initiating cause of this was a lifestyle that was in conflict with their Christian profession.

When cognizance is taken of the immoral activities referred to (5:11) and the specific connecting particles 'at the same time also' (ἅμα δὲ καί) (5:13),[48] it is right to draw the conclusion that there was a connection between the promiscuous activities of the indolent widows and what they did in going from household to household.[49]

They were 'learning to be idlers' rather than being industrious; this is stressed twice (5:13). An important public monument in the *Forum Transitorium* in Rome has a frieze that depicts women spinning and weaving.

---

45. A. T. Robertson, *A Grammar of the Greek New Testament in the Light of Historical Research*, 2nd ed. (London: Hodder & Stoughton, 1915), pp. 511-16.

46. Robertson, *A Grammar of the Greek New Testament*, p. 972.

47. A. Sand, "Witwenstand und Ämterstrukturen in den urchristlichen Gemeinden," *Bibel und Leben* 12 (1971): 196, argues that this refers to a vow of celibacy for devotion to God. Cf. also Rev. 2:4, ἡ ἀγάπη ἡ πρώτη. The reading back into the first century of an order of widows is rejected as it is clear that 1 Tim. 5:3-16 is intended to assist only those who qualify by reason of age for the assistance of the church.

48. See *BDF* #425,2.

49. In reading the discussion on the young widow, the earlier expectation of faith, love, holiness and modesty for any married woman would have applied equally to them (2:15).

D'Ambra, in her detailed work on the significance of life represented in statue types, comments, 'Rather than depicting weaving as a craft or industry, the wool working motif serves as a *topos* for the devout matron, the guardian of traditional society'.[50] She comments that this is a significant frieze and notes the use of statue types for imperial propaganda purposes. This was just as important at the beginning of the century in the Principate of Augustus as it was at the end under Domitian. 'In the Augustan period, the emblematic or iconic subject was employed to convey the proclaimed return to the *mores maiorum*. In particular, female protagonists . . . reflect the Augustan preoccupation with the morality of domestic life, and also cover the need for reform, so urgently desired by Augustus and expressed, in part, through his social legislation.'[51] This frieze in Rome was not an isolated instance — a similar portrayal of working women is represented in stone in the port of Ostia which was built by Claudius to facilitate the grain supply to Rome.[52]

In returning to the values of the ancients *(mores maiorum)* the industrious married woman was epitomised in the idealised domesticity of spinning and weaving. Idleness among rich women was therefore considered a vice and not a virtue, although men of status could boast that their hands had never known work.[53] In the household of Augustus, his immediate female family were said to have spun and woven, and he himself was clothed with the fruits of their labours.[54] It is interesting to note that in Crete, women who were divorced were entitled to half of the fruits of their labours which were to be returned to them.[55] Industriousness and not idleness was meant to be the hallmark of the first-century woman regardless of her rank, but this was not necessarily the case with 'new' women, as we have already noted.

The text tells us that 'not only' (οὐ μόνον δέ) were the young widows 'idlers going about the houses, but also (ἀλλὰ καί) gossips and busybodies, speaking that which was not becoming' (5:13).[56] 'The kind of things that

50. E. D'Ambra, "Women's Work," in *Private Lives, Imperial Virtues: The Frieze of the Forum Transitorium in Rome* (Princeton: Princeton University Press, 1993), p. 104.

51. D'Ambra, "Women's Work," in *Private Lives, Imperial Virtues: The Frieze of the Forum Transitorium in Rome*, p. 105.

52. N. Kampen, *Image and Status: Roman Working Women in Ostia* (Berlin: Gerb. Mann Verlag, 1981). For the activities of working women see S. Treggiari, "Jobs for Women," *AJAH* 1 (1976): 76-104.

53. On this boast among the sophists of knowing nothing of labour (πόνον οὐκ εἰδότες), see Philo, *Det.*, 34.

54. Suetonius, *Augustus*, 73.

55. See p. 142.

56. On the problems of gossip in a previous era see V. J. Hunter, "The Politics of Reputation," in *Policing Athens: Social Control in the Attic Lawsuits, 420-320 B.C.* (Princeton: Princeton

Romans reported saying to each other as gossip . . . were couched in nicer language than were graffiti and depended on implication rather than direct statement.'[57] Richlin proceeds to draw attention to the relationship between the obscene graffiti she had just discussed and obscene gossip. The latter, by implication, was the same as that found in graffiti.[58] On Clodia, 'Cicero indeed observes a certain urbane restraint: in accordance with his *recusatio* of obscenity in *Fam.* 9.22, he leaves out four-letter words; but he can still be quite crude.'[59] Richlin observes that the literature 'always portrays adultery as daring, never as normative. In the same way, malicious gossip establishes that one way to acquire a bad reputation is to have a reputation for adultery, yet it grants a certain cachet to both male and female sinners. Presumably this stems from the real issue involved — not marriage but power. . . . Gossip seems equally interested in both male and female peccadilloes'.[60] Such would also cover the affairs or casual liaisons of the young widow.

The other complaint is that the young widows were 'busybodies' (περίεργοι). The significance of the term is demonstrated from Menander's *The Arbitrators* where Onesimus who was a household slave revealed to his recently returned master that the child born by his wife in his absence was not fathered by him. He was told 'and you are a busybody', and even though that was the case, elsewhere he is told that the disclosure has not changed things — 'I love you, busybody though you are'. In one place he admits of himself, 'I am a busybody (περίεργός εἰμι)'. However, he later denies that he has been meddling, 'If anyone finds I am a busybody, I will let him castrate me.'[61]

The connection between the flighty young widows being gossips and busybodies and the content of their conversation is indicated (5:13). They are 'saying the things that are not right' (λαλοῦσαι τὰ μὴ δέοντα). The context is the semantic field of sexuality.[62] The nature of this sort of gossip is well illustrated from Juvenal, who provides a succinct picture of female gossip.

University Press, 1994), ch. 4, pp. 116-19, and esp. pp. 111-16 where gossip among women included malicious statements about sexual mores and the social status of other women.

57. Richlin, "Graffiti, Gossip, Lampoons and Rhetorical Invective," in *The Garden of Priapus*, ch. 4. On the issue of gossip, see pp. 83-86, *cit.* p. 84.

58. Richlin, "Graffiti, Gossip, Lampoons and Rhetorical Invective," pp. 81-83, 218.

59. Richlin, "Graffiti, Gossip, Lampoons and Rhetorical Invective," p. 84. On the nature of gossip she provides examples from Cicero's personal letters which, it has been argued, were intended for publication.

60. Richlin, "Graffiti, Gossip, Lampoons and Rhetorical Invective," pp. 81-83, 218.

61. Menander, *The Arbitrators*, *ll.* 262, 575; cf. *Samia*, *ll.* 299-300.

62. On the use of the neuter, see the entry in *Liddell & Scott*.

She knows who loves whom, what gallant is the rage; she will tell you who got the widow pregnant, and in what month; how every woman behaves with her lovers, and what she says to them.[63]

The comment about 'what month' points to a critical issue in the Empire. The surveillance of pregnant widows was a critical matter because a posthumous child would have the right to inherit from the deceased father's estate.

If a woman says that she is pregnant after her husband has died, she should take care to announce this twice within a month to those to whom this matter pertains . . . so that they, if they wish, can send those who will examine the womb . . . up to five free women are to be sent and these are all to examine together.[64]

Cicero speaks of 'the licentiousness of her [Clodia's] gossip'.[65] The inappropriate speech of the Christian widows seems to flow from the description of their lifestyle (5:11).

It was stipulated that the widow who qualified for financial support from the Christian community (5:9) was to be literally 'a woman of one man' (ἑνὸς ἀνδρὸς γυνή). The same was required of deacons (3:12) and overseers (3:2), who were to be 'a man of one woman' (μιᾶς γυναικὸς ἄνδρες). Does this reflect the ideal about which Tacitus wrote?

Still better is the practice of those societies in which only virgins marry and the hopes and prayers of a wife settled once and for all. Thus, just as they receive one body and one life, they receive one husband — this must be the limit of their thoughts and desires; marriage and not a husband must be their love.[66]

He was not commenting on his own generation, however much he might have wanted it to be like this, but he was repeating the purported situation in an early idealised society among the Germans. That the Christian widow at the age of sixty was to have been a 'one-man woman' cannot mean that she had been married only once. There has been a trend to translate or interpret the phrase by actually inserting a verb where there is none in the text. Had it read 'she had one husband', then the Greek would read γυνὴ ἔσχηκε ἕνα ἀνδρόν but it is literally 'a woman of one man' (ἑνὸς ἀνδρὸς γυνή). That

---

63. Juvenal, *Satires*, 6.405-6.
64. *The Digest*, 25.4.1.10. For an example see *BGU* IV.1104 (8 B.C.).
65. Cicero, *pro Caelio*, 31, 49.
66. Tacitus, *Germania*, 19.2.

would disbar the young widows who were encouraged to remarry (5:14) from doing so with any overseer or deacon, because the latter group qualified for office only if they were 'a man of one woman' (3:2). The reference is not to the older widow's marital history but to her moral conduct.[67]

Why did a promiscuous young widow now wish to marry and abandon her Christian profession and not simply marry a Christian man (5:11, cf. 14)? In the oration at the marriage bed Plutarch says how the wife must follow the gods of her husband and not embrace foreign divinities.[68] It is assumed that her desire to remarry was kindled by her enjoyment of her sexual promiscuity. She may have wished to abandon her faith in order to secure a husband who would not marry her if she remained a Christian.

III. To Marry and Have Children

There were legal, financial and social incentives 'to marry and have children' (γαμεῖν καὶ τεκνογονεῖν) (5:14). The Augustan laws, the *lex Julia de maritandis ordinibus* and related measures 'penalized unmarried men from the ages of twenty-five to sixty and unmarried women from twenty to fifty who did not have children and did not marry if they were divorced or widowed'.[69] Juvenal records that there were upper-class women who refused to have children.[70] Valerius Maximus writing in *c.* A.D. 30 notes that Septicia married an old man in the Principate of Augustus and was beyond menopause. There was a dispute and she excluded him from her will. The emperor forbade her husband 'to retain her dowry, since their marriage had not occurred "for the sake of procreating children"'.[71] 'If . . . a married couple had children, and three children in particular, they gained the *ius trium liberorum* (the right of three children), which gave them privileges such as advancement in the father's political career and financial autonomy for the mother.'[72] Widows who were

---

67. Cf. M. Dibelius and Hans Conzelmann, *The Pastoral Epistles* (Philadelphia: Fortress Press, 1972), 75, who argue that it refers to chastity whether married once or twice.

68. Plutarch, "Advice to the Bride and Groom," 19.

69. D'Ambra, *Private Lives, Imperial Virtues: The Frieze of the Forum Transitorium in Rome*, p. 99 *cit.*; Dixon, *The Roman Mother*, pp. 71-73, 84-103; and A. Wallace-Hadrill, "Family and Inheritance in the Augustan Marriage Laws," *Proceedings of the Cambridge Philological Society* (n.s.) 27 (1981): 58-80.

70. Juvenal, 6, *ll.* 592-609.

71. *Memorable Doings and Sayings*, VII.7.4. Cf. *CIL* VI.10.10230 (early first century A.D.) where a mother was lauded by the citizens for 'her equal treatment towards her children' and at the same time showing 'a pleasing and loyal spirit towards her husbands'.

72. D'Ambra, *Private Lives, Imperial Virtues: The Frieze of the Forum Transitorium in Rome*,

childless in their first marriage but remarried and had a child enjoyed benefits from an inheritance — such was the legal pressure to have children.[73]

A totally inequitable situation applied with the death of a spouse. 'Men are not compelled to mourn for their wives. This is no mourning for a fiancée.'[74] The required interval between the death of a husband and remarriage for the widow was to be a minimum of ten months.[75] This was an established convention in the early empire and enshrined in Roman law. When Seneca wrote to his widowed mother his argument was —

> our ancestors allowed widows to mourn their husbands for ten months, in order to compromise by public decree with the stubbornness of female grief. They did not prohibit mourning but they limited it.[76]

However, an important consideration was not so much that of propriety but 'he is accustomed to be mourned on account of a confusion of blood'.[77] *The Digest* indicated that 'it does not harm the woman who is mourning to have become engaged within the time limit'.[78] The encouragement to young Christian widows to remarry would have needed to take into account at least this minimum period for official mourning (5:14). Two years was the period set before a widow could remarry without incurring any financial or inheritance penalties under the *lex Papia Poppaea* of A.D. 9.[79]

If the only interest were in marriage and having children, then one would not have expected the call 'to manage their household' (οἰκοδεσποτεῖν). This requirement is also found in Titus 2:5 and the philosophical schools where there was the need for the wife to have taken 'the helm and steered the household's course'.[80] This instruction counters the lax lifestyle into which some of the young widows had drifted, for the enormous demands of running a household left no room for idleness.

---

p. 99. See also J. F. Gardner, *Women in Roman Law and Society* (London: Croom Helm, 1986), pp. 178-79.

73. L. F. Raditsa, "Augustus' Legislation concerning Marriage, Procreation, Love Affairs and Adultery," *ANRW* II 13 (1980): 323. D'Ambra, *Private Lives, Imperial Virtues: The Frieze of the Forum Transitorium in Rome*, p. 99.

74. *The Digest*, 3.2.9.

75. Hopkins, "The Age of Roman Girls at Marriage," p. 325, citing Plutarch, "Numa," 12.

76. Seneca, *Ad Helviam*, 16.1.

77. *The Digest*, 3.2.11.

78. *The Digest*, 3.2.10.

79. B. Rawson, "The Roman Family," in *The Family in Ancient Rome: New Perspectives* (London: Croom Helm, 1986), p. 31.

80. *Epigrammata Graeca*, 243b.

The verb, 'I wish' (βούλομαι), in 1 Timothy 5:14 is followed by four infinitives, the concluding one providing a compelling reason for the previous ones — 'to give (διδόναι) no occasion to the opponent [of the Christian message] on account of a reproach.' This is clearly related to her lifestyle giving the appearance of promiscuousness. How do marriage, childbearing and the management of the household rob the Christian's opponent of the opportunity to reproach the Christian message?[81] The following verse introduced by 'for' (γάρ) states that some have already turned aside to follow Satan, a description analogous to being against Christ by reason of promiscuous behaviour (5:11), which is clearly linked to the particular lifestyle described in 5:13.[82] This indicates such reproaches can justifiably be made as there are already some who have been promiscuous; this enabled outsiders to call into question the credibility of the Christian faith. A similar concern is expressed in Titus 2:5: 'that the Word of God may not be discredited' by the young Cretan Christian wives who had to be called back to their senses to love their husbands and children and to run their households.[83]

The remedial steps for this problem of regulating the support of real widows may seem somewhat draconian on an initial reading. However, notice needs to be taken of the unprecedented and unregulated institutional support of widows in the capital of the Province of Asia, and indeed the Graeco-Roman world, the exception being Judea and Diaspora Jewish communities. One can appreciate how enticing it would have been for a young widow, or any widow in fact, to join this 'welfare' association. Young widows could afford to be idle at the expense of the Christian community whose financial support also enabled them to be promiscuous. Furthermore, such inappropriate conduct was highly damaging to the credibility of the witness of the church as a whole in Ephesus. In effect, the church was paying the widows 'to shoot its cause in the foot'. If the issue of their lifestyle had not been addressed, it would have had effects which were far-reaching and highly compromising for the Christian witness before a watching world.

The appearance of the young widows could have put in jeopardy the very existence of the Christian church in Ephesus, giving its enemy the opportunity to 'revile us' (5:14). Prior to this, the Roman authorities had banned cults that appeared to promote sexual promiscuity as part of their tenets.[84] Tacitus records the case of Pomponia Graecina in the time of Claudius —

81. The predicate 'no occasion' is placed at the beginning of the clause for emphasis.

82. See *Liddell & Scott* on the special use of χάριν as a preposition following the noun and meaning 'for the sake of, on behalf of, on account of'.

83. See pp. 160-63.

84. O. F. Robinson, *The Criminal Law of Ancient Rome* (London: Duckworth, 1995), pp. 95-97.

a woman of high family, married to Aulus Plautius — whose ovation after the British campaign I recorded earlier — and now arraigned for alien superstition, was left to the jurisdiction of her husband. Following the ancient custom, he held the inquiry, which was to determine the fate and fame of his wife, before a family council, and announced her innocent.[85]

'Her creed, as was often the case, gave rise to immorality, on which she was tried and acquitted by the family council.'[86]

The extent of the financial problem for the support of widows *per se* is reflected in the fact that the church simply could not afford it. So that the church might be able to provide adequate care for those who were 'real' widows, not only immediate families were required to assist financially but also a believing woman with widowed relatives who needed support (5:4, 16).

It was suggested that 1 Timothy 5:11-14 contained descriptive, evaluative and prescriptive elements. The first two resonate with concerns expressed in the wider society. The prescriptive element required the church to refuse to enrol young widows for financial reasons so that the old widows who were by themselves could be 'honoured' with financial support.[87] The young widows were to marry, have children, and manage their households.[88]

In conclusion, some young widows in the church had been influenced by the values of the 'new' woman, whether the latter was married or widowed. The appearance of the young widows in terms of their lifestyle was such that it provided opponents of the Christian movement with the opportunity to discredit it.

---

85. Tacitus, *Annals,* 13.32.

86. J. Jackson, *Tacitus, Annals,* Loeb (1956), pp. 52, n. 3, 53 (cf. II.50).

87. The use of the verb 'to honour' (5:3), which was drawn from the semantic field of benefactions applied here to a widow given to good works. She was not seen as a liability as was the merry young widow but deserving of adequate support. For a discussion see my "Widows and Legal and Christian Benefactions, 1 Timothy 5:3-16," in *Seek the Welfare of the City: Early Christians as Benefactors and Citizens* (Grand Rapids and Carlisle: Eerdmans and Paternoster, 1994), ch. 4, esp. pp. 71-73.

88. See p. 124, including n. 5, on including this as an imperative.

CHAPTER 8

The Appearance of Young Wives, Titus 2:3-5

The terminology used in the injunctions to women in Titus 2:3-5 provides clues as to some of the problems the early Christian movement struggled with, given what is known of the first-century Cretan/Roman secular mores of both older and younger wives. This letter sent to Titus in Crete evaluates the consequences for Christian women of some of these cultural legacies.

I. The Legal Privileges of Cretan Women

Ancient Rights

Since *c.* 450 B.C. Cretan women had been in a more privileged legal position concerning their rights and matters relating to inheritance than their sisters in Athens — they had 'somewhat more independence' when contrasted with that of Athenian women.[1] The rights of both Cretan and Athenian women were recorded on the same inscription and provide important information on unique aspects of Cretan women's rights.[2] Lefkowitz and Fant recorded

---

1. S. Pomeroy, *Goddesses, Whores, Wives, and Slaves: Women in Classical Antiquity* (London: Random House, 1975), p. 42, notes, 'A chronological arrangement of the codes of Dorian Sparta and Gortyn [the capital of Crete] and the code of Ionian Athens shows that the Spartan code which antedated the Gortynian by a century or two, was the most favourable to women'. The Athenian was the most restrictive.

2. So note the editors M. R. Lefkowitz and M. B. Fant, *Women's Life in Greece and Rome* (Baltimore: Johns Hopkins University Press, 1992 [2nd ed.]), p. 55. For an English translation of part of the text of the *Gortyn Law Code* (*Inscr. Creticae* 4.72) see theirs on pp. 55-58. The citation is on p. 55. On the closeness of the Athenians and Cretans on their oath never to begin hostilities, see Plutarch, *Thes.*, 19.7.

the Cretan women's particular legal status they enjoyed with a citation from the inscription dealing with their legal code: 'She is to keep her property.'[3]

Even in the case of divorce and widowhood the woman's property rights were protected and in the division of other goods recognised. 'If a husband and wife divorce, she is to keep her property, whatever she brought to the marriage, and one-half of the produce from her property and half of whatever she has woven.... If a man dies and leaves children behind, if the wife wishes, she may marry, keeping her own property and whatever her husband gave her according to an agreement written in the presence of three adult free witnesses.... If a women dies without issue the husband is to give her property back to her lawful heirs and half of what she has woven within and half of the produce if it comes from her property.... If a female slave is separated from a male slave while he is alive or if he dies, she is to keep what she has.... If the mother dies leaving children, the father has power over the mother's estate, but he should not sell or mortgage it, unless the children are of age and give their consent. If he marries another wife, the children are to have power over their mother's estate.'[4]

The principle is also enunciated in the legal code: 'The mother's property shall also be divided if she dies, in the same way as prescribed for the father's.'[5] There were other rights unique to the women of Crete relating to inheritance: 'instead of the traditional dowry which was fixed at the time of the wedding, daughters had a specific portion of the inheritance equal to half that of the son.'[6]

Plutarch provides a contrast with what prevailed elsewhere. In a revealing comment in his wedding oration, he argued that 'a co-partnership in property is especially befitting of married people'. What that meant in reality he explained by way of analogy. 'As we call a mixture "wine", although the larger component part is water, so the property and the estate ought to be said to belong to the husband even though the wife contributed the larger share.'[7] Cretan women had long been ahead of their time in this respect and certainly would not have endorsed Plutarch's argument. According to Strabo, Cretans enshrined in their constitutions the belief that '... liberty is a state's greatest good, for this alone makes property belong specifically to those who have acquired it'.[8] This may well have accounted for the importance attached to the retention of a wife's property during her marriage.

3. Lefkowitz and Fant, *Women's Life in Greece and Rome*, p. 55.
4. Lefkowitz and Fant, *Women's Life in Greece and Rome*, p. 55.
5. *Gortyn Law Code*, 3.45.
6. Lefkowitz and Fant, *Women's Life in Greece and Rome*, p. 55.
7. Plutarch, "Advice on Marriage," 140F.
8. Strabo, *Geography*, 10.4.22.

Pomeroy notes that for Cretan women from the lower classes 'Marriage, divorce, birth, and possessions of chattels were subject to laws rivalling in complexity and comprehensiveness those affecting the upper classes. Extensive regulations were required concerning marriage of slaves. . . . A married female slave could herself possess property, for the divorce regulations state that she may take her moveables and small livestock'.[9]

Cretan legislation governing sexual offences such as rape sought to penalise the male perpetrator in some way. Even in the case where a slave had been raped, her testimony was given credibility. 'If a person deflowers a female household servant, he shall pay two staters. If she has already been deflowered, one obol if in the day-time, two obols at night. The female slave's oath takes precedence.'[10] The female rape victim's testimony was given credence and, however limited, the rapist suffered some financial penalties.

So the women in the Adriatic region of Crete possessed some measure of protection and enjoyed greater legal rights long before Roman rule. Mackenzie notes that even in the pre-Hellenic period they 'lived on a footing of greater equality with men than in any other ancient civilization. . . . We see in the frescoes of Knossos conclusive indications of an open and free association of men and women, corresponding to our idea of society, at the Minoan court'.[11] This measure of independence and power came in part through the retention of property in marriage and what was generated from their land for the duration of it.

The feminisation of the divinity in Crete in the forms of the snake-goddess, the dove-goddess and the lady of wild creatures meant 'that the conception of the Mother was an essential part of Cretan faith'.[12] That, however, was not peculiar to Crete.[13]

Plutarch, however, noted a phenomenon peculiar to Cretans. Their citizens referred to their country as the motherland — 'as the Cretans call it, our

---

9. See Pomeroy, *Goddesses, Whores, Wives, and Slaves*, pp. 41-42, for the legal regulations governing women of the lower classes, *cit.* p. 41.

10. *Gortyn Law Code*, 2.3.

11. D. A. Mackenzie, *Crete and Pre-Hellenic Myths and Legends* (London: Gresham, 1917; reprint, London: Senate, 1995), p. 71, endorses the view even from the early period.

12. Mackenzie, *Crete and Pre-Hellenic Myths and Legends*, p. 59. On female divinities, see generally R. Turcan, *The Cults of the Roman Empire* (E.T., Oxford: Blackwell, 1996).

13. Pomeroy, *Goddesses, Whores, Wives, and Slaves*, pp. 13-15, rightly cautions against drawing a conclusion about female dominance without the evidence of 'written documentation' and solely from the large number of female figurines. In the case of Crete we do have extant epigraphic evidence of a more privileged legal position for women, as she herself notes, pp. 39-42.

mother country (ματρίς), and not our fatherland unlike others'; and 'they possessed more privileges', for they had 'earlier and great rights'.[14]

The Coming of Roman Culture

The island of Crete was one of the last Greek strongholds to fall to Republican Rome in 71 B.C. As a result of a subsequent internal war it became a Roman province and was joined with Cyrene in North Africa. It was ruled by a senator of praetorian rank, and the provincial capital was Gortyn on Crete.

According to Sanders, the progress of Romanization on Crete was steady and this can be marked in part in the Julio-Claudian period by the number of Roman citizenship grants given, especially in the Principate of Claudius. The latter continued under the Flavian emperors. There was also increasing participation by Cretans in Roman affairs in the first century. The family of Aulus Larcius Lepidus Sulpicianus illustrates their integration into Roman culture and society. He was awarded Roman citizenship, and became a *quaestor* in Crete at the end of the Julio-Claudian dynasty, serving under Vespasian in Judaea. In first-century Crete there is ample extant evidence of the penetration of Roman culture and conventions.[15]

Strabo records that the administration of its affairs was carried on 'mostly by means of the decrees of the Romans, as is the case in other provinces' even though the constitution of the Cretans was worth noting 'on account of its fame'. He observed that naturally not many of the institutions endured after it was given provincial status.[16] From late Republican times through the first century and beyond, that did not change.

The coming of Roman values in no way diminished the gains Cretan women had secured. The change in Rome with married women able to hold property provided the inhabitants of the imperial capital with one of the powerful levers that secured for them greater financial independence from the late Republic onwards, and hence a measure of social freedom.[17] It will be suggested that the emergence of the 'new' Roman woman in the first century could only fortify the long-established legal gains that already provided a measure of independence for the women of Roman Crete.

14. Plutarch, "Old Men in Public Office," 792E.

15. I. F. Sanders, *Roman Crete: An Archaeological Survey and Gazetteer of Later Hellenistic, Roman and Early Byzantium* (Warminster: Aris & Phillips, 1982), esp. p. 132.

16. Strabo, *Geography,* 10:4.22.

17. See p. 21.

II. Cultural Conditioning and Cretan Christianity

What were the Cretan values that created problems for the Christian communities? The need for 'self-control' was stressed not only for the older and younger men but also for the younger wives (Titus 1:8; 2:2, 5, 6). A lack of personal restraint was also evidenced among older women with the uncontrolled consumption of wine and the slandering of others, but the term 'self-control' was not used (2:3). This term with its Latin equivalent, *pudicitia,* refers to a 'conscience which keeps a person from shameful [sexual] actions' and in relation to women refers to sexual fidelity. It is also sometimes associated with being 'faithful' *(fides)* to a husband.[18] This gives a hint of some of the personal ethics of the Cretans.

The concerns discussed here about 'self-indulgence', 'ungodliness' and 'worldly passions' were also the subject of comment in the philosophical schools.[19] We have already noted that virtues and the vices were recorded as part of the essential education of young men and women in first-century society. Some of these vices, especially self-indulgence, had gained a degree of acceptability among some married women and men in certain circles in the Roman world. (See ch. 2.)

Like any first-century Christians before their conversion, those on Crete had been brought up to act and respond to issues on the basis of culturally accepted patterns of behaviour. This chapter suggests that the reason for many of the difficulties listed concerning Christian conduct was the culturally determined responses to particular situations and certain relationships. Titus had been left on Crete to 'amend what was defective' (τὰ λείποντα ἐπιδιορθώσῃ) in the nascent Christian communities (1:5). He was now being urged to secure urgent changes in certain behaviour patterns of the local Christians.

Refusing to renounce some of these cultural responses, or seeing no need to teach converts to do this, would have resulted in a largely culturally driven Cretan Christianity. In the end that would have robbed the new movement of aspects of its distinctiveness. It may well be the reason why countering these responses is a central motif in the letter to Titus. The call to abandon certain traits that were antithetical to the Christian life is found either explicitly or implicitly in the ethical injunctions to both men and women alike (2:12; cf. 1:7; 2:3, 10; 3:1-2, 9). For example, Christians were not to be appointed elders if

---

18. S. Treggiari, *Roman Marriage: Iusti Coniuges from the Time of Cicero to the Time of Ulpian* (Oxford: Clarendon, 1991), p. 233.

19. See pp. 63-65.

they were 'arrogant', 'quick tempered', 'a drunkard', 'violent', or 'greedy for gain'. Furthermore, vices such as 'debauchery' and 'disobedience' among their children also disqualified potential teaching elders from office (1:6ff).

Instructors v. Elders

The appointment of suitable elders aimed at countering the unhelpful influence of certain instructors in the community, some of whom appear to have operated little differently from their secular counterparts. These Christian teachers were described as 'empty talkers and deceivers (ματαιολόγοι καὶ φρεναπάται) who had turned away from the truth' (1:10), and they were also accused of being motivated to teach for personal gain (1:11). These three criticisms had also been made of the *virtuoso* orators who had come to dominate first-century teachers in education, especially those at the tertiary level. Philosophers and others, including Philo, the first-century Hellenised Jew from Alexandria, made these charges.[20]

The first deficiency of 'empty talk' was also said to have characterised the content of the public declamations of many orators.[21] They focused on rhetorical technique rather than content, and their highly developed powers of persuasion were not used to transform their hearers, but to court the popularity of the crowd they sought to entertain with their vast arsenal of rhetorical tricks. The audiences paid admission fees to listen to their carefully crafted public orations which were largely empty in terms of content. They entertained but did not edify or improve the conduct of their audiences or their pupils.[22]

They were also accused of deception. Plato had long ago made a similar two-fold charge against the sophists. The first related to the 'magic' of rhetoric and the way it cast a hypnotic spell over its hearers, deceiving them into think-

20. Philo of Alexandria's indebtedness to philosophy is well documented by D. T. Runia, *Philo of Alexandria and the Timaeus of Plato* (Leiden: E. J. Brill, 1986), as is his training in oratory by A. Mendelson, *Secular Education in Philo of Alexandria* (Cincinnati: Hebrew Union College Press, 1982). His critique of the sophists is credible, being confirmed by late-first-century writers such as Dio Chrysostom, Plutarch, and Epictetus. The following discussion is a brief summary of that evidence and conclusions based on it from my *Philo and Paul among the Sophists: Alexandrian and Corinthian Responses to a Julio-Claudian Movement*, 2nd edition (Grand Rapids: Eerdmans, 2002). As the subtitle indicates, the New Testament discussion was restricted primarily to Corinth with a discussion about a similar situation in Thessalonica, but that on Crete was missed.

21. *Philo and Paul among the Sophists*, pp. 30-34, 118-21.

22. Philo, *Congr.* 67-68; *Philo and Paul among the Sophists*, pp. 74-75, 81-87.

ing that wisdom was being imparted to them.[23] Dio Chrysostom speaks of the activities of the sophists at the Isthmian games held close to Corinth with a similar analogy of 'jugglers showing their tricks'.[24] They were also charged with being deceiving with misleading merchandise. In the early Empire the orators had usurped the traditional role of philosophers as educators in the cardinal civic virtues of the young. While teaching the virtues of 'prudence', 'self-control', 'righteousness' and 'courage' as critical for the classical education of the rising generation, many of the teachers pursued a lifestyle that was marked by the opposite cardinal vices of 'folly', 'intemperance', 'injustice' and 'cowardice'.[25]

When challenged concerning their inconsistency some sophists actually rationalised their conduct by resorting to philosophical arguments that combined first-century Platonism and Hedonism.[26] No longer was the body Plato's 'prison house of the soul', but now its house was to be enjoyed by its occupant. The bodily senses were said to be the courtiers and guardians of the immortal soul, and nature meant them to be used and experienced to the full. The lifestyle of the sophists when compared with those they said were 'training for dying' validated their philosophical argument.[27] It was also said of these teachers of Cretan Christians that 'their minds and consciences are corrupted', for 'to the pure all things are pure, and to the corrupt and unbelieving nothing is pure' (1:15). There was a deep-seated inconsistency in the behaviour patterns of these Christian teachers, for theirs was not 'a knowledge of the truth that accords with godliness' (1:1). 'They profess to know God, but they denied God by their deeds' (1:16).

The third charge against sophists was that of 'greed'. The motivation of personal financial gain is mentioned of both potential elders and existing teachers in the Christian communities (1:7, 11). The first-century A.D. Cynic Epistles recorded that the sophists 'have little regard for education, but concern themselves with making money' as does Neilus, the Alexandrian student in his letter home to his father.[28] Dio also condemns sophists who 'for gain

---

23. J. de Romilly, *Magic and Rhetoric in Ancient Greece* (Cambridge, MA and London: Harvard University Press, 1975); for the first century Philo equates the magicians of Moses' day with the present-day sophists in their rhetorical practices. For evidence see *Philo and Paul among the Sophists*, pp. 88-91.

24. Dio Chrysostom, *Or.* 8.9.

25. For a discussion of the sophists' misuse of education for vice and deception, see *Philo and Paul among the Sophists*, pp. 81-91.

26. *Philo and Paul among the Sophists*, pp. 91-93. For a summary of their argument, see Philo, *Det.*, 32-34.

27. Philo, *Det.*, 34.

28. *Cynic Epistles*, "Of Socrates," 1.4 and 6.10; *P.Oxy.* 2190.

make false pretensions'.[29] In a comparable secular setting this took two forms. In the schools of the sophists, students were charged exorbitant tuition fees.[30] It has already been noted that the audience paid an entry fee to hear a one-off lecture or a series of public declamations by an orator. Sophists were among the rich and powerful first-century teachers, and increasing their wealth is what motivated much of what they did.[31]

Certain Christian teachers on Crete were singled out for censure, 'especially (μάλιστα) members of the circumcision party' (1:10). Jewish communities were known to have existed on the island from at least the first century B.C. Crete would not have been the only place where Christian teachers of Jewish origins had absorbed the values of secular orators or followed their conventions.[32] Philo testifies that his fellow Jews in Alexandria who were trained in rhetoric paraded their superiority among their compatriots or sought preferment in official positions under 'our rulers', the Romans in Egypt.[33] In Rome, a Jewish orator named Caecilius wrote on the superiority of the Attic style over the Asian as well as other literary works. This made him one the leading critics in the literary world of his day.[34] The Jewish/ Graeco-Roman divide in the Diaspora was not a sharp one in the field of education.[35]

The teachers were said to be upsetting 'whole families' (1:11). The convention of declaiming in a household was well established in the first century.[36] The role of tutors was critical in the education of the young, including the daughters of some households, and sometimes provided instruction for everyone. The personal benefits accruing to teachers were offset for some of them by their being put on the same level as others employed in the households, *viz.* the bondservants.[37] That would have created something of a prece-

29. Dio Chrysostom, *Or.,* 32.11.

30. Winter, *Philo and Paul among the Sophists,* pp. 91-94.

31. On the wealth and status of the sophists see E. L. Bowie, "The Importance of the Sophists," *Yale Classical Studies* 27 (1982): 29-59.

32. "Paul among the Christian Sophists," in *Philo and Paul among the Sophists,* ch. 10, where it is argued that some of the rhetorically trained teachers who were his critics in Corinth were Jews; see 2 Cor. 11:22-23.

33. Philo, *L.A.,* III.167.

34. G. A. Kennedy, *The Art of Rhetoric in the Roman World* (Princeton: Princeton University Press, 1972), pp. 364-69.

35. Winter, *Philo and Paul among the Sophists,* Part I.

36. Epictetus, *Discourses,* III.23.23. The editor noted the practice of inviting a popular scholar to lecture in one's house, which was widespread in both the Greek and Roman periods; W. A. Oldfather, *Epictetus, LCL,* II (1978): 177, n. 6.

37. On the denunciation of the motives and the conduct of teachers in households, see

dent for the activities in the early Christian families. This is recorded in both Titus 1:11 and in Acts 20:20 where instruction was given not only in a public gathering but also in households in Ephesus.

The preceding discussion noted that some of these Christian instructors were uncritical of Roman Cretan culture. They themselves had clearly been shaped and motivated by the academic fraternity of the first century. It seems that little emphasis had been given to the personal transformation of the lives of those they taught. It comes then as no surprise that instructors felt no compulsion to persuade those whom they taught of the need to renounce unacceptable patterns of conduct derived from their cultural surroundings. This may help explain the problem of minimal personal transformation that had occurred in the Cretan churches and the need for Titus to redress this malaise as a matter of urgency.

Cretans and Cretanizing

Although the text does not name the author, it has been assumed that it was Epimenides who was described as 'one of their own prophets' who succinctly epitomised the deficiencies of his compatriots by three vices.[38] 'Cretans are always liars, evil beasts, lazy gluttons (Κρῆτες ἀεὶ ψεῦσται, κακὰ θηρία, γαστέρες ἀργαί)' (1:12).[39] Just as the term to 'Corinthianize' in Greek meant 'to fornicate' given the sexual notoriety of the city in the Greek period, so too, 'to play the Cretan' (Κρητίζειν) had long been used to mean 'to lie'. Polybius records that conspirators discussed a plot 'from a thoroughly Cretan point of view'. When they met their victim they did not initially consider, 'as the saying is, "he was trying to play the Cretan with a Cretan" . . . although a Cretan and ready to entertain every kind of suspicion regarding others'.[40] Plutarch also quotes the saying: 'in thus "playing the Cretan against a Cretan", as the saying is, he misjudged his opponent'.[41] Strabo cites a proverb based on the

---

Lucian, "On Salaried Posts in Great Houses"; cf. his own defence when he himself later in life took up a salaried post in connection with Roman Administration (in his "Apology").

38. According to Plutarch, *Solon*, 12.1, Epimenides of Phaestus was summoned from Crete because he was 'reckoned the seventh Wise Man — a man beloved of the gods and endowed with a mystical and heaven-sent wisdom in religious matters'.

39. The attribution of the saying to Epimenides has been widely discussed. For a summary see W. Mounce, *Pastoral Epistles* (Nashville: Nelson, 2000), pp. 396-99; and I. H. Marshall, *The Pastoral Epistles*, ICC (Edinburgh: T&T Clark, 1999), pp. 200-201.

40. Polybius, 16.18.5–22.2.

41. Plutarch, *Lysias*, 20.2; cf. *Aemilius*, 23.

inhabitants of that island: '"The Cretans do not know the sea" is applied to those who pretend not to know what they do know.'[42] This suggests that Cretans regarded lying as culturally acceptable, and hence the use of the term 'to speak like a Cretan' came to mean 'to lie'. It may not be insignificant that in all the literature to the Pauline communities it is only in Titus that one particular aspect of the nature of God is spelt out. He is the God 'who never lies' (ὁ ἀψευδής). One implication of this is that Cretan Christians can be assured of the hope of eternal life because God keeps the promises he made ages ago with respect to this (1:2). If Cretans could not be relied to speak the truth, God could.

'Evil beasts' indicated their behaviour on an island that was said to be devoid of wild animals. The inhabitants and not the animals are the 'wild ones' intent on destroying life on this legendary beautiful island in the Aegean.[43]

'Lazy gluttons' refers to their 'self-indulgence' at feasts. Plutarch records a peculiarly Cretan phenomenon of the 'public mess' (ἀνδρεῖα), which was something like an 'association'. Each of the fifteen members who comprised the group donated a bushel of barley, eight gallons of wine, five pounds of figs and two and a half pounds of cheese. Young boys could attend such gatherings, in order, it was suggested, to benefit from the discussion of the adult men.[44] However much this might happen during the dinner, the example of fifteen men consuming one hundred and twenty gallons of wine per month at such dinners would provide an unhelpful paradigm when boys reached the age of eighteen and assumed the *toga virilis*. Excessive drinking at meals and afterwards went hand in hand with immorality. The term that Plutarch uses, ἀνδρεῖα, denoted 'courage' or 'manliness' which was also a euphemism for the male sexual organ.[45] Strabo writing of an earlier period refers to the same public messes and the effects these had on young Cretan boys moving towards manhood in terms of toughening them up, although he makes no mention of their social drinking, etc. He notes that 'even today, they are still called *Andreia*'.[46]

---

42. Strabo, *Geography*, 10.4.17.

43. On the absence of wild animals on Crete see Pliny, *Natural History*, 8.83; and Plutarch, "Progress in Virtue," 86C.

44. For something like this in terms of feasting in a neighbourhood association see Plutarch, *Lysander*, 12.1; O. M. van Nijf, *The Civic World of Professional Associations in the Roman East* (Amsterdam: J. C. Gieben, 1997), pp. 181-82. He does not classify Plutarch's reference thus.

45. = *membrum virile*, Artemidorus Tarsensis, *Grammaticus*, 1.45; J. N. Adams, *The Latin Sexual Vocabulary* (London: Duckworth, 1982), p. 69. For the significance of the *toga virilis*, see p. 68.

46. Strabo, *Geography*, 4.10.16, 18, 20. *Cit.* 18.

These uncomplimentary characterisations of the Cretans centuries before the coming of Christianity to the island were still regarded as valid, for 'This witness [of Epimenides] is true' (ἡ μαρτυρία αὕτη ἐστὶν ἀληθής) (1:13). The immediate discussion in the letter reflects Epimenides' summation — 'because of this (δι' ἥν)', i.e., his witness of the Cretans' lifestyle, Titus was to 'rebuke them sharply, in order that (ἵνα) they may be sound in the faith' (1:13). Sound faith was antithetical to Roman Cretan ethical norms.[47] In the letter to Titus liars and deceivers were contrasted with those who furthered the truth, evil doers with the lovers of good, and the self-indulgent with those who exercised self-control (1:9, 1:12, *cf.* 1:1, 3:8, 1:8, 2:1, 5, 6, 9-10). Towards the end of the letter there is a description of the vices said to be endemic in all humanity including Jews. 'For we ourselves were once foolish, disobedient, led astray, slaves to various kinds of passions and pleasures (δουλεύοντες ἐπιθυμίαις καὶ ἡδοναῖς), passing our days in malice and envy, hated by men and hating one another' (3:3). However, this letter distinguished between the negative characteristics of humanity as a whole (3:3) and specific cultural deficiencies of Cretans cited from Epimenides (1:12) that were to be subject to discussion (chs. 1-2).

There is an overall emphasis in this letter on ethical instructions for Christians of both genders. Certain ethical demands made of older and younger men were also required of older married women and younger wives. The nexus between older men and women is also clear — ethical injunctions to older men, and 'likewise' (ὡσαύτως) other instructions to older women (2:3). Older women were to help younger women in coping with married life and relationships. This is succinctly covered by a number of terms demanding the re-evaluation of their lifestyle and the restraint of their instincts (2:4-5). Then the younger men were immediately addressed, again with the same connective, 'likewise'; they were to have 'self-control' in all areas of their lives (2:6). For Titus to teach these ethical commands given to both men and women was part of the overall strategy to amend what was seen to be 'deficient' in the Christian communities; these were foils to the culturally determined norms of the inhabitants of first-century Roman Crete as the following section will show.

---

47. *Contra* A. C. Thiselton, "The Logical Role of the Liar Paradox in Titus 1:12, 13: A Dissent from the Commentaries in the Light of Philosophical and Logical Analysis," *Biblical Interpretation* 2 (1994): 207-23. He seeks to argue that the saying does not make a generalisation about Cretan society. However, his approach forces him to argue that the subsequent affirmation about the truthfulness of the witness 'is more likely to have been intended as a light touch underlining the absurdity of a regress *ad infinitum*', *cit.* p. 207.

III. Drunkenness among Older Married Women

Older women were not to be 'addicted to much wine' (μὴ οἴνῳ πολλῷ δεδουλωμένας) (2:3), implying a problem of drunkenness among them. Aulus Gellius in his early-second-century A.D. *Attic Nights* cites an excerpt from a speech by Marcus Cato (95-46 B.C.) on the life and drinking conventions of women of long ago.

> Those who have written about the life and culture of the Roman people say that women in Rome and Latium 'lived an abstemious life', which is to say that they abstained altogether from wine, called *temetum* in the early language, and that it was the custom to kiss their relatives so they could smell whether or not they had been drinking. Women, however, are said to have drunk the wine of the second press, raisin wine, myrrh-flavoured wine, a sweet drink. Marcus Cato reports that women were not only judged but also punished by a judge as severely for drinking wine as for committing adultery.

Gellius then revealed that he had 'copied Cato's words from a speech called *On the dowry*. . . . "The husband," he says, "who divorces his wife is her judge, as though he were a censor; he has power if she has done something perverse and awful; if she has drunk wine she is punished . . .".'[48]

In an extensive and sophisticated discourse on wine growing, on the quality of vintage and other wines and the problems of excessive drinking, Pliny notes the case of Egnatius where the offending husband was acquitted of his wife's murder because she drank wine from the vat.[49] He also records information from Fabius Pictor where a woman was starved to death by relatives for having broken open the casket containing the keys to the wine cellar. Pliny also notes Cato's explanation of the origins of the custom of women being kissed by male relatives to determine whether they had drunk wine. He explains that the origin of the word 'tipsy' was that women smelt of 'tipple', meaning 'wine'. The judge, Gnaeus Domitius, fined a woman the amount of her dowry for having 'drunk more wine than was required for her health'. Pliny also recorded 'that a great economy in the use of this commodity prevailed for a long time'. He reported that 'women were not allowed to drink wine' in former times in Rome.[50]

Almost a century earlier than Pliny, Valerius Maximus, who wrote in the

---

48. Gellius, *Attic Nights*, 10:23.
49. Pliny, *Natural History*, 14.89.
50. Pliny, *Natural History*, 14.89.

time of Tiberius, recorded that there had been a penalty for 'violating the laws of sobriety'. He also was aware of the case of Egnatius Mecennius from the reign of Romulus who for a 'much slighter cause' cudgelled his wife to death because she had drunk wine. He noted: 'All agreed that the penalty she paid to injured Sobriety was an excellent precedent.' At the end of his discussion Valerius Maximus discloses his own convictions about the nexus between excessive drinking and misconduct in his own day: 'and true it is that any female who seeks the use of wine closes the door on every virtue and opens it to every vice.'[51]

Unlike the Classical Greek and Hellenistic periods, women in Roman times could accompany their husbands to dinners.[52] For the wives, abstention was no longer the case, as Pliny himself went on to note.

> Think of the drinking matches! Think of the vessels engraved with scenes of adultery, as though tippling were not enough in itself to give lessons in licentiousness! . . . Then it is that greedy eyes bid a price for a married woman, and their heavy glances betray it to her husband; then it is that the secrets of the heart are published abroad . . . and truth has come to be proverbially credited to wine.[53]

The husband had not only turned a blind eye but also, in effect, acquiesced during the traditional drinking session that followed the meal to the sexual indiscretions of his wife in what was all part of the 'after dinners'.[54] These indiscretions were disclosed elsewhere by the eyewitnesses in an unguarded and drunken moment.

Philo recorded in the Julio-Claudian period that there were special tables reserved for 'the drink bouts which followed as part of but not the only event in "the after-dinners", as they call them'.[55] It was not only the single young men who, on donning the *toga virilis* as a sign of manhood, operated with no self-control, engaging in what has been described as 'the intimate and unholy trinity' of eating and drinking and sexual immorality at private dinners.[56] Both sexes might do so at these dinner parties. Female partners who had tra-

---

51. Valerius Maximus, *Memorable Doings and Sayings*, 6.3.9-12. Treggiari, *Roman Marriage: Iusti Coniuges from the Time of Cicero to the Time of Ulpian*, p. 461 n. 120.

52. See pp. 33-34 for the differences between the Greek and the Roman period.

53. Pliny, *Natural History*, 14.28.140-41.

54. See p. 22.

55. Philo, *Vit.*, 54.

56. A. Booth, "The Age for Reclining and Its Attendant Perils," in W. J. Slater, ed., *Dining in a Classical Context* (Ann Arbor: University of Michigan, 1991), p. 105.

ditionally been only the courtesans might now include those called 'new' wives.

Men and women alike in the first century were included in Epimenides' ancient epitaph of 'lazy gluttons'. In the Christian communities drinking to excess applied equally to men, for the Christian elder was not to be a drunkard (1:7) any more than the older women were to be given to 'much wine'. The injunction to younger men to exercise self-control in 'all things' would have included drinking bouts and sexual activities once they acquired the *toga* of manhood (2:6). Extant evidence shows that there could be a nexus between drunkenness and immoral conduct at the feasts of young men in the East as well as in Rome.[57]

In addition to the instruction not to be slaves to much wine, older women were not to be 'slanderers' (μὴ διαβόλους) (2:3). This activity was not totally unrelated to the gluttony at dinners and the subsequent excessive drinking. Epicharmus observed the nexus between drinking at banquets and slanderous comments: 'But after drinking comes mockery, and after mockery filthy insults, after insults a lawsuit . . .'.[58] The word 'slander' is part of the semantic field shared by the accepted legal convention called 'defamation' (διαβολή) in which one sought to 'bad mouth' an accused or defendant in public in advance of a civil or criminal trial.[59] The denigration of others with the tongue was associated with the loss of self-control. If present among older Christian women it would severely damage the whole tenor of the life of the various Christian communities on the island.

The connection, then, between gluttony, excessive drinking and slandering others as well as immorality among older women is well attested and provides the *Sitz im Leben* of this instruction to older women.

IV. Recalling Young Married Women to Their Responsibilities

'Reverend behaviour' was demanded of older Christian Cretan women. Like their Neo-Pythagorean sisters, they were to help younger wives live in marriage circumspectly in contrast to the current cultural laxness. (See pp. 72-74). The former could do this only if self-control and other virtues were evi-

---

57. See Winter, *After Paul Left Corinth*, pp. 82-85.

58. Athenaeus, *Deipnosophists*, 2.36.

59. For a discussion of διαβολή see K. M. D. Dunbabin and W. M. Dickie, "*Invidia rumpantur pectora*: Iconography of *Phthonos/Invidia* in Graeco-Roman Art," *JbAC* 26 (1983): 3-37. For the relevance of this for Phil. 1:12ff. see my *Seek the Welfare of the City: Christians as Benefactors and Citizens* (Grand Rapids: Eerdmans, 1993), p. 94.

denced in their own lives (2:3). The content of good teaching to be given by older women is explained in 2:4-5. More recently the Greek καλο- διδασκάλους, ἵνα σωφρονίζωσιν τὰς νέας εἶναι φιλάνδρους καὶ φιλοτέκνους has been rendered: 'They are to teach what is good, and so train the young women to love their husbands and children'.[60] It will be argued in this section that the verb, σωφρονίζω, in the clause has either not been translated, under-translated, or mistranslated.

The noun καλοδιδασκάλους means 'good teachers'. The running of two or three words together is certainly not unknown in Greek.[61] The sense is best secured by rendering this term as 'good teachers' and not 'teachers of what is good' and then by fully translating the ἵνα clause which expresses conscious purpose.[62] It indicates the aim as well as the content of the instructions that the good teachers give. Commentators have drawn the conclusion that the task of older women was 'to train', which would mean the Greek word used would be either παιδεύω 'I educate', or διδάσκω 'I teach' but certainly not σωφρονίζω. The verb 'to teach' does not appear in the text. Translators may have assumed it from 2:1 where again the sentence is addressed to Titus — lit-erally he is 'to speak that which befits wholesome teaching' (σὺ δὲ λάλει ἃ πρέπει τῇ ὑγιαινούσῃ διδασκαλίᾳ) and not literally 'to teach'. The role of teaching is contrasted with that of those who were denounced for not adorn-ing their instruction with a consistent life-style (1:10-16). While it is true that the older women were called upon to live a lifestyle appropriate to their Christian calling (2:3a), their role as good teachers (2:3b) is covered in the clause that follows (2:4a) with a series of ethical terms preceded by an impor-tant verb.

'Wakeup Calls'

Commentators have not reached a consensus in their interpretations of the meaning of the verb σωφρονίζω in the subordinate clause. Fee has suggested something of a dynamic equivalent: 'wise them up' as regards marriage and family responsibilities as if the problem being addressed was that of igno-rance; this does not really capture its meaning.[63] Marshall felt that Fee comes

---

60. *English Standard Version* (Wheaton: Crossways Publishers, 2002).

61. The joining of words is common, e.g., καλὸς καὶ ἀγαθός as καλὸς καγαθός and even καλοκαγαθία.

62. A. T. Robertson, *A Grammar of the Greek New Testament in the Light of Historical Re-search* (New York: Hodder & Stoughton, 1914), p. 981, citing this text on p. 985.

63. G. D. Fee, *1 and 2 Timothy and Titus* (Peabody, MA: Hendrickson, 1988), p. 187.

close to the force of the Greek word.[64] Mounce has suggested that this verse aims to 'encourage', but he adds the important observation — 'although this term does not carry the cognate's meaning to be self-controlled'.[65]

The entry in the latest edition of Bauer and Danker does not bring any more clarity to the issue. They begin the entry by citing the usual meaning in classical and *Koine* Greek (to 'bring to one's senses'), citing from sources as early as Xenophon and as late as Origen, and include the first-century writers Philo and Josephus. They then conclude that in Titus 2:4 it means to 'encourage, advise, urge' but precede this with the explanation 'to instruct in prudence or behaviour that is becoming and shows good judgement.' In support of this latter comment they cite this additional evidence. The second-century sophist, Maximus Tyrius, speaks of bringing people back to their senses but, he adds, 'not the Corinthians'. The late-first-century author, Dio Chrysostom, notes how the people of Sparta 'were brought back to their senses'. The much earlier Demosthenes provided a similar meaning where 'the utterly wicked . . . are only called back to their senses by suffering'.[66] These three sources are the basis for the three possible renderings given by Bauer and Danker, *viz.* 'encourage', 'advise' or 'urge'.

They also cite with approval Moulton and Milligan, who provided a late-second-century non-literary example, *viz.*, the imperial comment: 'we too are accustomed to bring to their senses those who are mad or beside themselves'.[67] Moulton and Milligan then noted 'cf. Titus 2:4 where, however, the RV understands the verb in the general sense "to train"'.[68]

Liddell and Scott from the earliest edition of their Greek-English Lexicon in 1843 provided two meanings for this verb: 'to chasten' and 'to recall a person to their senses'. In its twentieth-century editions they cite Titus 2:4 as an example of chastening. It will be argued in the light of the following first-century examples of the use of this verb that there is a very specific meaning.

---

64. Marshall, *The Pastoral Epistles*, p. 247.

65. W. D. Mounce, *Pastoral Epistles* (Nashville: Nelson, 2000), p. 411. The rendering of the verb as 'encourage' derives from the 1957 edition of Bauer, Arndt and Gingrich, *A Greek-English Lexicon of the New Testament and Other Early Christian Literature*, where 'to bring someone to his senses' is cited with appropriate references. However they add 'also simply *encourage, advise, urge*,' citing an article published in 1909.

66. Maximus Tyrius, 30.5g; Dio Chrysostom, *Or.*, 34.49; and Demosthenes, *Against Aristogeiton*, 93.

67. *P.Oxy.* 33, iv. *l.* 11.

68. F. W. Danker and W. Bauer, *A Greek-English Lexicon of the New Testament and Other Early Christian Literature*, 3rd edition (Chicago: University of Chicago Press, 2000), p. 986. J. H. Moulton and G. Milligan, *Vocabulary of the Greek Testament* (London: Hodder and Stoughton, 1929), p. 622.

It is re-enforced by terms used in the clause; the renderings offered by commentators and the latest lexicon of 'teaching' and 'encouraging' do not have the support of the ancient sources.

Long ago Ellicott concluded that the verb plus σώφρονας (2:5) to 'be somewhat tautologous' — he seems wrongly to have assumed that σωφρονίζω and not σωφρονέω was the verbal form of σώφρονας and went on to render 2:4: 'that they may school the young women to be . . . '.[69] Ellicott also cited Philo, who used the verb 'to admonish' (νουθετῆσαι) alongside σωφρονίζω, although the former does not appear in Titus 2:4 or anywhere else in the letter.[70]

Philo as a first-century witness provides a good starting point. A careful examination of his evidence provides a number of helpful examples of σωφρονίζω that cannot be translated 'I admonish' because the verb νουθετῆσαι appears alongside σωφρονίζω, and therefore the latter is rightly rendered as 'I recall a person to their senses'. It therefore has its own distinctive meaning over against the former verb, which indicates admonition. Philo makes mention of the need 'to admonish (νουθετῆσαι) those who could not otherwise "be brought to their senses" (σωφρονίζεσθαι)', 53.1 if ill-disciplined slaves 'cannot be brought to their senses and to wisdom by truth, they need to be brought to heel by fear'. 'The law imposes . . . an admonition and correction (νουθετεῖ καὶ σωφρονίζει) leading a person to improve his ways', i.e., to move back on the correct path. Philo speaks of shepherding by means of 'admonition' (νουθετῶν) and 'correcting' irrational powers. He notes elsewhere that fighting does not necessarily 'admonish' (νουθετῶν) or 'bring people back to their senses' (σωφρονίζων). Well-qualified teachers engage in the admonition and correction of those capable of receiving them. Elsewhere the fear of the sovereign has the force of correction to admonish the subject (ἀνάγκη σωφρονιζούσῃ νουθετεῖται), whereas a father's kindness has no such fear for a child. Philo's use of this word with the two other terms throws further light on its distinctive meaning to draw the person back to the appropriate way — 'reproving, admonishing and bringing them to their senses' (ἐπιτιμῶν, νουθετῶν, σωφρονίζων). So even the idea of chastening as a rendering of the verb used in Titus 2:4 should be called into question.[71]

Philo also uses the verb σωφρονίζω by itself. He noted that people flocked to Flaccus, who had been relegated, whenever he disembarked from his ship. Some came out of malice but the rest 'to find lessons of wisdom in the fate of others [so as] to be brought to their senses (σωφρονίζεσθαι)'. The punish-

---

69. C. J. Ellicott, *The Pastoral Epistles of St Paul* (London: Longmans, 1869), p. 193.

70. Ellicott, *The Pastoral Epistles of St Paul*, p. 194.

71. Philo, *Immut.* 53.1, 64.4, *Virt.* 115.3, *Det.* 3.3, *Conf.* 46.5, *Mig.* 14.5, *Fug.* 98.2, *Jos.* 73.4.

ment of others often admonishes the offenders and recalls them to wisdom. He even goes so far as to argue that in times of pestilence it is well that some of the guiltless should perish as a lesson that jolts all back to a wiser life (σωφρονίζωνται). It is the work of justice and the power of the law to bring men and women to their senses, according to Philo, as 'a father brings his son to his sense (σωφρονίζων) by way of a beating'. The aim of a ruler is to instil fear in his presence so that 'those who have no ears for reproof to come back to their senses (σωφρονίζονται) are controlled by fear'.[72]

An important conclusion can be made on the use of the verb σωφρονίζω in Philo's corpus. In all these instances the intention was either to bring a city, its inhabitants, sons and daughters or subjects back to their senses through persuasion, or for them to learn lessons through adverse circumstances. A clear distinction is to be drawn between 'reproof and admonition' and redirecting by the powers of persuasion a person back to the path from which he or she should not have deviated.[73] The other verb 'to admonish' or 'chasten' (νουθετῆσαι) is used on occasions where a sharp correction is undertaken, but σωφρονίζω is used with the hope of bringing about a return to an appropriate or a former way of operating. The fundamental meaning of the latter verb then is 'to recover one's senses' with respect to a particular matter or a course of action.

Philo wrote in the late Julio-Claudian era, and his use of this verb is confirmed in other literary sources at both the beginning and the end of the first century. The late Republican and early Empire writer, Dionysius of Halicarnassus, when discussing a siege recorded 'that those in the city neither showed gratitude nor were they brought to their senses by their misfortunes'.[74]

Dio Chrysostom at the end of the first century observed that severe and insuperable hardships help to bring men who are 'gluttonous' and 'folly-stricken' to their senses. In the rapidly changing alliances in Greece between Athens and Sparta, the inhabitants of the latter were called back to their senses, realising that nothing was more important to them than law and order whereby that city achieved its greatest prosperity.[75] A great city is one in which someone who

> admonishes with kindly intent is more beloved than he who speaks to flatter, [and] in which the masses are more eager to be called back to their

72. Philo, *Flacc.* 155.1, *Legat.* 7.4, *Prov.* 2.55.7, *Cong.* 179.4, *Det.* 49.5, *Gig.* 47.1.

73. M. Dibelius and H. Conzelmann, *The Pastoral Epistles* (Philadelphia: Fortress Press, 1972), p. 140, wrongly suggest in my opinion 'advise' in the sense of 'admonish', citing in the case of the latter the verb νουθετεῖν. which does not appear anywhere in Titus.

74. Dionysius of Halicarnassus, *Roman Antiquities*, 5.43.2.5.

75. Dio Chrysostom, *Or.* 8.12-13; *Or.* 34.49.

senses and to be restored (σωφρονίζεσθαι καὶ ἐπανορθοῦσθαι), than to be courted and live luxuriously, *Or.* 51.5.

His contemporary, Josephus, also used the term 'to bring his city to reason'.[76] Strabo challenged men to gentleness, calling them back (ἐσωφρόνιζε) to do certain things and forbidding them to do others.[77]

In the light of the above evidence it can be concluded that this key verb has not been correctly rendered in Titus 2:4, and its important role in the clause has not been fully appreciated. However, the general interpretation has become fixed — that the older women were simply to teach and/or to model a lifestyle or encourage. The intention was more than to seek 'to inculcate Christian values' or to teach women how to live as married women.[78] The idea of 'chastening' does not capture the significance of what is being said, but good teachers bringing their charges back to their senses does.

Lovers of Husbands and Children

The purpose of older married women undertaking this task with younger married women is for the recovering of what were seen as important perspectives on Christian marriage. The first focus of calling younger wives to their senses is their immediate family. They are 'to be lovers of their husbands and their children' (φιλάνδρους εἶναι καὶ φιλοτέκνους). These are qualities also recorded in epigraphic evidence of the good wife.

> Julius Bassus to Otacilia Polla, his sweetest wife, the lover of her husband and her children (τῇ γλυκυτάτῃ γυναικὶ φιλάνδρῳ καὶ φιλοτέκνῳ), she lived with him unblamably (ἀμέμπτως) for thirty years.[79]

On the tombstone of Pompeia Chia who died at twenty years was carved — 'I hope that my daughter will live chastely and learn by my example to love her husband'.[80]

---

76. Josephus, *Ant.* 5.256; *cf. Bell.* 3.445; 4.119. *Liddell and Scott* have cited the use of σωφρονίζω in Titus 2:4 followed by the infinitive meaning 'to chasten'.

77. Strabo, *Geography,* 9.3.11.17.

78. Marshall, *The Pastoral Epistles,* p. 247; A. T. Hanson, *The Pastoral Epistles* (London: Marshall and Pickering, 1982), p. 180.

79. *I.Perg.* II. 604, cited by A. Deissman, *Light from the Ancient East* (reprint, Grand Rapids: Baker, 1978), p. 315. See also Dibelius and Conzelmann, *The Pastoral Epistles,* 140 n. 11, for other epigraphic evidence of these qualities in a good wife.

80. *CIL* viii.8123 (North Africa).

Younger wives were also to live a life marked by 'self-control' (σώφρονας), which follows the requirement to love husbands and children. The embracing of this virtue was a primary concern for the women in the philosophical schools. Others with educative concerns were committed to instilling this one cardinal virtue that epitomised the modest wife. Among other things it covered sexual conduct in the context of relationships with the opposite gender. Its antonym, 'self-indulgence', related to inappropriate and unrestrained sexual behaviour that accompanied extravagant lifestyle.

To this was added the term 'pure' (ἀγνάς), the life to which younger wives were to be recalled (2:5; *cf.* 1:15 where the synonym for 'pure' [καθαρός] was used). The Latin language bears witness to the vast vocabulary of sexual terminology with foreign loan words for conduct of a particular sexual nature of which society did not approve. In addition there were a large number of seemingly ordinary terms that, when used in the semantic field of sexuality, epitomised a society where sexual innuendoes abounded in conversation.[81] Clearly, the call to purity on the part of younger wives touched this area of life which was marked not only by an infusion of sexual allusions into everyday terms be they in Greek or Latin, but also by impure sexual conduct.

Household Management

Strabo who wrote parts of his *Geography* in the reign of Tiberius visited Crete and recorded a marriage convention peculiar to that island. Husbands 'did not take their girls whom they married to their own homes immediately, but as soon as the girls were qualified to manage the affairs of the house' (ἀλλ' ἐπὰν ἤδη διοικεῖν ἱκαναὶ ὦσι τὰ περὶ τοὺς οἴκους).[82] This fits well with Titus 2:5. Young wives who had not been instructed in the management of their households are called to undertake that for which they were deemed qualified before they ventured into the marriage home. This further suggests that in Crete there was now an option of an alternative lifestyle for young married women — that which was promoted by the 'new' Roman women.

The young wife was to focus on the management of her household — she was to 'work at home' (οἰκουργούς).[83] Tacitus looked back to the 'good old days' when —

---

81. See Adams, *The Latin Sexual Vocabulary*, which also includes Greek terms.

82. Strabo, *Geography*, 10.4.20.

83. Dio Cassius, 56.3, draws a distinction between οἰκουρός = 'domestic' and οἰκονόμος = 'one who manages a household', but these same qualities were represented in the same woman.

every child born to a respectable mother was brought up not in the room of a hired wet-nurse but at his mother's knee. A mother could have no higher praise than that she managed her house and gave herself to her children. . . . With piety and modesty she regulated not only the serious tasks of her youthful charges, but supervised not only the boys' studies but also their recreation and games.[84]

He went on to relate a different situation which existed in the time when he lived.

. . . our children are handed over at birth to some silly little Greek servant maid. . . . The parents themselves make no effort to train their little ones in goodness and self-control; they grow up in an atmosphere of laxity . . . they come to lose all sense of shame, and all respect both for themselves and for other people.[85]

A moving inscription asks the reader to simply ponder the virtues of his wife including the fact that she kept house.

Friend, I have not much to say; stop and read. This tomb, which is not fair, is for a fair woman. Her parents gave her the name of Claudia. She loved her husband in her heart. She bore two sons, one of whom she left on earth, the other beneath it. She was pleasant to talk with, and she walked with grace *(sermone lepido, tum autem incessu commodo)*. She kept the house and worked in wool *(domum servavit, lanam fecit)*. That is all. You may go.[86]

A physician from Pergamum whose wife was named Pantheia and who lived in the second century A.D. recorded that she was not only the mother of his children and had cared for him and them but she also 'took the helm and steered the household's course and heightened the fame it had in the healing art'.[87] This reflects something of the complexities and diverse responsibilities, as well as the opportunities, in running the household.

The call is also to be 'kind' (ἀγαθάς) in her treatment of others, presumably to those who live in the household. This would encompass others beyond the confines of her family and include any of her household servants.

It should be noted that these injunctions to young wives which aimed to

---

84. Tacitus, 'A Dialogue on Oratory', 28.
85. Tacitus, 'A Dialogue on Oratory', 29.
86. *CIL* 1. 1211 (Rome, Gracchi).
87. *Epigrammata Graeca*, 243b.

bring them back to their senses culminated in the final call 'to be in submission to their own husbands' (ὑποτασσομένας τοῖς ἰδίοις ἀνδράσιν). Given that the preceding terms discussed were 'self-control', 'purity', and 'kindness' and 'lovers of their husbands and children', this last injunction sought at the very least to counter a prevalent view of marriage in which a wife might pursue a life of pleasure as some of the Roman wives did. It may also be aimed at the problem of adultery and, if that was the case, then the use of 'own' (ἰδίοις) contrasted with any sexual surrendering of themselves to another man. An inscription from the Roman period recording the virtues of a woman who was 'fair, good, gentle, and divinely beautiful' proudly adds that she was 'faithful to one husband' — the last term meant literally a woman of 'one marriage bed' (μουνολεχῆ).[88]

The Neo-Pythagoreans provide an interesting contrast between those who love their families and focus on their needs and the promiscuous wife whose deviousness forces her into deception which undermines the household as well:

Having mastery over appetite and high feelings, she will be righteous and harmonious; no lawless desires will impel her. She will preserve a loving disposition towards her husband and children and entire household. As many women as become lovers of alien beds become enemies of all at home, both the free members and the servants of the household (ἐλευθέρων τε καὶ οἰκετέων). Such a woman continually contrives lies and deceits for her husband and fabricates falsehoods about everything to him, in order that she may seem to excel in good will and, though she loves idleness, may seem to govern her house to such an extent.[89]

On the basis of this verse (2:4), Marshall suggests 'that one of the goals of the teaching is to prevent younger women from adopting patterns of careless, flighty living that would attract criticism'.[90] This goes some way to securing the sense but it was not primarily preventative but restorative in terms of the traditional role of women. The adjectives used help confirm that the concerns were not notional and primarily preventative. The significance of the verb is that older women were good teachers when they called their younger sisters back to their senses concerning their responsibilities in marriage to their hus-

---

88. *Epigrammata Graeca*, 272b, *ll.* 17-18. The word combines the word for 'marriage' bed λέχος and 'single' μοῦνος.

89. Thesleff, 1965, 143, 1ff., cited by R. Hawley and B. Levick, eds., *Women in Antiquity: New Assessments* (London: Routledge, 1995), p. 126.

90. Marshall, *Pastoral Epistles*, p. 247.

bands, their children, the management of their own households, and above all sexual faithfulness to their own husbands.

Debauchery among Older Children

The term 'debauchery' (ἀσωτία) had also been mentioned early in the letter as a vice among 'children' (1:6), and the existence of such behaviour by members of the families of potential elders ruled the father out of that role in Christian communities. The reference there must be to older and not younger children because they would have had to have reached puberty in order to engage in sustained sexual misconduct.[91]

Strabo refers to another Cretan peculiarity, *viz.* 'love affairs' which were limited to male homosexual liaisons as part of a rite of passage into manhood for Cretan citizens. Young men were sought out for sexual intercourse by their own gender and rewarded for submitting to them.[92] This conduct was not endorsed in Roman society for it was a criminal offence to sexually penetrate a male who was a Roman citizen, although no breach of the law occurred on the part of a Roman who penetrated a male who was not a citizen.[93]

The reference to 'debauchery' may refer in part to this and also a disease known in the ancient and modern medical terminology as 'priapism' or 'satyriasis' known to be suffered by Cretans. A plant, satyrion, was used as an aphrodisiac and the resulting condition if untreated could cause death. Themison in his work *Symptoms of Acute Diseases* recalled that 'often in Crete many men die of satyriasis [priapism] . . . because a plant called satyrion is often consumed in great quantities'.[94]

While it is known that soon after reaching puberty young women married, usually between the ages of fourteen and seventeen, the age at which

91. Sexual activity with females before menstruation was strongly discouraged by Soranus, the late-first-century gynaecologist from Ephesus, *Gynaecology*, 1:33.

92. Strabo, *Geography*, 10.4.20.

93. O. F. Robinson, *The Criminal Law of Ancient Rome* (London: Duckworth, 1995), pp. 70-71 and my appendix on Roman attitudes, "Roman Homosexual Activity and the Elite (1 Corinthians 6:9)," in *After Paul Left Corinth: The Influence of Secular Ethics and Social Change* (Grand Rapids: Eerdmans, 2001), pp. 110-20.

94. Themison, *Symptoms of Acute Diseases*, III, xvii, 185. For a discussion of this with citations by others in the ancient world, such as Rufus and Soranus (*Gynaecology*, III.3), the late-first-century gynaecologist, both from Ephesus, Caelius Aurelianus, *Acute Diseases*, Pseudo-Galen, Oribasius, and Aetius, see D. Gourevitch, "Women who suffer from a man's disease," in R. Hawley and B. Levick, eds., *Women in Antiquity*, ch. 10.

young men took the *toga virilis* was around eighteen. This transition was seen as providing the licence to 'sow their wild oats' with society's general acquiescence. In Athens when 'the new adult, aged eighteen, usually acquired the right to accept invitations to recline . . . he was considered sufficiently mature to cope with sexual advances'.[95] Tacitus records, 'The elegant banquet . . . along with the use of the *toga* . . . are the enticements of Romanization, to vice and servitude.'[96] Cicero would have sneered at the call to sexual purity on the part of young adults not yet married (Titus 2:6). He wrote:

> If there is anyone who thinks that youth [males] should be forbidden affairs even with courtesans, he is doubtless eminently austere, but his view is contrary not only to the licence of this age, but also to the custom and concessions of our ancestors.[97]

His appeal was to contemporary culture and ancestral conventions for young Roman men. Evidence produced shows that already in the first century some married women did compete with courtesans for the sexual favours of younger or other men at their debauched banquets.

The Behaviour of Husbands

There were no less rigorous demands made on 'older' men, i.e., married men who were not normally censured by society because of their adultery in the 'after dinners' or for their quarrelsome conduct.[98] On the latter Plutarch noted 'the practice of the Cretans, who often quarrelled with and warred with each other'.[99] However Titus 2:2 calls upon them to be 'temperate in the use of wine, worthy of respect, self-controlled, and sound in faith, love and patience'. The younger men did not escape the counter-cultural demands made of them, given the societal endorsement of their indulging themselves at din-

---

95. Booth, "The Age for Reclining and Its Attendant Perils," p. 117.

96. Tacitus, *Agr.* 21. This was also a problem among Christian young men in Corinth see 1 Cor. 6:12-20; and for a discussion of the evidence see my *After Paul Left Corinth*, pp. 86-93, 106-7.

97. Cicero, *Pro Caelio*, 20.48.

98. The term for older men πρεσβύτας in 2:2 is different from πρεσβυτέρους in 1:5. Dio Chrysostom writing at the end of the first century indicates the stages of males: 'just as one becomes successively a lad, a stripling, a youth and an old man by the passing of time' (παῖδα καὶ μειράκιον καὶ νεανίσκον καὶ πρεσβύτην χρόνος ποιεῖ), *Or.* 74:10.

99. Plutarch, "On brotherly love," 490B; he added, 'they made up their differences and united when outside enemies attacked'; and this it was which they called "syncretism" (συγκρητισμός).'

ners with wine and fornication or engaging in sexual liaisons with their own gender in the rite of passage to manhood. The single comprehensive imperative was sufficient to refute the Roman Cretan values of the self-indulgence of young men.[100]

Immediately after chapter 2:1-10, which also included instructions to older and younger men as well as slaves, the grace of God is declared to have brought salvation to all. Its intention involves

> instructing us that we should renounce ungodliness and worldly passions and to live self-controlled, upright and godly lives in the present age (παιδεύουσα ἡμᾶς ἵνα ἀρνησάμενοι τὴν ἀσέβειαν καὶ τὰς κοσμικὰς ἐπιθυμίας σωφρόνως καὶ δικαίως καὶ εὐσεβῶς ζήσωμεν). . . . [God's aim is] to purify for himself a people of his own who are zealous for good deeds (2:11-12, 14).

This theme is repeated in 3:3-8 where the goodness and loving-kindness of God our Saviour appeared for salvation. The purpose was not only that those Cretans who believed might be justified and have hope of eternal life but also that they would be godly and apply themselves to good works that were excellent and profitable to others (1:1, 2:14, 3:8). Christian virtues that manifested themselves in good works and that benefited others could be undertaken only if there was a renunciation of those Cretan values that were antithetical to them.

Traditional and Christian Values

In the city of Aphrodisias the wife of Pereitas Kallidedes, Tatu, was officially recognised in her death by 'the Council and the People'. They 'honoured' her on her sarcophagus as 'a woman who was modest (σώφρονα), who loved her husband and children (φίλανδρον καὶ φιλότεκνον), and who all her life was adorned with dignity and virtue (κοσμηθεῖσαν σεμνότητι καὶ ἀρετῇ)'.[101]

Some sixty years ago Lattimore argued on the basis of epigraphic material surveyed in his book: 'The world disclosed by the Greek epitaphs is mostly a woman's world, existing at a time when the old Athenian ideal had gone out of fashion even as an ideal. To be sure, it is mostly the old-fashioned virtues on which they are complimented; with beauty, they must have faith, honesty, seemliness, above all, affection for husband and family. They are

---

100. Plutarch, *Lysander*, 12.1; Strabo, *Geography*, 10.4.20.
101. *Monumenta Asiae Minoris Antiqua*, iii. 499 c. *ll.* 5-9.

praised because their children resemble their fathers, for being faithful to one husband, for loving their husbands in the good old way, for housekeeping, even for being γυνὴ φειδωλή [a thrifty wife].'[102]

The terminology used in 2:4-5 helps provide a composite picture of what young Christian married women were being called upon to abandon and what they were being summoned back to do. They were to operate with modesty primarily in the arena of the 'household' (τὰ ἴδια) which in the first century was distinguished from the other sphere, i.e., 'the public place' (πολιτεία).[103] Because the age for the consummation of marriage for young women in the first century could be immediately after puberty to mid or late teens, the temptation to look for casual liaisons was not peculiar to their husbands who normally were a decade older. For the latter group adultery was a social given but a husband was to be above reproach, being a 'one woman' man if he was to be considered for the eldership in the Christian community (1:6). The opening chapters of this book provided evidence of wives following their spouse's promiscuous example, and the legal steps taken to curb their unfaithfulness to their husbands was examined in chapter 3.

The tying of the virtues of the wife to salvation is unique in Titus. If Christian bonded servants (2:10) were required to live in such a way as 'to adorn the doctrine of God our Saviour', then in the final purpose clause younger women were not to engage in inappropriate conduct that caused the word of God to be blasphemed (2:5). It was not the husband who would be shamed by the wife's inappropriate conduct, but rather the word of God would be contradicted by it. Rome banned certain religious cults which were cloaks for political or promiscuous conduct. This may also have been an aspect of the background to this comment about discrediting the Christian faith by sexual and other forms of misconduct (2:5).[104]

In the light of the above discussion it is suggested that discrediting the Christian faith would occur for the following reasons: if young wives (i) did not return to their role of loving their husbands and children; (ii) did not exercise self-control but indulged in debauchery; (iii) were not pure, or committed to managing their own households; (iv) were not kind or submissive to husbands in the intimacy of marriage but engaged in casual sexual liaisons.

---

102. R. Lattimore, *Themes in Greek and Latin Epitaphs* (Urbana: University of Illinois Press, 1942), p. 292.

103. This is the dichotomy in the first-century description of life in the city. For a discussion see J. Bordes, *Politeia dans la pensée grecque jusquà Aristote* (Paris: Les Belles Lettres, 1982), pp. 116ff.; and C. Meier, *The Greek Discovery of Politics* (ET, Cambridge, MA: Harvard University Press, 1990), pp. 13ff.

104. O. F. Robinson, *The Criminal Law of Ancient Rome*, pp. 95-97.

Where this happened the credibility of the Christian message would be called into question. In terms of marital infidelity they would open themselves to judicial censure for adultery, but in terms of their religious profession their conduct would contradict their Christian confession.[105]

This divorce between faith and ethical conduct would deny the claims of Christianity and hold it up to ridicule. In the verses that immediately follow, the grace of God is said to train or discipline Christians to renounce ungodliness and worldly passions, to live self-controlled, upright and godly lives. Grace is spelt out in terms of redemption from all iniquity with the aim to create a community that would be zealous for good works (2:11-14), which included older and younger wives and did not exclude older or younger men.

V. Conclusions

What is to be concluded from the preceding evidence which explored the *Sitz im Leben* of Titus 2:3-5? 'Wives, be subject to your husbands, as is fitting in the Lord' was the simple injunction given to Colossian women (Col. 3:18). The following argument supplemented this apostolic tradition to wives in Ephesus: 'for the husband is the head of the wife as Christ is the head of the church, his body, and is himself its saviour. As the church is subject to Christ, so let wives also be subject to their husbands in everything' (Eph. 5:22-24). When this is compared with the teaching given to married women in Titus, it would be difficult to argue that Titus 2:3-5 simply reflected standard apostolic *paradosis* in 'all the churches' (cf. 1 Cor. 7:17) and therefore had no specific first-century *Sitz im Leben* in Crete. However, Dibelius and Conzelmann concluded, 'The following verses warn against vices which should be avoided by the Christian as a matter of course. That the warning is still presented, even though it would seem to be superfluous, is explained by the consideration that both the rules for the household and the list of virtues frequently use traditional material.'[106] Their conclusion, then, that there is no *Sitz im Leben*, is rejected.

When compared with the instructions to young wives by the older women in the Neo-Pythagorean tradition, the intention in Titus 2 is slightly different. In that case older women give the warmest commendation to those who underwent philosophical instruction on marriage of their own volition because they had been drawn to the Stoic or Neo-Pythagorean lifestyle.[107] As we com-

---

105. See ch. 3.
106. Dibelius and Conzelmann, *The Pastoral Epistles*, p. 140.
107. See pp. 72-73.

pare with patterns commended in the philosophical schools, a succinct and perhaps sharper contrast emerges between what was praiseworthy for young married women seeking instruction from older women in the philosophical schools and the role given to older women in relation to the younger wives in the Cretan Christian communities.[108] For the latter it was with a very specific task to recall them to their senses by means of a set of specific instructions.

The Cretan behaviour was succinctly epitomised in part by Epimenides' phrase 'lazy gluttons'. This is reflected in the behaviour of both men and women in Titus 2:2-6 with the older women's addiction to much wine and slanderous talk and the lack of self-control by younger married women and older and younger men alike.

In the light of the evidence produced in connection with the number of injunctions given to young Cretan Christian wives, it is suggested that they had been influenced by some of their secular married sisters. Terminology used in Titus to counter the situation in Crete fits well with what is known of the 'new' Roman women's conduct with their lack of interest in the welfare of the household which Cretan women had to demonstrate their ability to run before marrying. The neglect of her husband as well as her children presumably in favour of a social life that might involve casual extramarital affairs is also commented on. The call, therefore, was for the young Christian wives to come to their senses and no longer follow the secular trend. Just as such a promiscuous mindset earned the disapproval of the philosophical schools and might attract legal penalties under Roman law, so too there was a strong rebuke to be given to young Christian wives.

There could be no special pleading for those wives in the Christian communities on Crete. While their cultural traditions and legal provisions had long ago given them more independence than their sisters in the Eastern Mediterranean, they were not justified in embracing the *avant-garde* ground rules of the 'new women' with the coming of the Romans to their island. These new mores might also have furthered their freedom in another area — inappropriate liaisons with those not their husbands with the resulting neglect of their own spouses and children. In addition, there was the complex management of what was regarded as the backbone of first-century culture, *viz.* their households, where they were required to 'take the helm and steer the household's course'.[109] It was not the legal status in terms of their own prop-

---

108. See E. A. Judge, "A Woman's Behaviour," *New Documents Illustrating Early Christianity* 6 (1992), p. 19, on the domestic code *(Haustafel)* and its New Testament parallels including Titus 2:2-10 and his observation that it is conceived along different lines from the philosophical schools.

109. *Epigrammata Graeca*, 243b.

erty that was being curtailed in any way in the instructions given in Titus 2:3-5, but their conduct as married women that contradicted their confession of the grace of God that was bringing salvation to all. The aim was to recall them to their responsibilities with the implication that they had abandoned them for a lifestyle that replicated that of the new women whose values had found fertile ground with some in Cretan culture.

PART III

CHAPTER 9

The Appearance of Women
in the Public Sphere

Did women in the first century, unlike their earlier Greek sisters, have any place in the 'public' domain, what the ancients called *politeia* (πολιτεία)?[1] Thus far, this book has been concerned to trace the impact of the values of the 'new' woman on households, including Christian gatherings held there. The question now being explored is whether women functioned in commerce, in the courts, and in the forum. In this final chapter we will assemble epigraphic evidence that demonstrates that they were able to participate in and contribute to each of these areas of *politeia* in the first century.[2] The concluding section asks whether this social shift affected the way in which the women named in the Pauline communities were able to contribute to the Pauline mission in Corinth and Rome.

Bauman, a Roman legal historian, drew this conclusion. 'When Octavian "restored the Republic", that is, founded the Principate in 27 B.C., he initiated the most far-reaching change in Roman history. It was one that had a profound effect on every aspect of life, including women's role in public affairs. That role was still dominated by the upper echelons of society, but with a difference, for there was now an élite within the élite . . . women have a high profile in so many sectors of the Augustan kaleidoscope.'[3] He helpfully traces the

1. It is tempting to transliterate this Greek term into English and conclude that the question is about women's political involvement. But the ancients saw all activities outside the home as coming within the sphere of *politeia*.

2. R. MacMullen, "Women in Public in the Roman Empire," *Historia* 29 (1980): 208, n. 1, complains of the neglect of epigraphic material for the study of ancient women. He notes a similar concern of E. A. Judge for N.T. studies, "St. Paul and Classical Society," *JAC* 14 (1971): 28.

3. R. A. Bauman, *Women and Politics in Ancient Rome* (London: Routledge, 1992), pp. 99-100.

expanding role of women in the business of government, law and public affairs, and then looks at its connection with the activities of the imperial wives in Rome in the public sphere.[4]

Culham argues that there was a further effect of the Augustan reforms. 'Augustus' emphasis on the importance of élite political rank, and his own benevolent display, had the impact of opening new social and economic horizons for élite women, and that in turn had some impact on the lives of men and women outside the élite.'[5]

To explore this, we will examine the evidence for the role of women in (I) the commercial sphere; (II) the courts; and (III) the political sphere. We will then determine whether the contribution of Christian women was in any way facilitated by these important developments. Section III while recording the civic offices held by a number of women is a detailed discussion of Junia Theodora of Corinth whose composite inscription consists of five official commendations of her by leading cities in the Lycian Federation. It is the longest official extant testimony to the role of any woman in *politeia* in the first century, or indeed, in the early Empire.[6] Section IV is a comparative study of evidence from sections I to III and women in the Christian community.

I. Women in Commerce

As one would expect, this sort of evidence is naturally sparse given that there was little need to maintain records of transactions, but three areas are examined that provide insights into the participation of women in commercial activity from epigraphic and papyrological sources. Women contributed to commercial and other endeavours using their households as a base. For example, a physician who lived in Pergamum in the second century A.D. recorded that his wife, Pantheia, was not only the mother of his children who had cared for him and them, but she also 'took the helm and steered the household's course and heightened the fame it had in the healing art'.[7]

Jane Gardner in an important article on "Women in Business Life" has,

---

4. Bauman, *Women and Politics in Ancient Rome.*

5. P. Culham, "Did Roman Women Have an Empire?" in M. Golden and P. Toohey, eds., *Inventing Ancient Culture: Historicism, Periodization, and the Ancient World* (London: Routledge, 1997), p. 203. She cites in support MacMullen, "Women in Public in the Roman Empire," 208-18, on the visibility of priestesses and its impact.

6. This inscription and those officially authorised to other women in the East who held official positions have been recorded in the Appendix to this chapter (pp. 205-11).

7. *Epigrammata Graeca,* 243b.

among other things, undertaken a careful analysis of some 170 waxed wooden tablets discovered at Murecine near the Roman colony of Pompeii. They cover the period from March A.D. 26 to February A.D. 61 and relate to women's activities in business in the former city,[8] showing that women borrowed and lent money and went to court to recover it.[9]

She concludes that 'we find women operating in personal business matters in pretty much the same way as men, with their personal presence or absence being determined, as with men, by factors of social status and wealth. . . . What does emerge clearly is that the *tutela* system, in the first half of the first century A.D., is actively functioning in the daily commercial transactions of townsfolk around the Bay of Naples, without seeming to offer any particular hindrance to women's dealings'. Women were operating businesses, although there were restrictions on some of the legal aspects of commerce such as witnessing transactions. While she notes that women did not figure in that area of commercial interaction and therefore had a lower profile than men in the forum of Puteoli, nevertheless there was an important context in which women functioned in the business world.[10]

The port of Ostia was built in the time of Claudius to facilitate the grain supply to Rome, and the site contains six images of working women. Detailed discussion by Natalie Kampen shows how they were portrayed with the statue types falling into two categories. They are presented either realistically or in a subordinated, idealized way. They naturally reflect the tastes and interests of those who commissioned the work and under whose patronage they operated in Roman society. The statues portrayed in a passive pose re-enforce the view that labour was demeaning for those of the upper classes.[11] While upper-class women would not have approved of such manual activity for themselves, the fact is that they acknowledged that it did occur, and patrons in Ostia recorded it in sculpture in this busy feeder port for Rome.

MacMullen assembled a wide variety of evidence in his pioneering essay, "Women in Public in the Roman Empire". He concluded, 'At both the top and the bottom of society, women thus appear to take an active part in the common business of the city, at the former level because among them could be found, at the least, a lot of money and the ability to bestow it in one form or

---

8. J. F. Gardner, "Women in Business Life: Some Evidence from Puteoli," in P. Setälä and L. Savuen, eds., *Female Networks and the Public Sphere in Roman Society* (Rome: Institutum Romanum Finlandiae, 1999), pp. 11-27.

9. Gardner, "Women in Business Life: Some Evidence from Puteoli," pp. 17, 18.

10. Gardner, "Women in Business Life: Some Evidence from Puteoli," p. 27.

11. N. Kampen, *Image and Status: Roman Working Women in Ostia* (Berlin: Gerb. Mann Verlag, 1981), pp. 130-36.

another on those who sought it through their offers of flattery, respect and support; at the latter level, because women obviously wanted to take a part and no one told them it was useless or ridiculous. The fact carries its own implications.'[12] While his evidence is invaluable, his conclusion is speculative. The reason may have more to do for the upper class with the unexpected consequences of the legislation of Augustus and for all women with the example of the imperial wives who were not only fashion icons but also trend-setters in their participation in politics.

II. Women in the Courts

Valerius Maximus devotes a whole section to "Women who pleaded before magistrates for themselves and others" and prefaces it with the following comment:

> Nor should I be silent about those women whose natural condition and the modesty of the *stola* (*verecundia stolae,* i.e., the matron's dress) could not make them keep silent in the Forum and the courts of law.[13]

The sort of participation in the courts to which Valerius alludes was a far cry from that in the time of Cicero (106-43 B.C.). He recorded his response to women being forced against their own will to give evidence in the courtroom before a large gathering of men. In the trial he asks —

> Why did you force your friend's wife, and the mother of your friend's wife . . . to testify against you? See these modest and virtuous ladies, unwillingly facing the unaccustomed sight of this great gathering of men — why do you force them to do it?[14]

Fannia was the first woman recorded as having conducted her own defence in which she herself had initiated legal action. It revolved around the return of the dowry held by her husband who had married her clearly knowing

---

12. See MacMullen, "Women in Public in the Roman Empire," pp. 213-14 for a summary of evidence in Greek-speaking provinces, *cit.* p. 210. See esp. S. Dixon, "Reading the Public Face," in *Reading Roman Women* (London: Duckworth, 2001), Part III, where she is less sanguine. There are important caveats as one would expect given the enormous Empire and the diverse cultures, yet there can be no denying the evidence of women's public profile.

13. Valerius Maximus, *Memorable Doings and Sayings*, VIII.3. D. R. Shackleton Bailey translates it as the modesty of the matron's robe.

14. Cicero, *Against Verres*, 2.1.94.

that she had been an unchaste woman. He had done this in order to divorce her on the grounds of her unchastity and thereby to secure her property. 'The fact that it was held "in full public view" was specially noticed because a woman was appearing in person. Fania gave a new slant to the *actio rei uxoriae*.'[15]

Do we know the names of women who were engaged in debating where they sought to defeat the arguments of their male counterparts in the courts? Bauman has given the evidence of women who were learned in law, who emerged as legal advisers in the first century B.C. or A.D. and who placed their knowledge at the disposal of fellow citizens.[16]

He comments on the highly competent legal case presented by Maesia of Sentinum who so challenged the male-dominated courts that she was judged to be an 'Androgyne' (man-woman). The Senate sought her oracular help because of the good omen she might be for the city. 'The case is important, *inter alia*, because Maesia's great proficiency in the early first century was not acquired on the spur of the moment. It presupposes a line of women versed in at least the theory of the law, as we have already postulated, and possibly with some practical experience as well — if not in open court until Sempronia, then behind the closed doors of the family court and in private declamations.'[17]

According to Valerius Maximus, Carfania, a senator's wife who died *c*. 48 B.C., was —

> ever ready for a lawsuit and always spoke on her own behalf before the Praetor, not because she could not find advocates but because she had impudence to spare. So by constantly plaguing the tribunals with 'barking' *(latratus)*, to which the Forum was unaccustomed, she became a notorious example of female litigiousness, so much so that women of shameless habits are taunted [in Valerius' day] with the name Carfania by way of reproach.[18]

Carfania's actions produced a change in the law that forbade women from 'expounding one's own or a friend's claim before a magistrate or refuting the claim of another' (to cite Ulpian's definition of the term *postulare*). According to Roman legal history —

---

15. Bauman, *Women and Politics in Ancient Rome*, p. 231.
16. Bauman, *Women and Politics in Ancient Rome*, p. 51.
17. Bauman, *Women and Politics in Ancient Rome*, p. 50.
18. Valerius Maximus, *Memorable Deeds and Sayings*, 8.3.2; Bauman, *Women and Politics in Ancient Rome*, p. 50.

. . . the origin (of the prohibition) was introduced by Carfania, a very wicked woman, who, by bringing requests without shame and disturbing the magistrates, provided the reason for the edict. In this edict the praetor made particular mention of sex and misfortune, and likewise he marked with disgrace persons conspicuous due to shameful behaviour. In regard to sex: he prohibits women from bringing a request on behalf of others. And indeed there is a reason for prohibiting them: so that women do not get themselves mixed up in other people's lawsuits, contrary to the modesty *(pudicitia)* of their sex, and perform a male role by involving themselves in the cases of others.[19]

It is significant that in Roman law the term for the modesty *(pudicitia)* of married women was linked with the inappropriateness of their undertaking the public function of arguing in court. 1 Timothy 2:9, 15 records the equivalent Greek term, σωφροσύνη, at the beginning and the end of that particular discussion.

The Velleian decree of the Senate *(senatus consultum Velleianum)* which was enacted in the time of either Claudius or Nero 'attempted to discourage the practice of women "interceding" on behalf of another person'.[20] Remarkably after all that time the disruptive Carfania was still being held up as a negative example and was seen to provide the excuse for this change in the law. (See p. 93.) However, at the very time that the classical jurists were arguing most strongly that women were ignorant of the law, the latter were 'busily engaged in seeking rulings on the law from the imperial chancellery'.[21]

The Justinian Code contains hundreds of imperial responses to women litigants, many of which concerned civic status, obligations of freed condition, marriage, divorce, support, dowry, minority status and child custody — essentially private matters, though also among those most often of concern to men, too. It is worth noting, however, that financial affairs dominate in this collection, and they could involve substantial transactions. From just a single year MacMullen mentions cases involving women in litigation 'on "the income from estates (note the plural) given as a dowry", "the gift of slaves and other things given by a wife to her husband", "assessed estates given as a dowry", "fully equipped estates by bequest", one farm of which yields oil and wine for the market at the disposal of the mater familias, and finally, a certain

19. *The Digest,* 3.1.1.5. For discussion, see Bauman, *Women and Politics in Ancient Rome,* p. 51; and J. E. Grubbs, *Women in the Law in the Roman Empire: A Sourcebook on Marriage, Divorce and Widowhood* (London: Routledge, 2002), pp. 60-61.

20. Grubbs, *Women in the Law in the Roman Empire,* p. 55.

21. Bauman, *Women and Politics in Ancient Rome,* p. 51.

Marcia suing her debtors and getting hope of satisfaction even though she has lost the I.O.U's.'[22]

Juvenal (*c.* A.D. 60-100) makes an indefensible comment in his "The Ways of Women" —

> There are hardly any cases that were not set in motion by a woman. If Manilia is not the defendant, she's the plaintiff; she will herself frame and adjust the pleadings; she will be ready to instruct Celsus himself how to open his case, and how to urge his points.[23]

He also records women asking, 'Do we as women ever conduct cases? Are we learned in the civil law? Do we disturb your courts with our shouting?'[24] The answer to all these questions could have been 'Yes', even from the limited extant evidence. It was male malice as a response to feeling threatened by female legal competence that saw him blame women unfairly for the more litigious ethos of the late Republic.[25]

This brief survey demonstrates that, in a situation of legal wrangling and debate in the courts, some women competently conducted both their own prosecution and defence. The indelicate nature of some court cases involving sex and the embarrassment of misfortune were felt by men to be improper issues for women to debate in court. Was this the reason or an excuse for seeking to proscribe their endeavours? It is clear that there were women who were learned in law, and legal measures were subsequently enacted in an unsuccessful attempt to proscribe their activity. Strong feelings that they were trespassing into a male prerogative were expressed, but that did not inhibit them from representing themselves and others in what had previously been a male domain.

---

22. MacMullen, "Women in Public in the Roman Empire," p. 210.

23. Juvenal, *Satires*, 6.242-45. This was in his satire on "Moralists without Morals" in which he rightly sought to expose the hypocrisy of men.

24. Juvenal, *Satires*, 2.51-52.

25. D. F. Epstein, *Personal Enmity in Roman Politics, 218-43 B.C.* (London: Routledge, 1989), amply demonstrates how litigious that period was. The Empire was to prove no different in terms of disputes and vexatious litigation, in spite of the official appointment of private arbitrators in the Empire as well as in Republican times. For evidence and discussion see my "Civil Litigation, 1 Corinthians 6:1-11," in *Seek the Welfare of the City: Christians as Benefactors and Citizens,* First-Century Christians in the Graeco-Roman World (Grand Rapids: Eerdmans, 1994), ch. 6, esp. pp. 115-16.

III. Women in Politics

Election Propaganda in Pompeii

Painted on the walls of buildings facing the street in Pompeii are the equivalents of our political posters. They declared 'So-and-So asks you to make So-and-So *aedile*'. MacMullen observes, 'Quite a few of the supporters are women. . . . *Hilario cum sua rogat* is readily understood, in which the husband and his wife (not even named) ask the passer-by to vote for their candidate.' He comments further, 'it is also common to have a woman's name written ahead of the man's . . . an inversion of status explained by neither of the parties having any sense of status between them at all, or by the woman being free or freed, the man freed or slave.'[26]

Whereas a client was required to promote his patron's cause for election to public office, it is an interesting development that in the Roman colony of Pompeii women alongside their husbands were actively supporting candidates for civic office. Placing their name ahead of their husband would indicate that they were of either a higher rank or social status than he.

The Roman Forum and Italy

Valerius Maximus records that at least one married woman spoke in the Forum before the Triumvirs. He instances Hortensia who argued against the heavy tax imposed on women and not men. The latter would not come forward to plead the women's cause, and so she spoke and won the remission of the greater part of this discriminatory tax burden on her gender.[27] At the beginning of his twelve books on oratory Quintilian (*c.* A.D. 35–*c.* 95) records that her oration before the *Triumvirs* was still read in his day, and 'not merely as a compliment to her sex'. It was obviously a great oration, and her ability in this field is attributed to her father who had clearly passed on his skills to his daughter.[28]

Both inside and outside of Rome, there was the gradual integration of women into the local structure of political rank in Italian municipal settings over a period of time. Forbis has collected the inscriptions in Italy in which women are praised in the traditional public vocabulary of *munificentia*,

---

26. MacMullen, "Women in Public in the Roman Empire," p. 209.
27. Valerius Maximus, *Memorable Doings and Sayings*, VIII.3.6.
28. Quintilian, I.1.16.

liberalitas, beneficia and *merita,* not in the language of womanly virtues such as *castitas, pietas, pudicitia,* and *lanificium.*[29]

Woman Civic Patrons, Magistrates, and Gymnasiarch in the East

What was true of Italy in terms of the participation of women was also true in the East where 'similar practices even reached the Greek-speaking part of the Mediterranean eventually'. Just as imperial wives influenced the dress and conduct of women throughout the Empire through statues, so too they were a paradigm for the role of élite women in the *politeia,* and their contribution was given official recognition and recorded for posterity in stone.[30]

Rives commented on what was true for all the Empire when he wrote: 'The importance of women in civic life is another aspect of the ancient world that is known almost entirely from inscriptions, since literary and legal sources depict women as largely relegated to private life.'[31] The roles they played were extremely important for the city and the leagues. Unlike literary evidence these official inscriptions recorded the actual public offices held by these women in the East.

The first recorded instance of a city benefactress was that of Phile who was honoured in a first-century B.C. public decree in Priene.[32] Apart from her public benefactions of the city's aqueduct and reservoir, this inscription records that she was the first woman in Priene to hold the office of magistrate.[33]

Phile, daughter of Apollonius and wife of Thessalus, son of Polydectes, having held the office of magistrate (στεφανηφόρος) [a title of certain magistrates in Greek cities who had the right to wear crowns when in office],[34] the first woman [to do so], constructed at her own expense the reservoir for water and the city aqueduct.[35]

29. E. Forbis, "Women's Public Image in Italian Honorary Inscriptions," *American Journal of Philology* 111 (1990): 493-512.

30. S. E. Wood, *Imperial Women: A Study in Public Images, 40 B.C.–A.D. 69* (Leiden: E. J. Brill, 1999). See also pp. 78-80.

31. J. Rives, "Civic and Religious Life," in J. Bordel, ed., *Epigraphic Evidence: Ancient History from Inscriptions* (London: Routledge, 2001), pp. 135-36.

32. MacMullen, "Women in Public in the Roman Empire," p. 202.

33. *Contra* Grubbs, *Women in the Law in the Roman Empire,* p. 71, who asserts, 'At no time in Roman history could women themselves serve as senators or hold political magistracies on the imperial, provincial or local level'.

34. Aeschines, 1.19, of women; *IG* 12 (8). 526.7 (Thassos).

35. *Die Inschriften von Priene,* no. 208; S. Burstein, *The Hellenistic Age from the Battle of Ipsos to the Death of Kleopatra,* III (Cambridge: Cambridge University Press, 1985), p. 59, no. 45.

Rives speculates that the coincidence of Phile's benefactions and public office suggests that 'the increasing importance of wealth in public life, i.e., the ability to fund important public works, may have played a role in overcoming the traditional ineligibility of women for public offices.'[36] What the inscription recorded was the precedent of the appointment of Phile to this office and the distinction it was for her as the first woman to hold it in Priene.

From the imperial period comes Plencia Magna from Perge who held the magistracy for her city as well as the priesthoods of Artemis and the imperial cult.[37] She was honoured by 'the Council and the People' with two statues, and the pedestals recorded her public offices, with each describing her as a 'daughter of the city'. She proved that to be true by erecting a monumental gate adorned with statues of gods, the imperial family and her own. Each statue recorded her name as the benefactor as did the dedication on the main arch of the propylon.[38]

Then there is the highly influential Claudia Metrodora from Chios, named in three decrees and a contemporary of Junia Theodora. Her husband 'erected [this building in Ephesus] at his own expense and dedicated it together with his wife Claudia Metrodora'. Another refers to officials who 'held office in the second stephanephorate of Claudia Metrodora'. This was the highest magistracy in that city and she held it on two occasions. She was four times gymnasiarch, and president of the Heraklea Kaisareia and Romaia festival on three occasions. Described as 'queen *(basileia)* of thirteen cities of the Ionian federation . . . a lover of her homeland and priestess for life (ἱέρεια διὰ βίου) of the divine empress Aphrodite Livia', she undertook these liturgies in the federation 'by reason of her [civic] virtue and honourable civic mindness (καλοκἀγαθία)'. Greek in origin, hence her name Metrodora, she held Roman citizenship and undertook not only the highest office in her city on two occasions, but was a priestess for life of the imperial cult and also held a prestigious religious office in the wider Ionian federation.[39] She was a powerful woman in the public arena. (See pp. 210-11.)

From a later period we learn of Aurelia Leite of Paros who combined her role as gymnasiarch with the restoration of the gymnasium. She was re-

---

36. Rives, "Civic and Religious Life," p. 136.

37. For the importance of the imperial priesthood see D. Fishwick, *Imperial Cult in the Latin West: Studies in the Ruler Cult of the Western Provinces of the Roman Empire* (Leiden: E. J. Brill, 2002), vol. III.2, pp. 291-307, esp. pp. 296-98.

38. *L'Année épigraphique* (1958), 78; (1965), 209.

39. For a discussion of these women see R. Kearsley, "Women in Public Life in the Roman East: Iunia Theodora, Claudia Metrodora and Phoebe, Benefactress of Paul," *TynB* 50.2 (1999): 198-201.

warded by the Council and People who 'erected a marble statue of the wisdom-loving, husband-loving, children-loving woman [in verse]: "The glorious Faustus fully honoured Leite, his wisdom-bearing wife who bore the best children"'.[40] She was said to have combined her public office with the running of her household.

It is important to note that women holding these public offices did not cease after the first century, for there is numismatic evidence of seventeen of them known to have held the highest magistracy the city afforded (στεφανηφόρος) in thirteen cities in the East from A.D. 180 to 275.[41]

Junia Theodora, the Federal Patron in Corinth

To date, the only official Greek inscription found in first-century Corinth is to a high-class woman who was a Roman citizen residing there (*c.* A.D. 43 or 57). The public honouring of Junia Theodora occurs in five separate decrees or official letters that were recorded on a composite inscription erected in Corinth.[42] They are —

1. A decree of the Federal Assembly of the Lycian cities.
2. A letter from the Lycian city of Myra to the magistrates of Corinth.
3. A decree of the Lycian city of Patara.
4. A letter and decree of the Federal Assembly of Lycia.
5. A decree of the Lycian city of Telmessos.

With the exception of number 2 (which is an official letter) and the introduction of number 4, they were framed in the *genre* of the Greek benefaction in-

40. *IG* xii.5.292 (*c.* A.D. 300).

41. MacMullen, p. 213, citing K. W. Harl, *Civic Coins and Civic Politics in the Roman East, A.D. 180-275* (Berkeley: University of California Press, 1987).

42. For a discussion of Junia Theodora see MacMullen, "Women in Public in the Roman Empire," pp. 216-17; Kearsley, "Women in Public Life in the Roman East: Iunia Theodora, Claudia Metrodora and Phoebe, Benefactress of Paul," pp. 191-98; H.-J. Klauck, "Junia Theodora und die Gemeinde von Korinth," in M. Karrer, W. Kraus and O. Merk, *Kirche und Volk Gottes, Festschrift für Jürgen Roloff* (Neukirchen: Neukirchener Verlag, 2000), pp. 53-56; my *After Paul Left Corinth: The Influence of Secular Ethics and Social Change,* pp. 199-203; and A. D. Clarke, "Jew and Greek, Slave and Free, Male and Female: Paul's Theology of Ethnic, Social and Gender Inclusiveness in Romans 16," in P. Oakes, ed., *Rome in the Bible and the Early Church* (Carlisle and Grand Rapids: Paternoster and Baker, 2002), pp. 16-17. My discussion in this chapter is based on a paper prepared for the SNTS conference in Montreal in August, 2001.

scriptions in the long-established tradition from the classical period. They had become more elaborate in the Hellenistic period, and the expansive acknowledgement of the achievements of Junia Theodora in the Roman period reflects that trend. (For the full text, see pp. 205-10.)

The Greek benefaction inscriptions aimed to disclose three things for all to see in the forum — first, what the benefactor had done to deserve official recognition; second, what the Council and the People had awarded that person by way of honours; and third, what was the stated reason for the 'praising' or official acknowledgement of the person.

The first was preceded by an introduction which announced 'it is decreed (ἔδοχε) by the city of . . .' and the benefactions were then enumerated being introduced by 'since' (ἔπει) or 'whereas' (ἐπειδή). The honours agreed to by 'the Council and the People' are declared by the resolution of the city authorities — 'it has been decreed' (δεδόχθαι). The final clause 'in order that' normally began with either ἵνα or ὅπως and alerted all who read it that 'the Council and the People' (βουλὴ καὶ δῆμος) knew how to respond with civic honours to those who were its benefactors, past, present and, hopefully, future. It was important that all should read that the authorities had fulfilled their obligations to honour appropriately their benefactors, which was one of their traditional dual functions still operating in cities in the Roman Empire, the other being civic administration and civil law.[43]

Apart from a marble inscription, honours could also include a crown of gold leaf, a statue (normally in marble but it could be in the much prized bronze), and a seat of honour (with arm rests and therefore distinct from all other seats) for life in the theatre.[44] Finally there was a public proclamation that the persons by their benefaction had shown themselves to be 'good and noble' (καλὸς καὶ ἀγαθός), the 'three words' which Dio Chysostom noted were 'more precious to many than life itself'.[45]

A form-critical analysis of the official testimonials to the benefactress, Junia Theodora, assists in understanding what she had done in her role as a patron. She was rewarded with honours in the decree of the Federation of the Lycian cities and by three of her important cities which traditionally had two additional votes in the assemblies of the league.[46] Her benefactions were dis-

---

43. See A. S. Henry, *Honours and Privileges in Athenian Decrees: The Principal Formulae of Athenian Honorary Decrees* (Hildesheim and New York: G. Olms, 1983). The convention was followed in many instances for Greek inscriptions into the Roman period as the Junia Theodora example demonstrates.

44. Henry, "Crowns," in *Honours and Privileges in Athenian Decrees*, ch. II.

45. Dio Chrysostom, *Or.* 75.8.

46. Strabo, 14.664-65, Telmessos (Xanthus), Patara and Myra.

cussed, being introduced by the conventional 'since' (ἔπει),[47] the decreed honours were recorded 'it has been decreed' (δεδόχθαι),[48] and the purpose declared in the final clause 'in order that' (ἵνα or ὅπως) or 'that' (ὅτι).[49] The reason that number 2 does not have the first two classical elements of benefaction decrees is that it was a formal letter to the Corinthians. Number 4 is also an official letter to the magistrates, the council and the People of Corinth, and after the introduction that stresses the honours given by the federation, it records the traditional benefaction inscription in the standard classical *genre*. This form-critical analysis helps extrapolate information on the benefactions of Junia Theodora, who was a Roman citizen living in Corinth, and the nature of the honours bestowed upon her, together with the stated reasons in the official decrees and letters of this very important composite inscription.

Junia Theodora's Benefactions

Unlike most benefactions these inscriptions, which were incorporated into a single stone, make no mention of buildings, aqueducts, theatres or pavements. The first decree was passed by the Lycian federation and records that Junia Theodora has used her good 'offices' to secure 'the friendship of many of the authorities [on behalf of the federal league of Lycian cities], employing her assistance in all areas which most directly interest all Lycians; (and) by the will she has drawn up shows her desire to please the nation', no. 1 *ll.* 5-8. Reference was also made to her reception in her Corinthian home not only of private individuals but 'ambassadors sent by the nation [of the Lycians]', no. 4 *ll.* 50-51. An official letter was sent from the federal league to the magistrates, council and the People of Corinth, in which the same benefaction statement in no. 1 was largely replicated but important information was clearly added.[50] Her generosity towards the nation is further explained: 'Since also very many of our people in exile were welcomed by her with magnificence', no. 4 *ll.* 58-59. The letter from Myra refers to her devotion and hospitality to which she devoted herself to 'our people particularly at the time of their arrival in your city [Corinth]', no. 2 *ll.* 17-19. (See pp. 188-90 for a discussion of the exile.)

The decree of the city of Patara also provides additional information. She is a Roman citizen residing in Corinth. Apart from describing her as a woman of the greatest honour and possessing the great Roman virtue of 'modesty', it

47. Nos. 1. *ll.* 1-8, 3. *ll.* 22-30, 4. *ll.* 47-61, and 5. *ll.* 72-80.
48. Nos. 1. *ll.* 9-11, 3. *ll.* 36-37, 4. *ll.* 61-64, and 5. *ll.* 80-83.
49. Nos. 1. *ll.* 12-14, 2. *l.* 21, 3. *ll.* 37-39, 4. *ll.* 64-69, and 5. *ll.* 83-85.
50. Cf. 'since' (ἔπει) no. 4. *l.* 72 and 'since also' (ἔπει δέ) no. 4. *l.* 58.

adds, 'also offering hospitality to all the Lycians and receiving them in her own house, and she continues particularly to act on behalf of our citizens in regard to any favour asked', no. 3 *ll.* 23-29. The city of Telmessos calls her a patron; in this case she must have been a civic patron who was said to be 'supplying them with everything . . . displaying her patronage of those who are present', no. 5 *ll.* 76-77.

This information indicates that Junia was a Roman citizen with considerable wealth which she used to offer hospitality to ambassadors and to care for Lycian exiles in Corinth. She was perceived to have had 'ongoing influence' with the authorities.

Junia Theodora's Official Honours

Both decrees of the Lycian Federation contain standard resolutions 'to acknowledge and praise' (ἀποδεδέχθαι καὶ ἐπηνέσθαι) Junia Theodora, 1 *ll.* 9-10, 4 *l.* 62, and the same infinitives are found in no. 5 *ll.* 80-81, while praise also occurs in no. 3 twice and in the first instance 'to bear witness' (διαμαρτύρησαι) is added, *ll.* 32, 37, 'because the majority of our citizens have come before the Assembly to give testimony about her', *l.* 32, so 'the People' of Patara also formally affirm what she has done. In addition, the first Lycian Federation decree states that it will send her a crown of gold, also a standard honour for very generous benefactors, but it adds 'for the time when she will come into the presence of the gods', 4 *ll.* 9-11. In their second decree they resolve also to give her five minas of saffron for her burial and 'honour her with a portrait painted on a gilt background' and engraved with an inscription.

The acknowledgement of her benefaction and the 'praising' of her were a public event normally held in the theatre where she would have been declared a good and noble woman, and crowned with a crown of gold. It would seem that these honours were conferred *in absentia* by means of the official resolutions and were sent to her in Corinth and the civic officials of Corinth.

The Stated Purposes for Honouring Junia Theodora

All five inscriptions in one way or another indicate the reason for honouring her. The traditional final purpose clauses read, 'that all may see that the city of X knows how to reward with honours those who are its benefactors'. In its place the decree of the Lycian Federation sends her in effect the opening of a formal letter — 'The federal assembly of the Lycians to Junia Theodora, a Roman, fine and honourable woman and devoted to the nation', and indicates that 'our agent Sextus Iulius has equally been busy seeing to the engraving of the following inscription', 1 *ll.* 12-14. She is declared a public benefactress of the federation who is loyal to the nation of Lycia.

The letter from the city of Myra incorporates into it the standard final clause but it is for Junia Theodora — 'in order that you may know of the gratitude of the city' (ὅπως εἴδητε τὴν τῆς πόλεως εὐχαριστίαν) *l.* 21. The Myra decree specifies that the city of Corinth was also to be made aware of the honours for Junia with an official certified copy: 'So that (ἵνα δέ) Iunia herself, and the city of Corinth at the same time, may be aware of the loyalty of our city to her, and of the decree passed for her, the secretary of the council sends (40) to the people of Corinth this copy of the present decree after having sealed it with the public seal', no. 3 *ll.* 37-41.

The Lycian Federation in its letter incorporating the resolution indicates that she has been awarded a crown and an inscribed portrait that can accompany her to her grave — 'in order (ἵνα) that she may have it in readiness when she will reach the presence of the gods and to honour her with a portrait painted on a gilt background and engraved with the following inscription: "The federal assembly of the Lycians and the Lycian magistrates have honoured with a crown (68) and a portrait painted on a gilt background Iunia Theodora, a Roman, living at Corinth, a fine and honourable woman and constantly devoted to the nation by reason of her affection"', no. 4 *ll.* 64-69.

Finally the authorities of Telmessos revert to the ancient formula but with important variations. It is not only that passersby will see that she was appropriately rewarded. Their decree departs from the normal convention of honours for past benefactions and openly expresses the hope that she will continue to be their benefactress. They guarantee her that further civic honours can be assumed by her — 'and invite her, living with the same intentions, to always be the author of some benefit towards us, well knowing that in return our city recognises and will acknowledge the evidence of her goodwill', no. 5 *ll.* 83-85.

Junia Theodora and the Request of the Lycian Federation

To what did those who were welcomed by Junia 'with magnificence' as 'exiles' refer, no. 4 *ll.* 58-59? It has been attributed to the formation of Lycia as a Roman province in A.D. 43 which was preceded by civil discord and subsequent curtailing of rights in keeping with Rome's policy in the provinces; hence the dating of the inscription by some to this period.[51] The suggestion is feasible

51. Suetonius, *Life of Claudius*, 25.9; D. Pallas et al., "Inscriptions lyciennes trouvées à

because the Lycians were historically a fiercely independent nation, but discord preceded Rome's creation of the province of Lycia and Pamphylia and indeed was the cause of it.[52] Dio recorded the sequence:

> He [Claudius] reduced the Lycians to servitude because they had revolted and slain some Romans, and he incorporated them into the prefecture of Pamphylia. During the investigation of this affair, which was conducted in Latin, he put a question to one of the ambassadors who had originally been a Lycian citizen: and when the man failed to understand what he said, he took away his citizenship, saying that it was not proper for a man to be a Roman who had no knowledge of the Romans' language.[53]

B. Levick writes about 'the murder of Romans, possibly Italian business men who had misused their status to make a profit, more probably enfranchised natives deploying Roman citizenship as a weapon in local politics. Men trusted by Rome were assassinated or more probably became the victims of judicial murder, since the whole federation suffered. The Lycians sent an embassy but could not clear themselves.'[54]

It is possible that the help sought was in connection with this embassy to Rome, and that 'the ambassadors sent by the nation' came by way of the sea route to Corinth and on to Rome, no. 4 *ll.* 50-51.[55] The use of embassies to Rome was the major means of securing concessions and of seeking to reverse penalties incurred by Rome's use of the stick and carrot method of controlling the cities in the provinces.[56] Was it after this event that the patronage of Junia was invoked in the hope of reversing the fortunes of the Lycians?

It has also been suggested that the *Sitz im Leben* was the result of the unsuccessful case brought by the Lycian Federation against a former governor of the province for extortion, in A.D. 57. Tacitus succinctly records:

Solômos près de Corinthe," *Bulletin de correspondance héllenique* 83 (1959): 505-6; L. Robert, "Décret de la Confédération Lycienne à Corinthe," pp. 331-32.

52. See A. H. M. Jones, "Lycia," in *Cities of the Eastern Roman Provinces* (Oxford: Clarendon Press, 1937, reprint 1998), ch. 3, esp. p. 106.

53. Dio Cassius, 60.17.4.

54. B. Levick, *Claudius* (London: Batsford, 1990), p. 167. See also D. Noy, *Foreigners at Rome: Citizens and Strangers* (London: Duckworth with The Classical Press of Wales, 2000), p. 106.

55. See Noy, *Foreigners at Rome: Citizens and Strangers*, pp. 100-106, for a discussion of the extensive use of embassies.

56. C. Eilers, *Roman Patrons and Greek Cities* (Oxford: Oxford University Press, 2002), pp. 176-79.

The Lycians claimed damages from Titus Clodius Eprius Marcellus. But his intrigues were so effective that some of his accusers were exiled for endangering an innocent man.[57]

Governors of provinces could not be prosecuted for alleged misdemeanours while still holding the post. This could be done only after the completion of the term of office when a case could be initiated and heard in Rome.[58] The Lycian inscriptions mentioned Junia's welcoming ambassadors and 'very many of our people in exile' (*ll.* 50, 58).

Kearsley observes that the three cities which sent official letters or decrees were important seaports in Lycia in the Roman period, and therefore concludes that Junia was being honoured for her promotion of their commercial interests.[59] Such an arrangement was not without precedent.[60] However, the Lycians were asking Junia to use her influence to lobby the 'authorities' (ἡγεμόνες). That term could be used of provincial governors or in the singular of the emperor, and in this instance it could have also included the Senate in Rome. We do know of one provincial governor, Gallio.[61] He was a noted Roman jurist and was officially called 'my friend' by Claudius in the Delphi inscription. His brother, Seneca, was highly placed in the Principates of Claudius and Nero.[62] Gallio had held the governorship of Achaea in *c.* A.D. 51 and his brother was to play a leading role in Nero's administration. It was not unknown for ex-governors to exercise their influence in Rome on behalf of cities under their former control. It could be through contacts such as this that

---

57. *Annals*, 13.33.4. Kearsley, "Women in Public Life in the Roman East: Iunia Theodora, Claudia Metrodora and Phoebe, Benefactress of Paul," p. 191.

58. A. N. Sherwin-White, *Roman Society and Roman Law in the New Testament* (Oxford: Clarendon Press, 1963), p. 17; and D. Braund, "*Cohors*: The Governor and His Entourage in the Self-image of the Roman Republic," in R. Laurence and J. Berry, eds., *Cultural Identity in the Roman Empire* (London: Routledge, 1998), ch. 1.

59. Kearsley, "Women in Public Life in the Roman East: Iunia Theodora, Claudia Metrodora and Phoebe, Benefactress of Paul," p. 195. See my *After Paul Left Corinth: The Influence of Secular Ethics and Social Change* (Grand Rapids: Eerdmans, 2001), pp. 200-201, where I originally followed Kearsley that the issue concerned commercial interests between Lycia and Corinth.

60. See, for example, *CIL*, no. 8837 (A.D. 55) where a legate acted as the civic patron for the Roman colony of Julia Augusta Tupusuctu.

61. See Acts 18:12 and the Delphi inscription, *l.* 6, for the designation 'my friend and proconsul'. For text and discussion see J. Murphy-O'Connor, *St. Paul's Corinth: Texts and Archaeology* (Collegeville: Liturgical Press, 2002), pp. 161-69.

62. See J. H. Kent, *Corinth: The Inscriptions, 1926-1950* (Princeton: American School of Classical Studies, 1966), VIII.3, pp. 61-67 for extant evidence of governors in the Augustan and Flavian periods.

Junia was asked to plead the cause of the Lycian Federation in Rome, even though their attempt to indict a former governor of Lycia had backfired badly.

Her benefactions were not bricks and mortar but receiving exiles, ambassadors, and acting as the patron of the Federation as she had done in the past on its behalf and hopefully in the future. It is not possible to disconnect Junia's role as patron receiving the Lycian ambassadors and the exiles in her home, and the request to her to use her influence with the authorities. Had the exiles not been mentioned, then the arrival of ambassadors from one city to another seeking commercial concessions or trading arrangements would have been the obvious reason. The concerted official activity of the federation and leading Lycian cities in it suggests that there was something more afoot than trade.

Eilers in his recent book on Roman patronage in the Greek cities, which is the first extended treatment of this subject, records the nature of this patronage. However, in his extensive appendix 1 of inscriptions of Roman patrons he does not notice the one woman patron, Junia Theodora.[63] Hers is not the only evidence of the role of Roman patron of Lycia (*patronus provinciae*).[64] Eilers records that Proculus was honoured as the patron of Lycia, but his was not a provincial post as he held his magistracy (*praetor*) in Rome: 'Proculus, praetor, with a gold crown and bronze statue, a good and noble man, patron of the province, because of his virtue and goodwill (ἀρετὴ καὶ εὔνοια)', the latter being standard benefaction terms also used of Junia (*ll.* 20, 27, 35, 55, 56, 72). He was a Lycian senator either from the time of Augustus or the end of the same century.[65]

Proculus' designation parallels the patronage (προστασία) of Junia which the decree of the Lycian city of Telmessos officially acknowledged as federal and not civic for their city (*l.* 77). The reference is to an ancient league that had operated since *c.* 200 B.C. and continued to do so with reduced powers as part of the Roman province of Lycia and Pamphylia. Junia was therefore perceived by the Lycians to be a person of influence and could represent them. If the federation had fallen on difficult days in either A.D. 43 or 57, then the need

---

63. Eilers, *Roman Patrons and Greek Cities*. For an earlier discussion of the role of civic patrons see J. Nichols, "*Tabulae patronatus:* A Study of the Agreement between Patron and Client-community," *ANRW* 2.13 (1980), pp. 535-59.

64. On patrons of provinces see J. Nichols, "Patrons of Provinces in the Early Principate: The Case of Bithynia," *ZPE* 80 (1990): 101-81; and for a later period W. Williams, "Antoninus Pius and the Control of Provincial Embassies," *Historia* 16 (1967): 470-83.

65. Eilers, *Roman Patrons and Greek Cities*, p. 252. For the inscription see *L'Année épigraphique* (1981), no. 840.

for the right patron to represent their cause to Rome was critical. It has already been noted that it was not only for past support and benefactions she was officially praised but the expectation is made explicit, 'to invite her, living with the same intentions, to always be the author of some benefit towards us [as the patron]' (*ll.* 83-84). This points to the great importance of the patronage of Junia and reveals her Roman rank and status.[66]

Why was the highly unusual action being taken of addressing inscriptions 2-4 to city authorities of Corinth? She was not only a citizen of Lycia but also a Roman citizen who was now resident in Corinth (*l.* 17).[67] Corinth had long understood the importance of civic patrons, as did the Achaean League.[68] The governor of Achaea's *imperium* was restricted to his province and therefore he had no legal jurisdiction over the Lycians.

The extravagant outpouring of praise of her and the multiple 'testimonials' suggest that what was being sought was no commercial concessions, but her urgent help, whether the inscriptions are dated to *c.* 43 or 57. For the Lycians to have requested her aid indicates that she was a woman of considerable means as the mention of her will confirms, but she also had political influence in high places. Junia Theodora's contribution does not come under the category of business, or even civic patronage. The reason for the Lycians addressing the magistrates and people of Corinth in their official inscriptions remains an enigma if the latter view is taken; and if the former, then the very mention of exiles was unnecessary, given the sensitive nature of their political situation. She would have had to go to Rome to represent their political interests at some stage to retrieve their good standing with the authorities. Junia Theodora was no insignificant player in the wider realm of provincial *politeia*.

The Limits of Participation

Before turning to the next section it should be noted that not all will agree with this assessment of the independent and important role of Junia Theodora in *politeia*. J. E. Grubbs asserts somewhat boldly, 'At no time in Roman history could women themselves serve as senators or hold political mag-

---

66. See E. A. Judge, *Rank and Status in the World of the Caesars and St. Paul* (Christchurch: University of Canterbury Publications, 1982).

67. Multiple citizenship was possible in the empire. On the familiarity of the term *isopoliteia* see Sherwin-White, *Roman Society and Roman Law in the New Testament*, p. 178.

68. Imperial patrons Vipsanius Agrippa (Augustus), Iulius Spartiaticus (Nero), Iulius Severus (Hadrian), and patrons of the Achaean League, Quintus Ancharius (Vespasian) and Lucius Piso, are cited in Eilers, *Roman Patrons and Greek Cities*, pp. 281, 285, 192-93.

istracies on the imperial, provincial or local level'. For evidence to the contrary see pp. 181-83. She then goes on to concede that ancient evidence is stacked against her. 'The sources translated in this section "Women in public life: restrictions and responsibilities" demonstrate that there were dozens of laudatory inscriptions set up by communities in honour to élite women, demonstrate that women were in fact expected to play a role in public life, albeit to a much more limited extent than their fathers, brothers or husbands.' Her conclusion is, 'However, it should be stressed that this role, and the honour paid to these women, was contingent on their membership in wealthy, élite families. Just as women's role in legal matters was restricted to matters involving themselves or close family members, so their role in civic life was restricted to acting as part of, or on behalf of, their family.'[69]

In arguing thus, Grubbs follows the thesis of van Bremen that women could not operate except under the aegis of husbands or other males.[70] A patronising inscription to Aba from Histiaea in an introductory citation in Part 1 of her book and at the beginning of her conclusion influenced her because it read that this woman performed offices 'normally taken on by male benefactors, doing her best to imitate them . . .'.[71]

Unlike Eilers who in his *Roman Patrons and Greek Cities* fails to include Junia Theodora in his appendix, van Bremen relegates her contribution to three footnotes.[72] It may be significant that her inscription is still bypassed by many, as it is located in the farthest corner of the portico in the courtyard in the museum in Corinth, and on the right of the public toilet. It contains no significant information as to its uniqueness in the ancient world and goes unnoticed by most, even TV producers filming on site ancient material for documentaries on Paul and early Christianity.

This amazing first-century lady cannot be ignored. On the contrary she provides hard evidence of a woman operating as a patron, not of a single city but of the Lycian Federation, which has some thirty-six cities with voting rights in its deliberations.[73] The intensity of support for her at grassroots level is also seen because 'the majority of citizens [of Patara] have come be-

---

69. Grubbs, *Women in the Law in the Roman Empire*, p. 71.

70. R. van Bremen, *The Limits of Participation: Women and Civic Life in the Greek East in the Hellenistic and Roman Periods* (Amsterdam: J. C. Gieben, 1996).

71. *SEG* 24 (1969), 1112. Van Bremen, *The Limits of Participation;* the text is discussed on pp. 9, 297-99.

72. van Bremen, *The Limits of Participation*, pp. 164 n. 73, 165 n. 78, and 198 n. 11, referring to Junia's receiving the Lycians in her town house, her Roman citizenship and her legal status.

73. Pliny, *Natural History*, 5.101; and evidence cited by. A. H. M. Jones, *Cities of the Eastern Roman Provinces* (Oxford: Oxford University Press, 1937), p. 107.

fore the Assembly to bear testimony concerning her' (καὶ πλεῖστοι τῶν πολειτῶν ἡμῶν καταστάντες ἐπὶ τῆς ἐκκλησίας διαμεμαρτύρηκαν αὐτήν) (*ll.* 30-31).[74] In the minds of the Lycians she had the necessary political clout to warrant ambassadorial visits with the support of official honorific inscriptions that sought her intervention on their behalf. That is, she belonged to a new 'élite within the élite', to cite Bauman[75] — imperial women whose images were exported to the provinces as icons for modest women in terms of dress and hairstyles but whose achievements as successful operators in *politeia* also provided a paradigm.[76] Junia appears to be one who was able to emulate their example in the provinces.

IV. Women in *politeia* and Women in the Church

It is through the lens of the epigraphic sources discussed in the previous sections that it is proposed to look afresh at two New Testament texts on the participation of Christian women in *politeia*. As in previous chapters it is not proposed to enter into a full discussion but to see what light can thrown on them from the extant evidence we have from their world. It is an interesting feature of this material that the contribution of men and women alike in the Pauline churches is not specifically featured. In fact relatively few men are named, and even fewer women. This contrasts with *The Memorable Doings and Sayings* of Valerius Maximus where he often supplies details of rank and status as well as achievements.

It is proposed to add to our comparative investigation of women in the official non-literary field of inscriptions and coins a woman from Corinthians and another from Romans. It is proposed to compare Junia Theodora with Phoebe and Junia as they provide possible evidence of the filtering-down influence of the public role for women. It is not being argued that any women who are mentioned in the Pauline communities held public office or were of the same rank and status as Junia Theodora. The evidence we do have makes no comment on their secular rank or connection with specific areas of *politeia* we have just examined.

---

74. E. A. Judge drew my attention to the importance of this evidence of active participation by citizens in the assembly, given the received view that 'As time went on the assent of the people became more and more formal, and eventually, the assembly ceased to meet', A. H. M. Jones, *The Greek City from Alexander to Justinian* (Oxford: Clarendon Press, 1998), p. 177.

75. Bauman, *Women and Politics in Ancient Rome*, p. 99.

76. S. E. Wood, *Imperial Women: A Study in Public Images, 40 B.C.–A.D. 69* (Leiden: E. J. Brill, 1999).

The snapshots that exist provide some details, but we would have wished for further information. Some are so scant that no significant comment can be made by way of comparison with the evidence reviewed in the first three sections.

The number of Christian women whose names and sometimes whose contribution to the Pauline mission and churches we know of suggests that Christian women were not relegated to the private rooms in first-century households. That was an ancient Greek custom, as we have noted, but not the convention that operated in either of the Roman colonies of Corinth and Philippi or Rome itself.

Junia Theodora and Phoebe, Patron and Deacon

Apart from Junia Theodora of whom the term 'patronage' (προστασίαν) was used (*l. 77*), there were others who were officially recognised as having had this role at a provincial level in Achaea or at a civic one in Corinth.[77] There is also an inscription to a private patron in Corinth. 'Marcus Antonius Promachus (set up this monument to honour) the [his] friend and patron [——] because of his virtue and trustworthiness' (τὸν φίλιο[ν] καὶ π[ρο]οτάτην ἀ[ρετ]ῆς ἕνεκ[α] κ[αὶ] πίστεως).[78] Phoebe is called 'our sister, being a deacon of the church at Cenchreae', the satellite port of Corinth in the Aegean Sea, and is also called a 'patron'; her clients are indicated as being 'many, including myself' (Rom. 16:2).

The term 'patron' is a surprising one for Paul to have used in sending greetings from Corinth to the church in Rome. It is totally unexpected, given that he sought to undo not only the crucial fabric of the role of clients for Christians,[79] but also the traditional role of patronage, and that within the Corinthian community from which he was writing his letter to the Romans. The comment in 1 Corinthians 16:15 that the senior members of the house of Stephanas set themselves to serve the needs of their fellow Christians does not surprise us. However, in the first century a patron and his immediate family voluntarily placing themselves in a servile position represented a total cultural inversion in a critical domain in Roman society.[80]

77. For references see p. 191 n. 68.

78. Kent, *Corinth*, VIII.3, no. 265.

79. See my "From Secular Clients to Christian Benefactors, 1 Thessalonians 4:11-12 and 2 Thessalonians 3:6-13," in *Seek the Welfare of the City: Christians as Benefactors and Citizens*, First-Century Christians in the Graeco-Roman World (Grand Rapids: Eerdmans, 1993), ch. 3.

80. On the distinction in the use of the terms 'household' and 'house' of Stephanas in

Judge has argued this case thus: 'The Corinthian letters show him in head-on confrontation with the mechanisms [of patronage] by which it imposed social power. . . . His positive response to this collision was to build a remarkable new construction of social realities that both lay within the fabric of the old ranking system and yet transformed it by a revolution of social values.'[81] Elsewhere he defined them. '"Rank" is meant to denote any formally defined position in society, while "status" refers to positions of influence that may not correspond to the official pattern of the social order.'[82] Secular rank remained for the Christians in society, but now secular status could no longer do so in the Christian community. The maintenance of the latter could only adversely affect how one perceived relationships with others, how one acted towards them and the nature of the contribution that one could make to the welfare of all within the community.

Paul has promoted this radical transformation further by warmly commending Stephanas for taking a servile position, as he did others whom he mentioned in 1 Corinthians 16:16-17. I have argued elsewhere that this was part of Paul's final solution in 1 Corinthians to the underlying problem of social conflict that was endemic in Corinth. The initiators of social conflict, the patrons, were as Christians now to abandon that role and exchange that function for that of the servant, a paradigm from Jesus and commended as a mindset by Paul to the Philippians (Phil. 2:5). Stephanas has now adopted a servile position with those who formerly had existed primarily to serve his social standing and his political objectives. It is for this reason that the designation and the commendation of Phoebe as a patron is not a little surprising.[83]

Like Junia, Phoebe is 'patron' (προστάτις) but unlike Junia it is not in a civic or federal capacity that she acts, or with a particular ethnic group. It is to many individuals among whom presumably are 'the saints', for we are told that she 'has been a patron of many and myself also' (προστάτις πολλῶν ἐγενήθη καὶ ἐμοῦ αὐτοῦ) (Rom. 16:2). She may have been a host to many in her home as was Junia, and her sphere of influence was the church in Cenchreae in whose service she operated, possibly in her own home.

Had this been an issue of patronage connected to 'the politics of friend-

---

1 Cor. 1:16 and 16:15 see my "Secular Patronage and Christian Dominance (1 Corinthians 16:15-16)," and "The Meaning of οἰκία and οἶκος," in *After Paul Left Corinth*, Appendix, pp. 206-11, and ch. 9 for its implications for Stephanas and his ministry in 16:15.

81. E. A. Judge, "Cultural Conformity and Innovations," *TynB* 35 (1984): 23.

82. Judge, *Rank and Status in the World of the Caesars and St. Paul*, p. 9.

83. See my "The 'Underlays' of Conflict and Compromise in 1 Corinthians," in Trevor J. Burke and J. Keith Elliott, eds., *Paul and the Corinthians: Studies on a Community in Conflict. Essays in Honour of Margaret Thrall* (Leiden: E. J. Brill, 2003), ch. 7.

ship', to use Rawson's phrase,[84] then the other appropriate term to have used would have been 'friend' (φίλος, *amiculus*). Marcus Antonius Promachus described his patron in Corinth as also his 'friend'. No such relationship is claimed by Paul with Phoebe, as he uses a distinctively *familia* term, 'sister'. In fact, he appears to have studiously avoided the term 'friend', given the reciprocal obligations involved which were created by money.[85]

Phoebe is called a διάκονος of the church in Cenchreae in the same way the abstract noun 'service' (διακονία) was used to describe the intention of the ministry of Stephanas in 1 Corinthians 16:15. The term was not a status one, as was argued by Collins, but very much a service role, as Clarke has shown by means of his careful philological approach in his refutation of Collins' proposal.[86] That conclusion is important, for rank and status went hand in hand in Roman society.[87] Phoebe may have possessed the former. The comment on her servile role in the church suggests that she had voluntarily surrendered her secular status.[88] This was done in order to engage in the Christian service to others, as was the case in the ministry of Stephanas, Fortunatus and Achaicus, who had, in Paul's words when he wrote to the Corinthians, refreshed 'my spirit as well as yours' (1 Cor. 16:17-18).[89]

The recipients of her patronage were 'many' (πολλῶν) but the exact nature of it is not specified. It could have been financial or she may have used her contacts and her influence on their behalf. It would have included those residing in Cenchreae, but was not restricted to them. Paul went out of his way to stress to the Roman Christians that he himself had been the recipient of her patronage. His use of the double pronoun (καὶ ἐμοῦ αὐτοῦ) is a way in

---

84. B. Rawson, *The Politics of Friendship: Pompey and Cicero* (Sydney: Sydney University Press, 1978).

85. R. P. Saller, *Personal Patronage under the Early Empire* (Cambridge: Cambridge University Press, 1982), pp. 9-11.

86. See J. N. Collins, *Diakonia: Re-interpreting the Ancient Sources* (Oxford: Oxford University Press, 1990); and A. D. Clarke, "Pauline Ministry in the Church," in *Serve the Community of the Church*, First-Century Christians in the Graeco-Roman World (Grand Rapids and Carlisle: Eerdmans and Paternoster, 2000), ch. 9, esp. pp. 233-43, for a repudiation of Collins' thesis that it refers to someone of status, and for evidence that it is instead a term having low standing and involving a servant role to others.

87. Judge, *Rank and Status in the World of the Caesars and St. Paul.*

88. I am grateful to P. Williams who drew my attention to Pliny's description of the two female slaves whom he interrogated under torture and who then yielded the information that they were 'deacons'. The servile term, *ministra*, was used to describe their place in the church; Pliny, *Letters*, X, 96.

89. A. D. Clarke, "'Refresh the Hearts of the Saints': A Unique Pauline Context?" *TynB* 47.2 (1996): 277-300.

Koine Greek of strongly emphasising a point — in this case her patronage to him in his apostolic mission.[90] Can we assume that he has plundered the 'patronage' terminology to describe Phoebe's support of his mission, not only in Cenchreae and Corinth, but well beyond that Roman colony and its precincts? Elsewhere, he changes the use of the secular concepts of 'giving and receiving' in his letter to the Philippians to 'fellowship in the gospel' as a way of describing the significance of the gift of money from that church in relation to his ministry in Rome.[91]

Paul also commends Phoebe to the church in Rome for her visit, the purpose of which is not stated. Seneca, writing in the time of Claudius, gives the following reasons why people moved to Rome, either temporarily or permanently.

> From their *municipia* and *coloniae,* from the whole world they congregated here. Ambition has brought some; the requirements of public office (*necessitas officii*) has brought others. For some, it was an embassy imposed on them; for others, it was luxury, seeking a convenient and wealthy setting for its vices. Eagerness for liberal studies brought some; the shows (*spectacula*) brought others. Some were led by friendship, others by industry taking the ample opportunity for showing virtue. Some have brought beauty for sale, some have brought eloquence for sale. Every race of humans has flowed together into the city which offers great rewards for both virtues and vices.[92]

Noy indicates the reasons why many moved to Rome and some of the challenges facing those settled there. Phoebe's proposed visit might have related to business matters, given the importance of Cenchreae as the conduit for trade across the Aegean on to Rome overland by the Diolkos of Isthmia or around the Peloponnese.[93] The sea route from the other port for Corinth, Leichaion, the port on the other side of the Isthmus, was the fast route to Rome. Phoebe may have, like others, been going to Rome to reside there as a foreigner or citizen. Paul commended her because he wished the church to receive her, given that in her ministry she was the sort of person whose service they should also accept. Noy documents the need for local contacts and be-

---

90. Cf. 1 Cor. 11:13 ἐν ὑμῖν αὐτοῖς and the grammatical discussion on p. 92.

91. See G. Peterman, *Paul's Gift from Philippi: Conventions of Gift Exchange and Christian Giving* (Cambridge: Cambridge University Press, 1997).

92. Seneca, *ad Helviam,* 6.2-3.

93. Noy, "The Practicalities of Moving to Rome," in *Foreigners at Rome: Citizens and Strangers,* ch. 6, p. 147.

lieves of the early Christians that 'Members of the church gave access to a more regularized system of contacts for newcomers. A Christian, at least one of standing, could expect to receive hospitality from fellow-Christians at Rome. Roman members of the Jesus movement met Paul even before he reached the city.'[94] One senses that his comments on Christians of status could be a reading into that scene the evidence which he had just reviewed of others who sought to exploit the wealth of visitors in exchange for the promise of Roman networks and reciprocity. That is not to say that Paul would not have expected that Phoebe, who had been the patron of many up to that point, would not continue to serve the Christian cause there in Rome in the same way she had done in Cenchreae as a διάκονος.[95]

Finally, what significance should be attached to the fact that while Paul uses the feminine form of προστάτης for Phoebe, he does not do so for διάκονος? There is no Christian evidence of the feminine form for the latter before the third century.[96] There is a fascinating fourth-century Christian inscription where it was used.

<table>
<tr><td>Ἐνθάδε κῖται ἡ δούλη
καὶ νύμφη τοῦ Χριστοῦ
Σοφία, ἡ διάκονος, ἡ δεύ-
τερα Φοίβη, κοιμηθῖσα
ἐν εἰρήνη . . .</td><td>Here lies the slave,
and bride of Christ
Σοπηιε, τηε δεαφον, τηε
second Phoebe, who fell asleep
in peace . . .[97]</td></tr>
</table>

Sophia is called 'the second Phoebe' and is referred to as a 'servant' and 'a bride', both in the feminine; ἡ διάκονος is in the same gender form as Paul used in speaking of Phoebe as our sister and patron and διάκονος, but with the feminine article ἡ preceding the latter. Paul used the same gender for Phoebe as he did for himself in Romans as 'the servant' (διάκονος) to the Jews (16:1, 15:8), and as he had done for Apollos' and his ministry in Corinth (1 Cor. 3:5). From a list of male and female priests and διάκονοι from the cult of the

94. Noy, "Why did people move to Rome?" in *Foreigners at Rome: Citizens and Strangers*, ch. 5.

95. Paul's commendation of Phoebe should be read in part in the light of his concerns about the right reception of Timothy (1 Cor. 16:10).

96. C. F. Whelan, "*Amica Pauli:* The Role of Phoebe in the Early Church," *JSNT* 49 (1993): 84-85.

97. *Epigrafia greca*, IV, 445, cited G. Horsley, "Sophia, the Second Phoebe," *New Documents Illustrating Early Christianity* 4 (1979), no. 122, pp. 239-44.

Twelve gods Horsley cites two women, Elpis and Tyche, who are both referred to as διάκονος; and he also notes later Christian sources where that form was used for women. He suggests it shows that there was continuity in the use of this term from non-Christian to Christian cultic organization. However the use of the status term with respect to Phoebe is functional in terms of its servile orientation, which was seen as the essence of all Christian ministries (Mk. 10:42-45).[98]

There are clearly differences between Junia Theodora and Phoebe. In terms of her rank nothing is known, nor is that of the many whom she assisted as their patron, apart from Paul. It has been argued that the *Sitz im Leben* of the Lycian Federation relates to the relegation of certain members of that league from their homeland and the aim to reverse the unjust decision of Rome through the political networks of Junia Theodora. There is no specific situation known concerning help given to 'the clients' in the Christian situation of Phoebe. Both have operated from their own homes and have used them as the base for hospitality and, in the case of Junia, housing those they were connected with; in neither case is mention made of a living spouse.

It is suggested that this comparative approach has assisted in not only recapitulating the high-profile influence of Junia Theodora but also appreciating the significant personal help to many and to the Pauline mission as well as the ministry of Phoebe to the church in Cenchreae. Some have speculated that Phoebe supplied 'aid to others, especially foreigners, providing housing and financial aid and representing their interests before local authorities'.[99] We would wish for more information on Phoebe, who suddenly appears as a major player in a hitherto unknown Christian church, not unlike Poseidon's rising out of the Aegean Sea at Isthmia, just up the coast from Cenchreae where Phoebe lived. Her residence was in an important satellite and wealthy sea port for Corinth — the ruins of the houses on the seafront indicate its prosperity. The wealth of Junia Theodora suggests that she might have lived in the prosperous Corinthian suburb of Craneion,[100] as might Phoebe on the sea front of Cenchreae, but the texts disclose none of that information, for it was not germane to these women's significant contribution in their respective spheres.

---

98. *IEph.* 3218, *ll.* 4, 12-13; Horsley, "Sophia, the Second Phoebe," 240-41.

99. A. J. Köstenberger, "Women in the Pauline Mission," in P. Bolt and M. Thompson, eds., *The Gospels to the Nations: Perspectives on Paul's Mission* (Leicester and Downers Grove: Apollos and IVP, 2000), p. 229, citing D. J. Moo, *The Epistle to the Romans* (Grand Rapids: Eerdmans, 1996), p. 916.

100. Dio Chrysostom, *Or.* 8.5.

Junia Theodora and Junia

In Romans 16:7 mention is made of Andronicus and Junia. Junia is a Latin name, and Judge has noted that one third of the names of ninety-one individuals connected to Paul and the Pauline communities are Latin. He regards this figure as very high by comparison with three major collections representing an extensive group, in fact ten times higher.[101] The name Junia is well attested in Rome with more than two hundred and fifty examples, according to Lampe.[102] There is record of a Junia in Rome who came from Greece.[103]

Could the Junia of Romans 16:7 be the same person as Junia Theodora? This possibility deserves to be explored, as in the discussions of Junia and Junia Theodora to date the focus has been solely on Junia Theodora and Phoebe.[104] Is it possible that by the time Paul had written to the Roman Christians from Corinth Junia Theodora had moved to Rome, as Phoebe proposed to do? Since Junia Theodora had connections with those who were powerful, like Proculus, the other patron of Lycia who operated in Rome, she had every reason to locate herself near the seat of imperial power if she was to be their patron. Noy notes that one of the best-attested reasons for going to Rome was service on embassies, and the time spent in Rome for this purpose sometimes led to an extended stay.[105]

To what incident or incidents that resulted in Andronicus and Junia being Paul's fellow prisoners could he refer? Is it possible that it had been in some way linked to the near-death experience of Paul to which he refers in 2 Corinthians 1:8-10? This experience was such that he recorded 'but we ourselves had received the sentence of death' (ἀλλὰ αὐτοὶ ἐν ἑαυτοῖς τὸ ἀπόκριμα τοῦ θανάτου ἐσχήκαμεν) (2 Cor. 1:9).[106] It has been assumed that the reference was to Paul and Timothy in Ephesus, given that the letter comes addressed from both of them. This incident may have involved Andronicus and Junia. It could have

101. Judge, *Rank and Status in the World of the Caesars and St. Paul*, p. 13. See his n. 17 for the basis of his survey.

102. P. Lampe, *Die Städtrömischen Christen in den ersten beiden Jahrhundert* (Tübingen: J. C. Mohr, 1987), p. 139.

103. *IGUR*, 1239.

104. Kent, *Corinth*, VIII.3, provides literary evidence of similar names found in a number of inscriptions in his volume, so any examinations of this nature should not be dismissed, as ancient historians explore these possibilities as a matter of course.

105. Noy, "Why did people move to Rome?" in *Foreigners at Rome: Citizens and Strangers*, pp. 100-1.

106. *Liddell & Scott* cite 2 Cor. 1:9 as an example of a 'judicial sentence', 'condemnation', and in their *Supplement* to the 9th edition they cite *P. Tebt.* 286 (2nd century A.D.) and *P.Mich.* ix, 529 in the following century as judgements pronounced by the emperor after hearing a legal case.

been part of the reverberations from the assassination of Junius Silanus, pro-consul of Asia, at the instigation of Nero's mother, Agrippina.[107] Guilt by reason of association with leading figures in Ephesus would have been an indictable offence.[108] If the evidence of Acts 19:31 is added, then Paul himself had impor-tant connections, 'some of the Asiarchs also, who were friends of his, sent to him and begged him not to venture into the theatre', having 'despaired of life it-self' (2 Cor. 1:8). This could mean that in the subsequent imperial intrigue in Ephesus guilt by association was sufficient to implicate them in a criminal trial involving treason, especially since there was the precedent of the infamous trials involving Sejanus' conspiracy in the time of Tiberius. While the exact reason for the imprisonment of Andronicus and Junia is not spelt out, Junia Theodora's connections were not in that province but in the province of Lycia and Pamphylia. Her reception of Lycian ambassadors and those who were exiles by imperial decree whose federation was in disgrace in Rome could have preju-diced her position with the authorities in the East to whom she had access. That is a case for identification, but not a particularly strong one.

There are reasons that would rule against the identification of the two women as being one and the same person. Andronicus and Junia had long been Christians, in fact before Paul, and they had apostolic connections or knew the other apostles, yet the Lycian inscriptions to Junia Theodora sent gifts to her for when she would go into the presence of the gods (*ll.* 11, 65). It is possible that these gifts and the identification of her with the ancient gods reflect the Lycian Federation's perception of her religious attachment. If she had been a Christian before Paul's conversion, it is unlikely but not impossi-ble that they did not know this fact.

Andronicus and Junia were Jewish, Paul's 'kinsfolk', a wide term but Clarke rightly argues that the reference is to Jews (Rom. 9:3; cf. 16:7, 11). They were Paul's kinsfolk as were those who sent their greetings from Corinth, Lucius, Jason and Sosipater (16:21).[109] Noy found on the basis of the extensive survey of Roman epigraphic evidence that 'the Jews of Rome had Latin names more often than Greek ones, the Greek ones more often than Semitic ones. . . . Most people are recorded with only one name' in the first century.[110] So the use of a single Latin name for them, and Paul as well, was not unusual.

---

107. F. F. Bruce, *New Testament History* (London: Nelson, 1969), p. 331.

108. B. Levick, "Tiberius and the Law: The Development of *maiestas*," in *Tiberius, the Politician* (London: Thames and Hudson, 1976), ch. 11.

109. A. D. Clarke, "Jew and Greek, Slave and Free, Male and Female: Paul's Theology of Ethnic, Social and Gender Inclusiveness in Romans 16," in P. Oakes, ed., *Rome in the Bible and the Early Church* (Carlisle and Grand Rapids: Paternoster and Baker, 2002), p. 112.

110. Noy, *Foreigners at Rome: Citizens and Strangers*, p. 262.

Another reason for rejecting the possible identification is the fact that there is no husband named in the inscriptions for Junia Theodora, only a male relative, Sextus Iulius, who was a Roman described as 'our agent', and not Junia's, and also her heir (*ll.* 12, 54). The names Andronicus and Junia were linked by the connective 'and', just as Prisca and Aquila were (Rom. 16:3), who according to Acts 18:2 were married. This suggests that this male and female, who were Jews, long-standing Christians, prisoners together in detention with Paul in a place other than Corinth and now together in Rome, were also married to each other. The arguments on the present evidence are weighted against the identification of Junia Theodora and Junia.

If the two Junias referred to were not one and same person, what light might be shed on the role of Junia from the epigraphic evidence we have of her namesake? In a very well researched chapter in his book *Gospel Women*, Richard Bauckham has argued that the Junia of Romans 16:7 is to be identified with Joanna, the wife of Chuza, Herod's steward mentioned in Luke 8:3. That would make her a woman of status in the East, as was Junia Theodora. Part of Bauckham's grounds for so arguing was the practice in Jewish circles of adopting Latin names that sounded similar to their Semitic names, for which he provides good examples, including Acts 1:23, 'Joseph called Barsabbas, who was also called Justus.'[111] He argues that Joanna had acted in effect as a private patron, along with others, in financing the ministry of Jesus and his disciples from its beginning (Lk. 8:3). She was also a witness to the resurrection, as was Mary Magdalene who is also mentioned as one of the early supporters of that ministry (Lk. 24:10).

If this connection is correct, then we have in Junia someone with status, as the wife of Herod's steward, who had operated as a private patron to Jesus and his disciples and as a result was 'well known among the apostles' (οἵτινές εἰσιν ἐπίσημοι ἐν τοῖς ἀποστόλοις) (Rom. 16:7), if that is how that clause is to be read, according to Burer and Wallace.[112] Bauckham proposes a different reading, mounting a challenge to their recent article supporting their rendering.[113] He translates the clause as 'who are outstanding among the apostles' and concludes that Andronicus and Junia were the founding apostles of the church in Rome.[114] The church is not said to be meeting in their home, but in that of

---

111. R. Bauckham, "Joanna the Apostle," in *Gospel Women: Studies in the Named Women in the Gospels* (Grand Rapids: Eerdmans, 2002), ch. 5, and pp. 182-86 for a discussion of a list of names.

112. M. H. Burer and D. B. Wallace, "Was Junia Really an Apostle? A Re-examination of Rom 16:7," *NTS* 47 (2001): 76-91, which is a substantial linguistic study with a careful annotation of the recent secondary discussion.

113. Bauckham, *Gospel Women: Studies in the Named Women in the Gospels*, pp. 172-80.

114. Bauckham, *Gospel Women: Studies in the Named Women in the Gospels*, p. 181.

Aquila and Prisca (Rom. 16:5). Their actual role is not specified, and up to this point there is a single Christian meeting which Paul is anxious to maintain as part of God's purposes (Rom. 14-15, esp. 15:5-6).

If the nexus between Joanna and Junia is correct, then as Bauckham notes, his thesis requires that Chuza also changed his name to a Greek one, Andronicus.[115] He defends the Jewishness of Chuza who would be circumcised as a convert when he married Joanna, as this was the established protocol of marriage for those Gentiles connected to Herod's court.

Even if Joanna and Junia were not one and the same person, it is suggested that some conclusions can be drawn from Romans 16:7. Junia is a married woman, who along with her husband has been a long-standing Jewish Christian. Together they have been imprisoned with Paul, presumably for their identification with his cause. They are at the very least known to the apostolic band, or on Bauckham's thesis they are prominent apostles and are now residing in Rome.[116] They clearly have a considerable sphere of influence among Christians, and while Junia is unlike Phoebe in that she has a husband, both she and Andronicus are connected to the leading authorities in this movement.

Again, we would wish for more information, but this ancient snapshot, however indistinct in places, shows that she had a role and it was not a case of Andronicus simply travelling with a wife who was an appendage (1 Cor. 9:5). She has shared imprisonment with him because she was identified as a significant player herself in the Christian cause. Not unlike Junia Theodora, Junia had her sphere of influence in the circle in which she operated.

In the case of Aquila and his wife, Prisca, who were Jews, there is evidence that they were expelled from Rome, located next in Corinth, then Ephesus, and finally returned to Rome, where the church was to meet in their house. Acts 18:3 records that Paul resided with them because Paul and Aquila had the same trade skills, and would have operated in one of the shop houses of Corinth. However, there is no record that Prisca engaged in her husband's trade.[117] If

---

115. Bauckham, *Gospel Women: Studies in the Named Women in the Gospels*, pp. 186.

116. Bauckham with his vast knowledge of Second Temple Judaism has mounted a substantial case, and it is not possible in any way to do full justice to it in relation to Joanna in this final chapter. The expansion of the meaning of the term 'apostle' cannot be denied. However, did it occur in so short a time after writing that the apostles had the right to carry about a wife, 1 Cor. 9:5 — the inference being that they were all men — that in Rom. 16:7 the term included not only Andronicus but also his wife Junia?

117. Noy, *Foreigners at Rome: Citizens and Strangers*, p. 259, has assumed that both husband and wife engaged in the trade of tentmaking, but Acts 18:3 is silent on the issue, while Paul and Aquila shared the same trade.

she had done so, then it would be appropriate to compare Prisca with Pantheia, the wife of a physician in Pergamum in the second century A.D. who was not only the mother of his children and cared for them all, but also 'took the helm and steered the household's course and heightened the fame it had in the healing art'.[118] It is interesting that Aquila and Prisca were mentioned in relation to their ministry in the church in the same way that Andronicus and Junia were.

V. Conclusions

The parameters of this chapter were set for a comparison between the public role of women officially recorded in inscriptions and leading Christian women.[119] While the results demonstrate that both Phoebe and Junia were able to operate in a wider sphere, one would have wished for more information than the texts supply, not least of all their secular rank and status to assist in comparisons with the women mentioned in the epigraphic material. We long for more details about other women (and men) mentioned in the Pauline communities but they have not been included in the letters.[120]

Christian women did operate in a grey area, for the church met in the main reception room of homes, which was its public area. However, it is clear that women were not relegated to the private rooms in the house in the first century, any more than their secular sisters were. MacMullen has noted that one unexpected effect of the legal moves of Augustus against new women in the Empire was the loosing of social convention that allowed élite women to participate in *politeia*. Phyllis Culham observed that it also resulted in a relaxation for others. Limited though the evidence may be for Christian women, the filtering down of the new roles for women enabled Christian women to contribute to a wider sphere of service.

---

118. *Epigrammata Graeca*, 243b.

119. See n. 2 and the challenge of MacMullen and Judge on the use of epigraphic evidence.

120. For the most recent discussions see M. Y. MacDonald, "Reading Real Women through the Undisputed Letters of Paul," and "Rereading Paul: Early Interpreters of Paul on Women and Gender," in R. S. Kraemer and M. R. D'Angelo, eds., *Women and Christian Origins* (Oxford: Oxford University Press, 1999), chs. 9, 11, and A. D. Clarke, "Jew and Greek, Slave and Free, Male and Female: Paul's Theology of Ethnic, Social and Gender Inclusiveness in Romans 16," ch. 4.

Women in Civic Affairs

Iunia Theodora[1]

1. A Decree of the Federal Assembly of the Lycian Cities

Ἔδοξε Λυκίων τῶι [κοινῶ]ι. Ἐπεὶ Ἰουνία Θεοδώρα κατοικοῦσα ἐν Κορίνθωι γυνὴι καλὴι καὶ ἀγαθὴι καὶ εὔνους
τῶι ἔθνει διὰ παντὸς ἐνδείκνυται τὴν ὑπὲρ τοῦ ἔθνους σπουδὴν
4 καὶ φιλοτειμίαν καὶ τοῖς καθ' ἕνα Λυκίων καὶ κοινῶς ἅπασιν συμπαθῶς
διακειμένηι πλείστους τε τῶν ἡγουμένων φίλους κατεσκεύακεν
τῶι ἔθνει, συνλαμβανομένηι περὶ πάντων τῶν μάλιστα διηκόντων
ἅπασι Λυκίοις, διά τε ἧς τέθειται διαθήκης ἐνδέδεικται τὴν εἰς τὸ
8 ἔθνος ἀρέσκειαν, καλῶς δὲ ἔχον ἐστὶν καὶ τὸ ἔθνος τὰς προσηκού-
σας αὐτῆι ἀποδοῦναι μαρτυρίας, δεδόχθαι Λυκίων τῶι κοινῶι ἀποδεδέχθαι καὶ ἐπηνέσθαι Ἰουνίαν Θεοδώραν στέφανόν τε αὐτῆ χρυ-
σοῦν, ὅταν εἰς θεοὺς ἀφίκηται, ἀποστεῖλαι· μεριμνήσει δὲ ὁ φροντι-

---

1. D. Pallas *et al.*, 'Inscriptions lyciennes trouvées à Solômos près de Corinthe', *Bulletin de correspondance héllenique* 83 (1959): 496-508; *SEG* 18 (1962): 143 with supplements at *ll.* 54-55, 64-65, 74-75 by L. Robert, 'Décret de la Confédération Lycienne à Corinthe', *Revue des études anciennes* 62 (1960): 331, n. 1; 332; 326, n. 3 = *Supplementum Epigraphicum Graecum* 22 (1967), no. 232; *Supplementum Epigraphicum Graecum* 23 (1968), no. 176; *contra* Robert G. Klaffenbach, 'Miscellanea epigraphica', *Klio* 48 (1967): 54, n. 3, who proposes κρατε[ύοντα] at *l.* 55. Line 65: . . . αὐτὴν] τ[ιμῆσαι . . . (Kearsley).

The translations appearing in this appendix are by Dr R. Kearsley, "Women in Public Life in the Roman East: Iunia Theodora, Claudia Metrodora and Phoebe, Benefactress of Paul," *TynB* 50.2 (1999): 203-9 with amendments. Reproduced with the permission of the Editor, *Tyndale Bulletin*.

12 στῆς ἡμῶν Σέξτος Ἰούλιος καὶ ἐπιγράψαι ἐπιγραφὴν τήνδε· Λυκίων
τὸ κοινὸν Ἰουνίᾳ Θεοδώρᾳ Ῥωμαίᾳ γυναικὶ καλῆι καὶ ἀγαθῆι καὶ εὐνό-
ωι τῶι ἔθνει.

It was decreed (ἔδοξε) by the federal assembly of the Lycians: since (ἐπεί) Iunia
Theodora, living in Corinth, a fine and worthy woman, and devoted to the nation,
continuously shows her zeal and her munificence towards the nation and (4) being
full of goodwill both to individual Lycians and to all in general has gained for the nation the friendship of many of the authorities, employing her assistance in all areas
which most directly interest all the Lycians; (and) by the will which she has drawn up
shows her desire to (8) please the nation; it has been decreed (δεδόχθαι) that the nation in its turn returns to her these appropriate testimonies. The assembly of the
Lycians is pleased to acknowledge and to praise Iunia Theodora, and to send her a
gold crown for the time when she will come into the presence of the gods. (12) Our
agent Sextus Iulius has equally been busy seeing to the engraving of the following inscription: 'The federal assembly of the Lycians to Iunia Theodora, a Roman, fine and
honourable woman and devoted to the nation.'

2. A Letter from the Lycian City of Myra to Corinth

Μυρέων ἡ βουλὴ καὶ ὁ δῆμος Κορινθίων ἄρχουσι χαίρειν. Πλεῖστοι τῶν
16 ἡμετέρων γεγονότες ἐν τοῖς καθ' ὑμᾶς τόποις ἐμαρτύρουν Ἰουνίᾳ Λευκί-
ου Θεοδώρᾳ τῆι πολείτιδι ὑμῶν τὴν εὔνοιαν καὶ σπουδὴν ἣν εἰσενήνε-
κται ὑπὲρ αὐτῶν, προνοουμένη διὰ παντὸς τῶν ἡμετέρων καὶ παρα-
γενομένων εἰς τὴν πόλιν ὑμῶν· ἡμεῖς οὖν ἀποδεχόμενοι αὐτὴν ἐφ' ἧ
20 ἔχει πρὸς τὴν πόλιν εὐνοίᾳ ἔχομεν ἐν τῆι πλείστηι καταλογῆι, ἐχρεί-
ναμεν δὲ καὶ ὑμῖν γράψαι, ὅπως εἴδητε τὴν τῆς πόλεως εὐχαριστίαν.

The council and people of Myra greet the magistrates of Corinth. Many of (16) our
(citizens) who travelled in your territory testified concerning a citizen of yours, Iunia
Theodora, daughter of Lucius, and the devotion and zeal which she used on their behalf, occupying herself continually for our people particularly at the time of their arrival in your city; this is why, according her our approval for (20) her loyalty to the
city, we hold her in the greatest esteem, and have decided at the same time to write to
you as well in order that (ὅπως) you may know of the gratitude of the city.

3. A Decree of the Lycian City of Patara

Ἔδοξε Παταρέων τῷ δήμῳ. Ἐπεὶ Ἰουνία Θεοδώρα Ῥωμαία τῶν κατοι-
κουσῶν ἐν Κορίνθῳ, γυνὴ τῶν ἐν πλείστῃ τειμῇ καθεστηκειῶν, ζῶ-

24 σα σωφρόνως καὶ φιλολύκιος οὖσα καὶ ἀνατεθεικυῖα τὸν ἑαυτῆς βίον
   εἰς τὴν πάντων Λυκίων εὐχαριστίαν, πολλὰ καὶ πλείστοις τῶν ἡμετέρων πολειτῶν ἐπ' εὐεργεσίαν παρέσχηται καὶ τὸ ἑαυτῆς μεγαλοπρε-
   πὲς τῆς ψυχῆς ἐνδεικνυμένη ἐξ εὐνοίας οὐ διαλείπει ξένην τε ἑαυ-
28 τὴν πᾶσιν Λυκίοις παρεχομένη καὶ τῇ οἰκίᾳ δεχομένη καὶ μάλιστα τοῖς
   ἡμετέροις πολείταις οὐ διαλείπει ὑπερτιθεμένη τὰς εἰς πάντας χάρι-
   τας, δι' ὃ καὶ πλεῖστοι τῶν πολειτῶν ἡμῶν καταστάντες ἐπὶ τῆς ἐκκλησίας διαμεμαρτύρηκαν αὐτῇ· καθήκειν οὖν καὶ τὸν ἡμέτερον δῆμον
32 εὐχάριστον ὄντα ἐπαινέσαι τε τὴν Ἰουνίαν καὶ διαμαρτυρῆσαι αὐτῇ
   ἣν ἔχει παρὰ τῇ πατρίδι ἡμῶν ἀποδοχὴν καὶ εὔνοιαν καὶ ὅτι παρακαλεῖ
   αὐτὴν προσεπαύξειν τὴν εἰς τὸν δῆμον εὔνοιαν, εἰδυῖαν ὅτι καὶ ὁ δῆμος
   ἡμῶν πρὸς οὐθὲν ἐνλείψει τῆς εἰς αὐτὴν εὐνοίας καὶ χάριτος, πάντα δὲ
36 πράξει τὰ πρὸς ἀρετὴν αὐτῇ καὶ δόξαν διήκοντα· δι' ὅ, τύχῃ ἀγαθῇ, δεδόχθαι ἐπηνέσθαι αὐτὴν ἐπὶ πᾶσιν τοῖς προγεγραμμένοις· ἵνα δὲ καὶ αὐτὴ Ἰουνία καὶ ἡ Κορινθίων πόλις ἐπιγνῷ τὴν ἐκ τῆς πόλεως ἡμῶν εἰς αὐτὴν εὔνοιαν καὶ τὸ γεγονὸς αὐτῇ ψήφισμα, τὸν γραμματέα τῆς βουλῆς τοῦδε
40 τοῦ ψηφίσματος τὸ <δὲ> ἀντίγραφον σφραγισάμενοι τῇ δημοσίᾳ σφραγεῖδι' πέμψασθαι πρὸς τὸν Κορινθίων δῆμον.

It was decreed (ἔδοξε) by the people of Patara: since (ἐπεί) Iunia Theodora, a Roman, living at Corinth, a woman of the greatest honour, (24) living modestly, who is a friend of the Lycians and has dedicated her life to earning the gratitude of all the Lycians, has bestowed numerous benefits also on many of our citizens; and, revealing the generosity of her nature, she does not cease, because of her goodwill, from offering hospitality to (28) all the Lycians and receiving them in her own house and she continues particularly to act on behalf of our citizens in regard to any favour asked — so that the majority of our citizens have come before the Assembly to give testimony about her. Therefore, our people (32) in gratitude agreed to vote to commend Iunia and acknowledge her generosity to our native city and her goodwill, and to invite her to extend her loyalty to the people in the certainty that in its turn our people will not show any negligence in its devotion and gratitude to her, and (36) will do everything for the excellence and glory she deserves. This is why, with good fortune, it has been decreed (δεδόχθαι) to commend her for all the aforesaid reasons, in order that (ἵνα δέ) Iunia herself, and the city of Corinth at the same time, may be aware of the loyalty of our city to her, and of the decree passed for her, the secretary of the council sends (40) to the people of Corinth this copy of the present decree after having sealed it with the public seal.

4. A Letter of the Federal Assembly to Corinth
Introducing a Second Decree in Favour of Iunia Theodora

Λυκίων τὸ κοινὸν καὶ οἱ ἄρχοντες Κορινθίων ἄρχουσι, βουλῇ, δήμῳ χαίρειν. Τοῦ γεγονότος ψηφίσματος φιλανθρώπου καὶ στεφανώσεως χρυ-
44 σῷ στεφάνῳ καὶ ἀναθέσεως εἰκόνος εἰς ἀποθέωσιν μετὰ τὴν [ἀπ]α[λ]λα-
γὴν Ἰουνίᾳ Θεοδώρᾳ κατοικούσῃ παρ' ὑμεῖν ἐξαπεστάλκαμεν ὑμεῖν τὸ ἀντίγραφον σφραγισάμενοι τῇ δημοσίᾳ σφραγεῖδι ὅπως ε[ἴ]δητ[ε] τα[ῦτα].
Ἔδοξε Λυκίων τῷ κοινῷ· ἐπεὶ Ἰουνία Θεοδώρα κατοικοῦσα ἐν [Κορ]ίν-
48 θῳ γυνὴ καλὴ καὶ ἀγαθὴ καὶ εὔνους τῷ Λυκίων ἔθνει διὰ παν[τὸ]ς ἐνδέδεικται τὴν ὑπὲρ τοῦ ἔθνους σπουδὴν καὶ φιλοτειμίαν πᾶ[σι] τοῖς
παρεπιδημήσασιν ἰδιώταις τε καὶ [πρ]έσβεσιν τοῖς ἀ[πο]στελλομ[έν]οις
ὑπό τε τοῦ ἔθνους καὶ ἰδίᾳ κατὰ πόλιν συ[μ]παθῶς διακειμ[ένη ἡρέ]σ-
52 κευται πᾶσιν συνκατασκευάζουσα τοὺς ἡγ[ε]μόνα[ς ε]ὐνο[υστάτο]υς
ἡμεῖν γείνεσθαι ἀρεσκευομένη τούτοις κατὰ πάντα πρόπον τό[ν τε δ]ιά-
δοχον αὐτῆς Σέκτον Ἰούλιον Ῥω[μαῖ]ον ἄνδρα ἀγαθὸν ὄ[ν]τ[α καὶ τῇ
ὑ]περβαλλούσῃ εὐνοίᾳ κρατέ[οντα καὶ] σπουδῇ πρὸς τὸ ἔθνος [ἡμ]ῶ[ν σ]τοι-
56 χοῦντα τῇ ἄνωθεν Ἰουνίας πρὸς ἡμᾶς εὐνοίᾳ· ᾧ κατὰ τὸν [αὐτὸν] και-
ρὸν πεμφθήσεται ἡ ἀπὸ τοῦ ἔθνους Λ[υ]κίων ψήφισμα Ἰο[υνίᾳ Θεοδώ]ρᾳ
ἔτι δὲ καὶ πλείστους τῶν ἡμε[τέρ]ων ἐκπεσόντας ὑπεδ[έξατο μεγα]λο-
μερῶς, διά τε ἧς τέθειται διαθήκ[ης ἐν]δέδ[εικ]ται τὴν [ἑαυτῆς εὔνοι]αν·
60 καλῶς δὲ ἔχον ἐστὶν καὶ τὸ κοινὸ[ν ἡ[μῶν ἐφ' οἷς ἐπιμένο[υσα *ca.* 5 εὖ]
ποιεῖ ἀποδιδόναι αὐτῇ μαρτυρία[ς καὶ χ]άριτας· δεδόχθαι Λ[υκίων τῷ κ]οι-
νῷ ἀποδεδέχθαι καὶ ἐπηνέσθαι [ἐπὶ πᾶσι] τοῖς προγεγ[ραμμένοις Ἰου]νί-
αν Θεοδώραν Ῥωμαίαν κατοικοῦ[σαν ἐ]ν Κορίνθῳ στέφανόν τ[ε] αὐτῇ [χρυ]-
64 σοῦν ἀποστεῖλαι καὶ κρόκου μνᾶς πέντε [ἃ]ς [ἀ]ποθ[έσθαι ἐν τῇ οἰκίᾳ ἵνα ἐν
ἑ]τοίμῳ ἔχῃ, ὅταν εἰς θεοὺς ἀφικνῆται, κα[ὶ αὐτὴν] τ[ιμῆσαι εἰκόνι γραπτῇ
ἐ]πιχρύσῳ καὶ ἐπιγράψαι ἐπιγραφὴν τή[νδε· Λυκίων τὸ κοινὸν καὶ οἱ ἄρχοντες]
Ἰουνίαν Θεοδώραν Ῥωμαίαν κατοικοῦσαν ἐν Κορίνθῳ [ἐτίμησαν στεφά]-
68 νῳ καὶ εἰκόνι γραπτῇ ἐπιχρύσῳ γυναῖ[κα κα]λὴν καὶ [ἀ]γαθὴ[ν κ]αὶ ε[ὔνουν]
διὰ παντὸς τῶι ἔθνει φιλοστοργίας ἕνεκεν κα[ὶ *ca.* 10] ΕΙΣΛΛ [*ca.* 3-4].

Greetings from the federal assembly of the Lycians and the Lycian magistrates to the magistrates, the council and the people of Corinth. By an honorific decree made in favour of Iunia Theodora, living among you, it is voted to grant her both the crowning with a (44) golden crown and the offering of a portrait for her deification after her death, and we have sent you a copy (of the decree) sealed with the public seal so as to inform you at the same time.

It was decreed (ἔδοξε) by the federal assembly of the Lycians: since (ἐπεί) Iunia Theodora, living in Corinth, (48) a fine and honourable woman and devoted to the Lycian nation, has not ceased to show her zeal and generosity towards the nation and is full of good will to all travellers whether private individuals or ambassadors sent by the nation or by various cities, and has procured the gratitude (52) of all of us by assuring the friendship of the authorities which she seeks to win by every means, and making well-disposed her heir Sextus Iulius, a Roman, a good man also behaving with surpassing goodwill and with zeal towards our nation, imitating (56) the devotion of Iunia towards us which was mentioned above. To that man will be sent on the same occasion the decree of the Lycian nation in honour of Iunia Theodora. Since also very many of our people in exile were welcomed by her with magnificence, and that by the will she has made she shows her loyalty, it has been decreed (δεδόχθαι) therefore that, in its turn, (60) our assembly make testimony on her behalf and register its gratitude for her continual benefits, . . . it pleases the Lycian federal assembly to give honour and praise for all the above-mentioned reasons to Iunia Theodora, a Roman, living at Corinth, and to send her a crown of gold (64) and five minas of saffron to be set aside in her house in order that she may have it in readiness when she will reach the presence of the gods and to honour her with a portrait painted on a gilt background and engraved with the following inscription: 'The federal assembly of the Lycians and the Lycian magistrates have honoured with a crown (68) and a portrait painted on a gilt background Iunia Theodora, a Roman, living at Corinth, a fine and honourable woman and constantly devoted to the nation by reason of her affection.'

5. A Decree of the Lycian City of Telmessos

Ἔτους τεσσαροκοστοῦ, ἐπὶ ἱερ(έ)ως Διονυσοφά[ν]ου το[ῦ *ca.* 1-2] Α [*ca.* 12-13
ἔδοξε] Τελμησέων τῇ βουλῇ καὶ τῶι δήμωι, πρ[υ]τάνεω[ν *ca.* 2-3] Ο [*ca.* 16]
72 γνώμη. Ἐπὶ Ἰουνία Θεοδώρα Ῥωμαία γυνὴ ὑπάρχουσ[α ἐν πλείστῃ εὐνοί]-
ᾳ τοῦ τε κοινοῦ τῶν Λυκίων καὶ τῆς πόλεως ἡμῶν πο[λ]λὰ[ς *ca.* 5 εὐεργεσί]-
ας τετέλεκεν τῷ τε κοινῶι καὶ τῇ πατρίδ[ι ἡ]μῶν, [κατοικοῦσα δὲ ἐν τῇ Κορινθί]-
ων πόλει τοὺς παρεπιδημοῦντας Λυκίων καὶ τῶν πολ[ειτῶν ἡμῶν *ca.* 7 δέχε]-
76 ται τῇ ἰδίᾳ οἰκίᾳ παρεχομένη αὐτοῖ[ς πάν]τα [*ca.* 23]
τῶν παραγεινομένων προστασίαν [ἐν]δ[εικνυμένη *ca.* 17]
ἰδίας φιλοδοξίας καὶ ἐκτενείας Α Ο [*ca.* 2-3] ΑΘ [*ca.* 17 καλῶς]
δὲ ἔχον ἐστὶ καὶ τὴν πόλιν ἡμῶν ἀποδοῦναι α[ὐτῇ τὴν καθήκουσαν μαρτυ]-
80 ρίαν, τύχῃ ἀγαθῇ, δεδόχθαι Τελμ[ησ]σ[έων] τῶ[ι] δήμω[ι ἀπ]ο [δεδέχθαι καὶ
ἐ]πῃνῆσθαι ἐπὶ πᾶσι τοῖς προγεγραμμένοις Ἰουνίαν Θ[ε]οδώραν [τὴν προγε]-
γραμμένην, παρακαλεῖν τε αὐτὴν μένουσαν ἐπ[ὶ] τῆς αὐτῆς ὑποσ[τάσεως]
ἀεί τινος ἀγαθοῦ παραιτίαν γείνεσθαι πᾶσιν ἡμεῖν εἰδυῖαν ὅτ[ι καὶ ἡ πόλις]
84 ἡμῶν εὐχάριστος ὑπάρχουσα ἀποδώσι αὐτῇ πάλιν τὰς καθηκο[ύσας] μαρτυρίας.

In the fourth year, when Dionysophanes, son of . . . was priest, it was decreed (ἔδοξε) by the council and people of Telmessos, the proposal of the prytaneis . . . : (72) Since (ἐπεί) Iunia Theodora, a Roman, a benefactress of the greatest loyalty to the Lycian federation and our city, has accomplished numerous . . . benefits for the federation and our city, and, dwelling in the city of the Corinthians, (76) welcomes in her own house Lycian travellers and our citizens, . . . supplying them with everything . . . ; dis-

playing her patronage of those who are present . . . of her own love of fame and assid-
uousness . . . , it has been decreed (δεδόχθαι) that our city in its turn testify to her according to her deserts; (80) by good fortune, it pleases the *demos* of Telmessos to give
honour and praise for all the above reasons to the above-mentioned Iunia Theodora
and to invite her, living with the same intentions, to always be the author of some
benefit towards us, well knowing that in return our city (84) recognises and will acknowledge the evidence of her goodwill.

Claudia Metrodora from Chios

1. *Claudia Metrodora as Magistrate (stephanephoros)*[2]

Οἱ πολέμαρχ]οι καὶ ἐξετασ[ταὶ οἱ]
[ἄρξαντες ἐ]ν τῷ ἐπὶ στεφανη[φό]-
[ρου Κλαυδ]ίας, Σκυθείνου θυ-
4 [γατρὸς, Μητ]ροδώρας τὸ β' (ἐνιαυτῷ) στεφα-
[νοῦσι τ]ὸν ἑαυτῶν συνάρ-
[χοντα Λε]ύκιον . . .

The polemarchs and the financial officials who held office in the second
stephanephorate of Claudia Metrodora, daughter of Skytheinos, crown their co-
archon, Lucius . . .

2. *Claudia Metrodora and Her Many Other Public Offices*[3]

---------------------- Κλαυδί-
[αν Σκυθείνου θυ]γατέρα [Μητροδώραν] γυμνασιαρ-
[χήσασαν τε]τράκις καὶ δὶς ἀλείψασαν τὴν
4 [πόλιν κατὰ τ]ὴν τῶν Ἡρακλήων ἀγώνων πανή-
[γυριν τρ?]ὶς ἀγωνοθετήσασαν τῶν Ἡρα-
[κλήων Ῥωμ]αίων καὶ Καισαρήων καὶ βασιλεύσα-
[σαν τοῦ τρισκα]ιδεκαπολειτικοῦ τῶν Ἰώνων
8 [κοινοῦ, φ]ιλοδοξοῦσα[ν περ]ὶ τὴν πόλιν
[---------------- φ]ιλόπατριν [καὶ ἱ]έρειαν δ[ιὰ]
[βίου Σεβαστ]ῆς θεᾶς Ἀφροδίτης Λιβίας

2. L. Robert, 'Inscriptions de Chios du Ier siècle de notre ère', *Études épigraphiques et philologiques* (Paris: Champion, 1938), 133-34.
3. J. and L. Robert, 'Bulletin épigraphique', *Revue des études grecques* 69 (1956): 152-53, no. 213.

ἀρετῆς ἕνεκα καὶ καλοκαγαθί-
12 ας τῆς εἰς ἑαυτόν.

... for Claudia Metrodora, daughter of Skytheinos, gymnasiarch (4) four times
(who) twice distributed oil to the city on the occasion of the festival of the Heraklea
games; agonothete three (3) times of the Heraklea Romaia and Kaisareia; queen of the
thirteen cities of the Ionian (8) federation, being desirous of glory for the city, ... a
lover of her homeland and priestess for life of the divine empress Aphrodite Livia, by
reason of her excellence and admirable behaviour (12) towards it.

3. Claudia Metrodora from Ephesos[4]

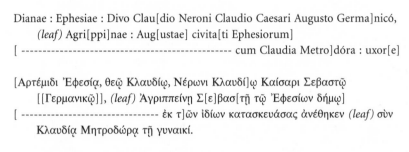

Dianae : Ephesiae : Divo Clau[dio Neroni Claudio Caesari Augusto Germa]nicó,
      (leaf) Agri[ppi]nae : Aug[ustae] civita[ti Ephesiorum]
[--- cum Claudia Metro]dóra : uxor[e]

[Ἀρτέμιδι Ἐφεσίᾳ, θεῷ Κλαυδίῳ, Νέρωνι Κλαυδί]ῳ Καίσαρι Σεβαστῷ
      [[Γερμανικῷ]], *(leaf)* Ἀγριππείνῃ Σ[ε]βασ[τῇ τῷ Ἐφεσίων δήμῳ]
[----------------------------- ἐκ τ]ῶν ἰδίων κατασκευάσας ἀνέθηκεν *(leaf)* σὺν
Κλαυδίᾳ Μητροδώρᾳ τῇ γυναικί.

For Ephesian Artemis, the deified Claudius, Nero Claudius Caesar Augustus
Germanicus, Agrippina Augusta, and the people of Ephesos, ... erected (this building) at his own expense and dedicated it together with his wife Claudia Metrodora.

4. J. Keil, 'Inschriften', in *Forschungen in Ephesos* III (Vienna, 1923), 94-95, no. 3; R. Meriç,
R. Merkelbach, J. Nollé, and S. Sahin, eds., *Die Inschriften von Ephesos* (*Inschriften griechischer
Städte aus Kleinasien* 17/1; Habelt: Bonn, 1981), VII.1, no. 3003.

Bibliography

Adams, J. N. *The Latin Sexual Vocabulary.* London: Duckworth, 1982.

Alcock, S. E. Graecia Capta: *The Landscapes of Roman Greece.* Cambridge: Cambridge University Press, 1993.

Allen, A. W. "Elegy and the Classical Attitude towards Love: Propertius I,1," *Yale Classical Review* 11 (1950): 255-77.

Amunsen, D. W., and C. J. Diers, "The Age of Menopause in Classical Greece and Rome," *Human Biology* 42 (1970): 79-88.

Ando, C. *Imperial Ideology and Provincial Loyalty in the Roman Empire.* Berkeley: University of California Press, 2000.

Aubert J.-J. "Conclusion: A Historian's Point of View," in J.-J. Aubert and B. Sirks, eds., Speculum Iuris: *Roman Law as a Reflection of Social and Economic Life in Antiquity.* Ann Arbor: University of Michigan Press, 2002, pp. 182-92.

Aubert, J.-J. "Direct Management and Public Administration: Four Case Studies," in *Business Managers in Ancient Rome: A Social and Economic Study of* Institores, *200 B.C.–A.D. 250.* Leiden: E. J. Brill, 1994, ch. 5.

Badian, E. *Publicans and Sinners: Private Enterprise in the Service of the Roman Republic.* Oxford: Blackwell, 1972.

Baldwin, H. S. "αὐθεντέω in Ancient Greek Literature," in A. Köstenberger, T. R. Schreiner and H. S. Baldwin, eds., *Women in the Church: A Fresh Analysis of 1 Timothy 2:9-15.* Grand Rapids: Baker, 1995, pp. 269-305.

Balsdon, J. P. V. D. *Roman Women: Their History and Habits.* London: Bodley Head, 1974.

Barrett, A. A. *Livia: First Lady of Imperial Rome.* New Haven: Yale University Press, 2002.

Bauckham, R. "Joanna the Apostle," in *Gospel Women: Studies in the Named Women in the Gospels.* Grand Rapids: Eerdmans, 2002, ch. 5.

Bauer, Arndt and Gingrich. *A Greek-English Lexicon of the New Testament and Other Early Christian Literature.* Chicago: University of Chicago Press, 1957.

Bibliography

Baugh, S. M. "A Foreign World: Ephesus in the First Century," in A. Köstenberger, T. R. Schreiner, and H. S. Baldwin, eds., *Women in the Church: A Fresh Analysis of 1 Timothy 2:9-15.* Grand Rapids: Baker, 1995, ch. 1.

Bauman, R. A. *Lawyers and Politics in the Early Roman Empire: A Study of Relations Between the Roman Jurists and the Emperors from Augustus to Hadrian.* Munich: C. H. Beck, 1989.

Bauman, R. A. *Women and Politics in Ancient Rome.* London: Routledge, 1992.

Blundell, S. "Clutching at Clothes," in L. Llewellyn-Jones, ed., *Women's Dress in the Ancient Greek World.* London and Swansea: Duckworth and University Press of Wales, 2002, ch. 9.

Bond, R. P. "Anti-feminism in Juvenal and Cato," in C. Deroux, ed., *Studies in Latin Literature and Roman History.* Brussels: 1979.

Bookidis, N., and R. S. Stroud, *The Sanctuary of Demeter and Kore: Topography and Architecture.* Part 3. Princeton: American School of Classical Studies in Athens, 1997.

Booth, A. "The Age for Reclining and Its Attendant Perils," in W. J. Slater, ed., *Dining in a Classical Context.* Ann Arbor: University of Michigan Press, 1991, pp. 105-20.

Bordes, J. *Politeia dans la pensée grecque jusquà Aristote.* Paris: Les Belles Lettres, 1982.

Bowie, E. L. "The Importance of the Sophists," *Yale Classical Studies* 27 (1982): 29-59.

Braund, D. "*Cohors:* The Governor and His Entourage in the Self-image of the Roman Republic," in R. Laurence and J. Berry, eds., *Cultural Identity in the Roman Empire.* London: Routledge, 1998, ch. 1.

Braund, D., ed. *The Administration of the Roman Empire, 241 BC–AD 193.* Exeter: Exeter University Press, 1988.

Braund, S. H. "A Woman's Voice — Laronia's Role in Juvenal Satire 2," in R. Hawley and B. Levick, eds., *Women in Antiquity: New Assessments.* London: Routledge, 1995, ch. 14.

Bruce, F. F. *New Testament History.* London: Nelson, 1969.

Brunt, P. A. *Italian Manpower, 225 B.C.–A.D. 14.* Oxford: Oxford University Press, 1971.

Buckland, W. W. *A Text-book of Roman Law from the Time of Cicero to the Time of Ulpian.* Oxford: Clarendon Press, 1991.

Burer, M. H. and Wallace, D. B. "Was Junia Really an Apostle? A Re-examination of Rom 16:7," *NTS* 47 (2001): 76-91

Burstein, S. *The Hellenistic Age from the Battle of Ipsos to the Death of Kleopatra,* III. Cambridge: Cambridge University Press, 1985.

Cairns, F. "Propertius on Augustus Marriage Law," *Grazer Beiträger* 8 (1979): 185-205.

Cairns, F. "The Meaning of the Veil in Ancient Greek Culture," in L. Llewellyn-Jones, ed., *Women's Dress in the Ancient Greek World.* London and Swansea: Duckworth and University Press of Wales, 2002, ch. 5.

Cameron, A. "Women in Ancient Culture and Society," *Altsprachliche Unterricht,* 32.2 (1989): 6-17.

Cartledge, P. "Spartan Wives: Liberation or Licence?" *CQ* n.s. 31 (1981): 84-109.

Cartledge, P., and A. Spawforth, *Hellenistic and Roman Sparta: A Tale of Two Cities*. London: Routledge, 1989.

Cherry, D. "Gifts between Husband and Wife: The Social Origins of Roman Law," in J.-J. Aubert and B. Sirks, eds., Speculum Iuris: *Roman Law as a Reflection of Social and Economic Life in Antiquity*. Ann Arbor: University of Michigan Press, 2002, pp. 34-45.

Chrimes, K. *Ancient Sparta*. Manchester: Manchester University Press, 1949.

Clarke, A. D. "Jew and Greek, Slave and Free, Male and Female: Paul's Theology of Ethnic, Social and Gender Inclusiveness in Romans 16," in P. Oakes, ed., *Rome in the Bible and the Early Church*. Carlisle and Grand Rapids: Paternoster and Baker, 2002, ch. 4.

Clarke, A. D. *Serve the Community of the Church*. Grand Rapids and Carlisle: Eerdmans and Paternoster, 2000, ch. 9.

Collins, J. N. *Diakonia: Re-interpreting the Ancient Sources*. Oxford: Oxford University Press, 1990.

Corley, K. E. *Private Women, Public Meals: Social Conflict in the Synoptic Tradition*. Peabody, Mass.: Hendrickson, 1993.

Cotter, W. "The *Collegia* and the Roman Law: State Restrictions on Voluntary Associations, 64 BCE–200 CE," in J. S. Kloppenborg and S. G. Wilson, eds., *Voluntary Associations in the Graeco-Roman World*. London: Routledge, 1996, ch. 5.

Crisafulli, T. "Representations of the Feminine: The Prostitutes in Roman Comedy," in T. W. Hillard, R. A. Kearsley, C. E. V. Nixon, A. M. Nobbs, eds., *The Ancient Near East, Greece, and Rome*, Ancient History in a Modern University. Grand Rapids: Eerdmans, 1998, I, pp. 222-29.

Crook, J. A. "Augustus: Power, Authority, Achievement," in A. K. Bowman, E. Champlin and A. Lintott, eds., *The Augustan Empire, 43 BC–AD 69*, 2nd edn., vol. X. Cambridge: Cambridge University Press, 1996, ch. 3.

Crook, J. A. *Law and Life of Rome, 90 B.C.–A.D. 212*. New York: Cornell University Press, 1967.

Crook, J. A. "Legal History and General History," *BICS* 41 (1996): 31-36.

Croom, A. T. *Roman Clothing and Fashion*. Stroud: Tempus, 2000.

Culham, P. "Did Roman Women Have an Empire?" in M. Golden and P. Toohey, eds., *Inventing Ancient Culture: Historicism, Periodization, and the Ancient World*. London: Routledge, 1997, ch. 10.

Dalby, A. *Empire of Pleasures: Luxury and Indulgence in the Roman World*. London: Routledge, 2000.

Dalby, A. "Levels of Concealment: The Dress of the *Hetairai* and *Pornai* in Greek Texts," in L. Llewellyn-Jones, ed., *Women's Dress in the Ancient Greek World*. London and Swansea: Duckworth and University Press of Wales, 2002, ch. 7.

D'Ambra, E. "Virgins and Adulterers," in *Private Lives, Imperial Virtues: The Frieze of the* Forum Transitorium *in Rome*. Princeton: Princeton University Press, 1993.

Danker, F. W., and W. Bauer, *A Greek-English Lexicon of the New Testament and Other Early Christian Literature*, 3rd edn. Chicago: University of Chicago Press, 2000.

Bibliography

Daube, D. *Roman Law: Linguistics, Social and Philosophical Aspects*. Edinburgh: University of Edinburgh Press, 1969.

Davies, G. "Clothes as Sign: The Case of the Large and Small Herculaneum Women," in L. Llewellyn-Jones, ed., *Women's Dress in the Ancient Greek World*. London and Swansea: Duckworth and University Press of Wales, 2002, ch. 12.

Deissmann, A. *Light from the Ancient East: The New Testament Illustrated by Recently Discovered Texts of the Graeco-Roman World*. ET reprint, Grand Rapids: Baker, 1978.

Desideri, P. "City and Country in Dio," in S. Swain, ed., *Dio Chrysostom: Politics, Letters, and Philosophy*. Oxford: Oxford University Press, 2000, ch. 3.

Dibelius, M., and H. Conzelmann, *The Pastoral Epistles*. Philadelphia: Fortress Press, 1972.

Dixon, S. *Reading Roman Women*. London: Duckworth, 2001.

Dixon, S. *The Roman Mother*. 2nd edn. London: Routledge, 1990.

Doriani, D. "A History of the Interpretation of 1 Timothy 2," in A. J. Köstenberger, T. R. Schreiner, and H. S. Baldwin, eds., *Women in the Church: A Fresh Analysis of 1 Timothy 2:9-15*. Appendix 1. Grand Rapids: Baker, 1995.

Dunbabin K. M. D. and W. M. Dickie, "*Invidia rumpantur pectora*: Iconography of *Phthonos/Invidia* in Graeco-Roman Art," *JbAC* 26 (1983): 3-37.

Edwards, C. *The Politics of Immorality in Ancient Rome*. Cambridge: Cambridge University Press, 1993.

Eilers, C. *Roman Patrons and Greek Cities*. Oxford: Oxford University Press, 2002.

Ellicott, C. J. *The Pastoral Epistles of St Paul*. London: Longmans, 1869.

Epstein, D. F. *Personal Enmity in Roman Politics, 218-43 B.C.* London: Routledge, 1989.

Eyben, E. *Restless Youth in Ancient Rome*. London: Routledge, 1993.

Falk, Z. W. *Introduction to Jewish Laws of the Second Commonwealth*. Leiden: E. J. Brill, 1978.

Fantham, E., et al. "The 'New Woman': Representation and Reality," in *Women in the Classical World*. Oxford: Oxford University Press, 1994, ch. 10.

Fee, G. D. *1 and 2 Timothy and Titus*. Peabody, Mass.: Hendrickson, 1988.

Fishwick, D. *Imperial Cult in the Latin West: Studies in the Ruler Cult of the Western Provinces of the Roman Empire*. Leiden: E. J. Brill, 2002, vol. III.2.

Forbis, E. "Women's Public Image in Italian Honorary Inscriptions," *American Journal of Philology* 111 (1990): 493-512.

Gardner, J. F. "Women in Business Life: Some Evidence from Puteoli," in P. Setälä and L. Savuen, eds., *Female Networks and the Public Sphere in Roman Society*. Rome: Institutum Romanum Finlandiae, 1999, pp. 11-27.

Gardner, J. F. *Women in Roman Law and Society*. Oxford: Clarendon, 1986.

Gill, D. "The Importance of Roman Portraiture for Head-coverings in 1 Corinthians 11:2-16," *TynB* 41.2 (1990): 245-60.

Goette, H. R. *Studien zu römischen Togadarstellungen*. Mainz am Rhein, 1990.

Gourevitch, D. "Women who suffer from a man's disease," in R. Hawley and B. Levick, eds., *Women in Antiquity: New Assessments*. London: Routledge, 1995, ch. 10.

Greene, E. *The Erotics of Domination: Male Desire and the Mistress in Latin Love Po-etry.* Baltimore: Johns Hopkins, 1998.

Griffin, J. "Augustan Poetry and the Life of Luxury," *JRS* 67 (1977): 87-105.

Griffin, J. "Propertius and Antony," *JRS* 66 (1976): 17-26.

Grubbs, J. E. *Women in the Law in the Roman Empire: A Sourcebook on Marriage, Divorce and Widowhood.* London: Routledge, 2002.

Hands, A. R. *Charities and Social Aid in Greece and Rome.* London: Thames and Hudson, 1968.

Hanson, A. T. *The Pastoral Epistles.* London: Marshall and Pickering, 1982.

Harris, W. V. "The Roman Father's Power of Life and Death," in R. S. Bagnall and W. V. Harris, eds., *Studies in Roman Law in Memory of A. A. Schiller.* Leiden: Brill, 1986, 81-95.

Hawley, R. "Marriage, Gender, and the Family in Dio," in S. Swain, ed., *Dio Chrysostom: Politics, Letters, and Philosophy.* Oxford: Oxford University Press, 2000, ch. 5.

Hemelrijk, E. A. Matrona Docta: *Educated Women in the Roman Elite from Correlia to Julia Domna.* London: Routledge, 1999.

Henry, A. S. *Honours and Privileges in Athenian Decrees: The Principal Formulae of Athenian Honorary Decrees.* Hildesheim and New York: G. Olms, 1983.

Hoff, M. C. and S. I. Rotroff, *The Romanization of Athens: Proceedings of an International Conference,* Oxbow Monograph 94. Oxford: Oxbow Books, 1997.

Hopkins, M. K. "The Age of Roman Girls at Marriage," *Population Studies* 18.3 (1965): 309-27.

Hopkins, M. K. "Contraception in the Roman Empire," *Comparative Studies in Society and History* 8 (1965): 124-51.

Hopwood, K. "Aspects of Violent Crime in the Roman Empire," in P. McKechnie, ed., *Thinking like a Lawyer: Essays on Legal and General History for John Crook on His Eightieth Birthday,* Mnemosyne Supplements ccxxxi. Leiden: E. J. Brill, 2002, pp. 63-80.

Horsley, G. "Sophia, the Second Phoebe," *New Documents Illustrating Early Christianity* 4 (1979), no. 122.

Hunter, V. J. *Policing Athens: Social Control in the Attic Lawsuits,* 420-320 B.C. Princeton: Princeton University Press, 1994.

Jacoby, F. *Die Fragmente der griechischen Historiker,* II. 90. Berlin: Weidmannsche Buchhandlung, 1926.

Jones, A. H. M. *The Greek City from Alexander to Justinian.* Oxford: Clarendon Press, 1998.

Jones, A. H. M. "Lycia," in *Cities of the Eastern Roman Provinces.* Oxford: Clarendon Press, 1937, reprint 1998, ch. 3.

Judge, E. A. *Rank and Status in the World of the Caesars and St. Paul.* Christchurch: University of Canterbury Publications, 1982.

Judge, E. A. "St. Paul and Classical Society," *JAC* 14 (1971): 19-36.

Judge, E. A. "A Woman's Behaviour," *New Documents Illustrating Early Christianity* 6 (1992), no. 2.

Kampen, N. *Image and Status: Roman Working Women in Ostia.* Berlin: Gerb. Mann Verlag, 1981.

Kaster, R. A. "The Shame of the Romans," *TAPA* 127 (1997): 1-19.

Kearsley R. A., and T. V. Evans, *Greeks and Romans in Imperial Asia: Mixed Language Inscriptions and Linguistic Evidence for Cultural Interaction until the End of AD III.* Bonn: Habelt, 2001.

Kearsley, R. A. "Women in Public Life in the Roman East: Iunia Theodora, Claudia Metrodora and Phoebe, Benefactress of Paul," *Tyndale Bulletin* 50.2 (1999): 189-211.

Kennedy, G. A. *The Art of Rhetoric in the Roman World.* Princeton: Princeton University Press, 1972.

Kent, J. H. *Corinth: The Inscriptions, 1926-1950.* 8.3. nos. 128, 199. Princeton: American School of Classical Studies, 1966.

Klauck, H-J. "Junia Theodora und die Gemeinde von Korinth," in M. Karrer, W. Kraus and O. Merk, *Kirche und Volk Gottes, Festschrift für Jürgen Roloff.* Neukirchen: Neukirchener Verlag, 2000, pp. 42-57.

Knight III, G. W. "ΑΥΘΕΝΤΕΩ in Reference to Women in 1 Timothy 2.12," *NTS* 30.1 (1984): 143-57.

Köstenberger, A. J. "Ascertaining Women's God-Ordained Roles: An Interpretation of 1 Timothy 2:15," *BBR* 7 (1997): 107-44.

Köstenberger, A. J. "Women in the Pauline Mission," in P. Bolt and M. Thompson, eds., *The Gospels to the Nations: Perspectives on Paul's Mission.* Leicester and Downers Grove: Apollos and IVP, 2000, ch. 16.

Krause, J.-U. *Witwen und Waisen im Römischen Reich.* Stuttgart: F. Steiner, 1994-95. Vols. I-IV.

Lacey, W. K. *The Family in Classical Greece.* London: Thames and Hudson, 1968.

La Follette, L. "The Costume of the Roman Bride," in L. Bonfante and J. L. Sebesta, eds., *The World of Roman Costume.* Madison: University of Wisconsin Press, 1994, ch. 3.

Lambropoulou, V. "Some Pythagorean Female Virtues," in R. Hawley and B. Levick, eds., *Women in Antiquity: New Assessments.* London: Routledge, 1995, ch. 8.

Lampe, P. *Die Städtrömischen Christen in den ersten beiden Jahrhundert.* Tübingen: J. C. B. Mohr, 1987.

Lattimore, R. *Themes in Greek and Latin Epitaphs.* Urbana: University of Illinois Press, 1942.

Lawrence, R., and J. Berry, eds., *Cultural Identity in the Roman Empire.* London: Routledge, 1981.

Lee, D. A. "Decoding Late Roman Law," *Journal of Roman Studies* XCII (2002): 185-193.

Lefkowitz, M. R. and M. B. Fant, *Women's Life in Greece and Rome,* 2nd edn. Baltimore: Johns Hopkins University Press, 1992.

Levick, B. *Claudius*. London: Batsford, 1990.

Levick, B. "Tiberius and the Law: The Development of *maiestas*," in *Tiberius, the Politician*. London: Thames and Hudson, 1976, ch. 11.

Llewellyn-Jones, L., ed. *Women's Dress in the Ancient Greek World*. London and Swansea: Duckworth and University Press of Wales, 2002.

Lutz, C. E. "Musonius Rufus, 'The Roman Socrates,'" *Yale Classical Studies* 10 (1947): 3-147.

Lyne, R. O. A. M. "Horace in the First Augustan Period; The Adoption of the Role of Public, Moral Poet: Literary Strategies" and "The Resumption of the Role: 17-12 B.C.," in *Horace: Behind the Public Poetry*. New Haven: Yale University Press, 1995, chs. 4, 11.

Lyne, R. O. A. M. *The Latin Love Poets from Catullus to Horace*. Oxford: Clarendon Press, 1980.

Ma, J. "Public Speech and the Community in the Euboicus," in S. Swain, ed., *Dio Chrysostom: Politics, Letters, and Philosophy*. Oxford: Oxford University Press, ch. 4.

MacDonald, M. Y. "Reading Real Women through the Undisputed Letters of Paul," and "Rereading Paul: Early Interpreters of Paul on Women and Gender," in R. S. Kraemer and M. R. D'Angelo, eds., *Women and Christian Origins*. Oxford: Oxford University Press, 1999. chs. 9, 11.

Mackenzie, D. A. *Crete and Pre-Hellenic Myths and Legends*. London: Gresham, 1917; reprint London: Senate, 1995.

MacMullen, R. "Women in Public in the Roman Empire," *Historia* 29 (1980): 208-18.

Malherbe, A. J. *Moral Exhortation: A Greco-Roman Sourcebook*. Philadelphia: Westminster Press, 1986.

Manning, C. E. "Seneca and Stoics on the Equality of the Sexes," *Mnemosyne* 4, 26 (1973): 170-77.

Marshall, A. J. "Roman Ladies on Trial: The Case of Maesia of Sentium," *Phoenix* 44 (1990): 46-59.

Marshall, I. H. *The Pastoral Epistles*. Edinburgh: T&T Clark, 1999.

Mason, H. J. *The Greek Terms for Roman Institutions — A Lexicon and Analysis*, ASP 13. Toronto: Hakkert, 1974.

McCrum, M., and A. G. Woodhead, *Select Documents of the Principates of the Flavian Emperors*, no. 458. Cambridge: Cambridge University Press, 1961.

McGinn, T. A. J. "The Augustan Marriage Legislation and Social Practice: Elite Endogamy versus Male 'Marrying Down,'" in J.-J. Aubert and B. Sirks, eds., *Speculum Iuris: Roman Law as a Reflection of Social and Economic Life in Antiquity*. Ann Arbor: University of Michigan Press, 2002, pp. 46-93.

McGinn, T. A. J. *Prostitution, Sexuality and the Law in Ancient Rome*. Oxford: Oxford University Press, 1998.

McGinn, T. A. J. "Widows, Orphans and Social History," *Journal of Roman Archaeology* 12 (1999): 617-32.

Meier, C. *The Greek Discovery of Politics.* ET, Cambridge, Mass.: Harvard University Press, 1990.

Melville, A. D. *Ovid, Sorrows of an Exile.* Oxford: Clarendon Press, 1992.

Mendelson, A. *Secular Education in Philo of Alexandria.* Cincinnati: Hebrew Union College Press, 1982.

Mitchell, S., ed. "The Administration of Roman Asia from 133 B.C. to A.D. 250," in W. Eck, ed., *Lokale Autonomie und römische Ordnungsmacht.* München: R. Oldenbourg, 1999, pp. 17-46.

Moo, D. J. *The Epistle to the Romans.* Grand Rapids: Eerdmans, 1996.

Mounce, W. D. *Pastoral Epistles.* Nashville: Thomas Nelson, 2000.

Murphy-O'Connor, J. *St. Paul's Corinth: Texts and Archaeology.* Collegeville: Liturgical Press, 2002, 3rd ed.

Nichols, J. "*Tabulae patronatus:* A Study of the Agreement between Patron and Client-community," *ANRW* 2.13 (1980): 535-59.

Nickle, K. F. *The Collection: A Study in Paul's Strategy,* SBT 48. London: SCM, 1966.

Nicols, J. "Patrons of Provinces in the Early Principate: The Case of Bithynia," *ZPE* 80 (1990): 101-181.

North, H. "Canons and Hierarchies of the Cardinal Virtues in Greek and Latin Literature," in L. Wallach, ed., *The Classical Tradition: Literary and Historical Studies in Honor of Harry Caplan.* New York: Cornell University Press, 1966, pp. 165-83.

North, H. *Sophrosyne: Self-Knowledge and Self-Restraint in Greek Literature,* Cornell Studies in Classical Philology, 35. Ithaca, N.Y.: Cornell University Press, 1966.

Noy, D. *Foreigners at Rome: Citizens and Strangers.* London: Duckworth with The Classical Press of Wales, 2000.

Ogden, D. "Controlling Women's Dress: *gynaikonomoi,*" in L. Llewellyn-Jones, ed., *Women's Dress in the Ancient Greek World.* London and Swansea: Duckworth and University Press of Wales, 2002, ch. 11.

Oldfather, W. A. *Epictetus, LCL,* II. Cambridge, Mass.: Harvard University Press, 1978.

Pallas, D., et al. "Inscriptions lyciennes trouvées à Solômos près de Corinthe," *Bulletin de correspondance héllenique* 83 (1959): 496-508.

Papanghelis, T. D. *Propertius: A Hellenistic Poet on Love and Death.* Cambridge: Cambridge University Press, 1987.

Peterman, G. *Paul's Gift from Philippi: Conventions of Gift Exchange and Christian Giving.* Cambridge: Cambridge University Press, 1997.

Petrochilos, N. *Roman Attitudes to the Greeks.* Athens: National and Capodistrian University of Athens, 1974.

Pomeroy, J. *Arius Didymus: Epitome of Stoic Ethics,* Texts and Translations, Graeco-Roman Series 14. Atlanta: Society of Biblical Literature, 1999.

Pomeroy, S. B. *Goddesses, Whores, Wives, and Slaves: Women in Classical Antiquity.* London: Random House, 1975.

Pomeroy, S. B. *Spartan Women.* Oxford: Oxford University Press, 2002.

Pomeroy, S. B. *Women in Hellenistic Egypt: From Alexander to Cleopatra.* Detroit: Wayne State University Press, 1990.

Pomeroy, S. B., ed. *Plutarch's Advice to the Bride and Groom and A Consolation to His Wife: English Translations, Commentary, Interpretive Essays and Bibliography.* Oxford: Oxford University Press, 1999.

Raditsa, L. F. "Augustus' Legislation concerning Marriage, Procreation, Love Affairs and Adultery," *ANRW* 2.13 (1980): 278-339.

Rawson, B. "From 'daily life' to 'demography'," in R. Hawley and B. Levick, eds., *Women in Antiquity: New Assessments.* London: Routledge, 1995, ch. 1.

Rawson, B. *The Politics of Friendship: Pompey and Cicero.* Sydney: Sydney University Press, 1978.

Rawson, B. "The Roman Family," in B. Rawson, ed., *The Family in Ancient Rome: New Perspectives.* London: Croom Helm, 1986.

Rawson, E. "*Discrimina ordinum:* The *lex Julia theatricalis*," *PBSR* (1987): 83-114.

Richardson, P. "Early Synagogues as *collegia* in the Diaspora and Palestine," in J. S. Kloppenborg and S. G. Wilson, eds., *Voluntary Associations in the Graeco-Roman World.* London: Routledge, 1996, ch. 6.

Richlin, A. *The Garden of Priapus: Sexuality and Aggression in Roman Humor,* 2nd edition. Oxford: Oxford University Press, 1992.

Richlin, A. "Graffiti, Gossip, Lampoons and Rhetorical Invective," in *The Garden of Priapus,* ch. 4. Oxford: Oxford University Press, 1992.

Rickman, G. *The Corn Supply of Ancient Rome.* Oxford: Clarendon Press, 1980.

Rist, J. M. "Seneca and Stoic Orthodoxy," *ANRW* 36.3 (1989): 1992-2018.

Rives, J. "Civic and Religious Life," in J. Bordel, ed., *Epigraphic Evidence: Ancient History from Inscriptions.* London: Routledge, 2001.

Robertson, A. T. *A Grammar of the Greek New Testament in the Light of Historical Research,* 2nd edition. New York: Hodder & Stoughton, 1914.

Robinson, O. F. *The Criminal Law of Ancient Rome.* London: Duckworth, 1995.

Roche, P. A. "The Public Image of Trajan's Family," *Classical Philology* 97.1 (2002): 41-60.

Romilly, J. de. *Magic and Rhetoric in Ancient Greece.* Cambridge, MA and London: Harvard University Press, 1975.

Runia, D. T. *Philo of Alexandria and the* Timaeus *of Plato.* Leiden: E. J. Brill, 1986.

Russell, D. A. *Dio Chrysostom, Orations VII, XII, XXXVI,* Cambridge Greek and Latin Classics. Cambridge: Cambridge University Press, 1992.

Saller, R. P. "Men's Age at Marriage and Its Consequences for the Roman Family," *Classical Philology* 82.1 (1987): 21-34.

Salmon, E. T. *Roman Colonisation under the Republic.* London: Thames and Hudson, 1969.

Sand, A. "Witwenstand und Ämterstrukturen in den urchristlichen Gemeinden," *Bibel und Leben* 12 (1971): 196.

Sandbach, F. H. *The Stoics.* London: Chatto and Windus, 1975.

Sanders, I. F. *Roman Crete: An Archaeological Survey and Gazetteer of Later Hellenistic, Roman and Early Byzantium.* Warminster: Aris & Phillips, 1982.

Scherrer, P. *Ephesus: The New Guide.* Turkey: Austrian Archaeological Institute, 2000.

Bibliography

Schnaps, D. M. *Economic Rights of Women in Ancient Greece.* Edinburgh: Edinburgh University Press, 1979.

Schofield, M. *The Stoic Ideal of the City.* Cambridge: Cambridge University Press, 1991.

Schuhmann, E. "Der Typ der *Uxor Dotata* in den Komödien des Plautus," *Philologus* 121 (1997): 45-65.

Schürer, E. *The History of the Jewish People in the Age of Jesus Christ* II. Edinburgh: T&T Clark, 1979.

Sebesta, J. L. "Symbolism in the Costume of the Roman Woman," in L. Bonfante and J. L. Sebesta, eds., *The World of Roman Costume.* Madison: University of Wisconsin Press, 1994, ch. 2.

Shaw, B. D. "The Age of Roman Girls at Marriage: Some Considerations," *JRS* 77 (1987): 43-44.

Sherwin-White, A. N. *Roman Society and Roman Law in the New Testament.* Oxford: Clarendon Press, 1963.

Sirks B. "Conclusion: Some Reflections," in J.-J. Aubert and B. Sirks, eds., Speculum Iuris: *Roman Law as a Reflection of Social and Economic Life in Antiquity.* Ann Arbor: University of Michigan Press, 2002, pp. 169-81.

Stahl, H.-P. "'Betrayed Love: Change of Identity' (1.11 and 1.12)" and "'Love's Torture: Prophetic Loneliness' (1.1)," in *Propertius: 'Love' and 'War'; Individual and State under Augustus.* Berkeley: University of California Press, 1985, chs. 1 and 2.

Stout, A. M. "Jewelry as a Symbol of Status in the Roman Empire," in L. Bonfante and J. L. Sebesta, eds., *The World of Roman Costume.* Madison: University of Wisconsin Press, 1994, ch. 5.

Stuckenburch, J. T. "Why should women cover their heads because of the angels?" *Stone Campbell Journal* 4.2 (2001): 205-34.

Syme, R. *The Augustan Aristocracy.* Oxford: Clarendon Press, 1986.

Syme, R. "The Error of Caesar Augustus," in *History in Ovid.* Oxford: Clarendon Press, 1978.

Taubenschlag, R. *The Law of Greco-Roman Egypt in the Light of the Papyri, 332 B.C.–640 A.D.* Warsaw: Panstwowe Wydawnictwo Naukowe, 1955.

Thibault, J. C. *The Mystery of Ovid's Exile.* Berkeley: University of California Press, 1964.

Thiselton, A. C. *The First Epistle to the Corinthians: Commentary on the Greek Text.* Grand Rapids and Carlisle: Eerdmans and Paternoster, 2000.

Thiselton, A. C. "The Logical Role of the Liar Paradox in Titus 1:12, 13: A Dissent from the Commentaries in the Light of Philosophical and Logical Analysis," *Biblical Interpretation* 2 (1994): 207-23.

Thiselton, A. C. *The Two Horizons: New Testament Hermeneutics and Philosophical Description with Special Reference to Heidegger, Bultmann, Gadamer and Wittgenstein.* Exeter: Paternoster Press, 1980.

Treggiari, S. "Jobs for Women," *AJAH* 1 (1976): 76-104.

Treggiari, S. *Roman Marriage: Iusti Coniuges from the Time of Cicero to the Time of Ulpian.* Oxford: Clarendon, 1991.

Turcan, R. *The Cults of the Roman Empire.* E.T. Oxford: Blackwell, 1996.

van Bremen, R. *The Limits of Participation: Women and Civic Life in the Greek East in the Hellenistic and Roman Periods.* Amsterdam: J. C. Gieben, 1996.

Van Nijf, O. M. *The Civic World of Professional Associations in the Roman East.* Amsterdam: J. C. Gieben, 1997.

Veyne, P. "The Roman Empire," in P. Veyne, ed., *Histoire de la vie privée,* ET, *A History of Private Life.* Cambridge, MA: Harvard University Press, 1987, ch. 1.

Walcot, P. "On Widows and Their Reputation in Antiquity," *Symbolae Osloenses* lxvi (1991): 5-26.

Wallace, R., and W. Williams. "Roman Rule in the Near East," in *The Three Worlds of Paul of Tarsus.* London: Routledge, 1998, ch. 6.

Wallace-Hadrill, A. "Family and Inheritance in the Augustan Marriage Laws," *Proceedings of the Cambridge Philological Society* n.s. 27 (1981): 58-80.

Wallach, L., ed. *The Classical Tradition: Literary and Historical Studies in Honor of Harry Caplan.* New York: Cornell University Press, 1966.

Wardman, A. *Rome's Debt to Greece.* New York: St. Martin's Press, 1977.

Watson, A. *The Law of Obligations in the Later Roman Republic.* Oxford: Clarendon, 1965.

Whelan, C. F. "*Amica Pauli:* The Role of Phoebe in the Early Church," *JSNT* 49 (1993): 67-85.

Wilkinson, L. P. *Classical Attitudes to Modern Issues.* London: William Kimber, 1979.

Williams, G. "Poetry in the Moral Climate of Augustan Rome," *JRS* 52 (1962): 28-46.

Wilshire, L. "The TLG computer and further references to ΑΥΘΕΝΤΕΩ in 1 Timothy 2.12," *NTS* 34 (1988): 120-34.

Winter, B. W. "*Christentum und Antike:* Acts and the Pauline Corpus as Ancient History," in T. W. Hillard, R. A. Kearsley, C. E. V. Nixon, and A. M. Nobbs, eds., *Ancient History in a Modern University,* Vol. 2. Grand Rapids: Eerdmans, 1998.

Winter, B. W. "The 'New' Roman Wife and 1 Timothy 2:9-15: The Search for a *Sitz im Leben,*" *TynB* 51.2 (2000): 285-94.

Winter, B. W. "On Introducing Gods to Athens: An Alternative Reading of Acts 17:18-20," *TynB* 47.1 (1996): 71-90.

Winter, B. W. *Philo and Paul among the Sophists: Alexandrian and Corinthian Responses to a Julio-Claudian Movement,* 2nd ed. Grand Rapids: Eerdmans, 2002.

Winter, B. W. "The Problem with 'church' for the Early Church," in D. Peterson and J. Pryor, eds., *In the Fullness of Time: Biblical Studies in Honour of Archbishop Robinson.* Sydney: Lancer, 1992.

Winter, B. W. "*Providentia* for the Widows of 1 Timothy 5.3-16," *TynB* 39 (1988): 83-99.

Winter, B. W. "Roman Law and Society in Romans 12–15," in P. Oakes, ed., *Rome in the Bible and the Early Church.* Carlisle and Grand Rapids: Paternoster and Baker, 2002.

Winter, B. W. *Seek the Welfare of the City: Christians as Benefactors and Citizens.* Grand Rapids and Carlisle: Eerdmans and Paternoster, 1993, ch. 3.

Winter, B. W. "The 'Underlays' of Conflict and Compromise in 1 Corinthians," in

Bibliography

Trevor J. Burke and J. Keith Elliott, eds., *Paul and the Corinthians: Studies on a Community in Conflict. Essays in Honour of Margaret Thrall*. Leiden: E. J. Brill, 2003, ch. 7.

Winter, B. W. "Veiled Men and Wives and Christian Contentiousness (1 Corinthians 11:2-16)," in *After Paul Left Corinth: The Influence of Secular Ethics and Social Change*. Grand Rapids: Eerdmans, 2001.

Wiseman, T. P. *Catullus and His World: A Reappraisal*. Cambridge: Cambridge University Press, 1985.

Wood, S. E. *Imperial Women: A Study in Public Images, 40 B.C.–A.D. 69* Leiden: E. J. Brill, 1999.

Woolf, A. *Becoming Roman: The Origins of Provincial Civilization in Gaul*. Cambridge: Cambridge University Press, 1998.

Wyetzner, P. "Sulla's Law on Prices and the Roman Definition of Luxury," in J.-J. Aubert and B. Sirks, eds., Speculum Iuris: *Roman Law as a Reflection of Social and Economic Life in Antiquity*. Ann Arbor: University of Michigan Press, 2002, pp. 15-33.

Wyke, M. "Mistress and Metaphor in Augustan Elegy," in I. McClure, *Sexuality and Gender in the Classical World: Readings and Sources*. Oxford: Blackwell, 2002, ch. 7.

Wyke, M. *The Roman Mistress*. Oxford: Oxford University Press, 2002.

Zanker, P. *Power of Images in the Age of Augustus*. Ann Arbor: University of Michigan Press, 1988.

Zimmerman, R. *The Law of Obligations: Roman Foundations of the Civilian Tradition*. Cape Town: Juta, 1990.

Index of Subjects

Adultery, of wives
  as a criminal offence, 20-21, 24, 39-58
  and cropping or cutting off of hair,
    82-83
  and the courts, 40-41, 67, 84, 167
  and divorce, xi, 19, 23-24, 29, 41-43, 48,
    81, 106, 124, 137, 142-43, 177-78
  dress prescribed. *See* Dress code
  family punishments, 19, 41
  husband must prosecute within 60
    days, 24, 42, 55-56, 84
  husbands turning a blind eye, 23, 27-
    28, 36-37, 130, 153
  judicial punishments of, 42, 82-83, 84,
    108, 125
  of Julia. *See* Augustus
  justification for, 27-28, 36-37
  legislation on. *See* Augustus
  official policing of, 85-88
  posing as prostitutes, 56
  property and dowry, 19, 21, 42, 57, 106,
    126, 142-43, 176-78
  prostitutes exempt from prosecution,
    27
  and removal of marriage veil, 42-43,
    82, 91, 96
  significance of legislation against, 29-
    30, 35, 45, 51-52
  statute of limitation, 47
Adultery, of husbands
  denounced, 68-69, 137, 166
  inequitable treatment of husbands and
    wives, 19, 20, 22, 41, 68, 164
  and pimping, 28, 42, 84
  punishment of adulterers, 41-42
  socially acceptable, 20, 27-28, 36-37, 68,
    72, 98-99, 135, 162, 164, 166
Angels. *See* Messengers
Associations and the Christian community, 90-91, 122, 139
Augustus
  adultery of, 57
  adultery of his daughter Julia, 29-30,
    51-52
  adultery of his granddaughter
    Vipsania Julia, 29-30
  domesticity of his household, 134
  error of, 28-29
  the family and Rome, 46
  imperial wives as statue and coin
    icons, 5, 7, 34-35, 56, 89-90, 104, 134,
    176, 181-82, 193
  marriage legislation, xi, 20, 22, 28, ch.
    3, 84, 111, 134, 174, 204
  closing of loopholes, 54-55
  created inequality before the law,
    50-51
  defends his legislation, 52-54
  opposition to, 28-30, 47-50, 99

propaganda against 'new' women, 5, 7, 35, 133-34

restrictions on marriage, 44, 39-58

Roman propaganda, 5, 7, 33, 36, 38, 144

social engineering of, 5, 10, 31, 40, 42-46, 49-50, 52-54, 56-58, 91, 127, 173-74, 204

sumptuary laws, 40, 85, 103

Class. *See* Augustus: social engineering of; Rank and status of women

Divorce, xi, 48, 106, 142-43, 177-78. *See also* Adultery, of wives

Dowry, 21, 31, 73, 125-27, 142. *See also* Adultery, of wives; Widows
loss of, 42, 137, 152, 176-78

Dress code
Christians dress like prostitutes, 82, 108, 121, 132-33

of convicted adulteress, 42-43, 82, 84, 100

of high class prostitutes (*hetairai*), 4, 42-43, 72, 80-81, 84-85, 105

of immodest wives, 4, 11, 42-43, 60, 80-81, 85-86, 97-122, 132

on imperial statues and coins, 5, 11, 56, 77-78, 89-90, 181, 193

and marriage veil, xiii, 11, 18, 36, 42-43, 77-96, 100

of modest wives, 4-5, 11, 18, 39, 42, 63, 72-73, 78, 81, 84-85, 86-87, 90, 97-122, 176

official policing of, 12, 85-91

and Roman law, 4-5, 42-43, 77, 83-85, 90, 92, 96, 97-99, 108, 121-22

of the unmarried, 78, 101

of young men, 48, 62, 68, 71, 101, 150, 153-54, 163-64

Education
of daughters and wives, 29, 59, 62-68, 71, 88, 112-16, 145, 148, 160

of sons and men, 62, 67, 71, 88, 112-13, 115-16, 145, 148

Gold jewellery, xiv, 72-74, 81, 103-5, 107-8, 119-20, 122
crowns, 184, 186, 190, 206, 209

forbidden, 86, 97, 100, 105

Hair, xiii, xiv, 7, 34, 36, 74, 82-84, 86, 96, 97, 100, 103-4, 108, 113, 120, 122, 129, 193

Hetairai. See Prostitute

Husbands
affectionate, 18-19, 71, 101, 161

authority of, 19, 24, 41-42, 55-56, 81, 84, 105, 118, 130, 152, 167

criminal charge of pimping, 28, 42, 84

fidelity of, 19, 59, 67, 70, 166

infidelity allowed. *See* Adultery, of husbands

punishers of wife's adultery, 19, 41, 152, 177

Junia, 4, 14, 192, 200-203

Junia Theodora, 182-95, 199, 200-202

Marriage
age for men, 54, 131

age for women, 53-54, 109, 131-32, 163-64, 166

break-up of. *See* divorce

ceremony, 78

dowry, 21, 31, 73, 125-27, 142

forbidden to particular classes, 39, 41, 50,

gifts before, 106

speech at nuptial bed, 19-20, 24, 101, 103, 137

veil. *See* Dress code

Men. *See* Adultery, of husbands; Husbands; Young men

Messengers, 89

Modesty
artistic representation of, 5, 18, 35-36, 61, 78-79, 193

dress code of, 18, 80, 84, 99-100, 107-8, 176

of Livia, Augustus's wife, 29, 89-90, 104

modest and immodest behaviour contrasted, xi, 4, 29, 42, 72, 80-81, 100, 108, 114-15, 121

Pudicitia, Roman cult of, 46
and Roman law, 83-84, 96, 178
and widows, 133, 137
a wife's cardinal virtue, 45, 35-36, 60, 72-73, 97-98, 100-102, 109, 112, 160-61, 165, 178, 185, 207

'New' woman
and abortion and contraception, 60, 98, 109-12
and 'after-dinners', 22, 71, 91, 153-54
appearance of, xi, 4, 42-44, 60, 82-83, 99-101, 104-6, 122, 139-40
and the Christian community, xi, xii, 4, 5, 8, 11, 12, 14, 77-169 *passim,* 173, 194-204
contrasted with modest wife, xi, 4, 5, 23, 29, 42-43, 61-62, 74, 80-81, 83-85, 96, 97-104, 107-8, 114, 121, 132-33, 162
'emancipation' of, 8-9, 56-57
emergence of, 4, 6, 21-22, 25, 32-38, 144, 177
evidence of in the East, 32-37, 90, 99, 102, 202
financial independence of, 21-22, 173-204
imperial wives as, 29-30
and infidelity, 5, 26-27, 30, 37, 56, 167
morals of, 3, 5, 12, 24-25, 29, 36-41, 47-48, 50, 52, 55, 63, 66-67, 85, 95, 97-99, 108, 110, 119, 121, 124, 128-30, 132-33, 135, 138, 152, 160, 168
and the philosophical schools, xii, 10-11, 59-74
in public, 4-6, 11, 33-34, 173-204
refusing or aborting children, 40, 109-12
in the theatre, 5, 30-31, 121

Pearls, xiv, 60, 97-98, 100, 104-8, 122
Phoebe, 193-200, 203, 204
Politics, women and, 180-91
Priscilla (Prisca), 4, 203-4
Promiscuity, 7, 12, 23, 37-38, 40, 51-52, 57, 80, 82, 84, 93, 108, 121-24, 128, 129, 131-33, 137, 139, 150, 153-54, 162-66
Prostitute (high class, *hetairai*)

appearance of, 4, 42-43, 72, 80-81, 84-85, 105
and Augustus's legislation, 37, 42-43, 47, 55-57, 107
competition for wives, 22
as dinner companion, 19, 22, 71, 80-81, 132, 153-54
and high class woman, 47, 55-56
and married men, 20, 164
and pimps, 28, 42, 84
and poets, 26, 29
wives acting as, 37, 56, 82, 132
Public roles of women. *See* Wives

Rank and status of women, 4, 8, 38, 41, 44, 54, 112, 134, 174, 180, 191, 193, 195-96, 199, 204
accidentally given status, 42, 44, 58, 174
Roman law, xii, 11-12, 39-58, 67, 91-92, 106, 122-25, 132, 138, 168, 178. *See also* Dress code
inequality before the law, 50-51
society built on, 2-3, 4-5, 83

Theatre
Augustus's legislation on, 31, 44
popularity of, 31
promotion of values, 30-31
seating by classes, 5, 31
seats of honour, 184
upper class forbidden to marry actors, 44

Veil: significance of unveiling, 43, 81-83, 94-96. *See also* Dress code: marriage veil
Virtues, cardinal, 61-68, 102, 112, 147. *See also* Modesty

Widows, xiv, 123-40
age, 125, 131-32, 136
and dowry, 12, 126-27
'new', 41, 123, 129, 131-32, 137, 139
remarriage of, 124, 138
'young', 125
Wives
and commerce, 174-76

at dinners with husbands, 27-28, 34, 105, 114-15, 130, 153-54
educators of sons and daughters, 66-67, 115-16
as lawyers, 176-79
and magistrates, 176, 180
managers of households, 66-67, 138, 140, 160
and politics, 183-91
public roles of, 4-6, 11, 33-34, 173-204
speaking in public, 93, 115-16, 176-79

Women. *See* Adultery, of wives; 'New' woman; Prostitute; Rank and status of women; Widows; Wives

Young men
chaste, 11, 59, 131, 164-65
education of, 62, 67, 71, 88, 112-13, 115-16, 145, 148
not marrying, 26, 40, 48-49, 52-54, 57
unchaste, 29, 56, 59, 61, 68, 101, 108, 131, 153-54, 163-66

Index of Modern Authors

Adams, J. N., 80, 109, 150, 160
Alcock, S. E., 33
Allen, A. W., 25, 26
Amunsen, D. W., 125
Ando, C., 33, 97
Aubert, J.-J., 2, 32, 83

Badian, E., 33
Baldwin, H. S., 117
Balsdon, J. P. V. D., 126
Barrett, A. A., 90
Bauckham, R., 13, 202-3
Baugh, S. M., 98
Bauman, R. A., 21, 29, 30, 39, 41, 46-48, 52, 173, 177, 178
Blundell, S., 79
Bookidis, N., 88
Booth, A., 153, 164
Bordes, J., 166
Bowie, E. L., 148
Braund, D., 33, 189
Braund, S. H., 105
Bruce, F. F., 201
Brunt, P. A., 49
Buckland, W. W., 41
Burer, M. H., 202
Burstein, S., 181

Cairns, F., 46, 94
Cameron, A., 8

Cartledge, P., 85-88
Cherry, D., 106
Chrimes, K., 87
Clarke, A. D., 183, 196, 201, 204
Collins, J. N., 196
Conzelmann, H., 137, 158-59, 167
Corley, K. E., xii
Cotter, W., 90
Crisafulli, T., 31
Crook, J. A., 2-3, 8, 40, 83, 108
Croom, A. T., 42, 77, 84, 100, 104-6, 121
Culham, P., 44, 58, 174, 204

Dalby, A., 81, 103, 105
D'Ambra, E., 21, 134, 137
Davies, G., 78-79
Deissmann, A., 7-8
Desideri, P., 37
Dibelius, M., 137, 158-59, 167
Dixon, S., 8, 125, 176
Doriani, D., 13, 98
Dunbabin, K. M. O., 154

Edwards, C., 105
Eilers, C., 188, 190-91
Ellicott, C. J., 157
Epstein, D. F., 179
Eyben, E., 43

Falk, Z. W., 126

Fant, M. B., 141, 142
Fantham, E., 3, 5, 6, 21-22, 39, 42
Fee, G. D., 155
Fishwick, D., 90, 182
Forbis, E., 181

Gardner, J. F., 9, 125, 175
Gill, D., 91
Gourevitch, D., 163
Greene, E., 24, 28, 119
Griffin, J., 26, 27, 30, 34
Grubbs, J. E., 93, 106, 108, 178, 181, 192

Hands, A. R., 127
Hanson, A. T., 159
Harris, W. V., 17
Hawley, R., 37, 162
Hemelrijk, E. A., 66, 112-13, 115, 116
Henry, A. S., 184
Hoff, M. C., 33, 36
Hopkins, M. K., 20, 110, 125, 138
Hopwood, K., 3
Horsley, G., 198
Hunter, V. J., 134

Jacoby, F., 57
Jones, A. H. M., 188, 192, 193
Judge, E. A., 12, 62, 121, 168, 173, 191, 193, 195-96, 200

Kampen, N., 134, 175
Kaster, R. A., 83
Kearsley, R. A., 97, 102, 182-83, 189, 205
Kennedy, G. A., 148
Kent, J. H., 35, 90, 189, 194, 200
Klauck, H.-J., 183
Knight, G. W., III, 117
Köstenberger, A. J., xii, 109, 110, 199
Krause, J.-U., 9, 56, 123-24, 131

La Follette, L., 78, 80
Lacey, W. K., 126
Lambropoulou, V., 102
Lampe, P., 200
Lattimore, R., 165-66
Lawrence, R., 13
Lee, D. A., 2

Lefkowitz, M. R., 141, 142
Levick, B., 91, 162, 188, 201
Llewellyn-Jones, L., 77
Lutz, C. E., 62, 63, 64, 65, 66-67, 69-70, 114
Lyne, R. O. A. M., 34, 45

Ma, J., 37
MacDonald, M. Y., 204
Mackenzie, D. A., 143
MacMullen, R., 36, 80, 173-74, 176, 179-81, 183
Malherbe, A. J., 73
Marshall, A. J., 8
Marshall, I. H., 102, 119, 121, 156, 159, 162
Mason, H. J., 88
McCrum, M., 127
McGinn, T. A. J., 2, 5, 8, 9, 42, 43, 56, 58, 77, 84-85, 100, 108, 121, 123, 124
Meier, C., 166
Melville, A. D., 27-28
Mendelson, A., 146
Mitchell, S., 33
Moo, D. J., 199
Mounce, W. D., 149, 156
Murphy-O'Connor, J., 189

Nichols, J., 190
Nickle, K. F., 127
North, H., 60, 61
Noy, D., 188, 197, 198, 200, 203

Ogden, D., 85, 86
Oldfather, W. A., 148

Pallas D., 187-88, 205
Papanghelis, T. D., 26
Peterman, G., 197
Petrochilos, N., 34
Pomeroy, S. B., 19, 64, 72, 73, 74, 77, 85, 110, 141, 143

Raditsa, L. F., 40, 41, 47, 50-51, 55, 138
Rawson, B., 1, 20, 138, 195-96
Rawson, E., 31
Richlin, A., 131, 135
Rickman, G., 127

Rist, J. M., 70
Rives, J., 181, 182
Robertson, A. T., 82, 93, 95, 133, 155
Robinson, O. F., 90, 122, 139, 163, 166
Roche, P. A., 7
Romilly, J. de, 147
Runia, D. T., 146
Russell, D. A., 37

Saller, R. P., 20, 131, 196
Salmon, E. T., 32
Sand, A., 133
Sandbach, F. H., 63
Sanders, I. F., 144
Scherrer, P., 104
Schnaps, D. M., 126
Schofield, M., 110
Schuhmann, E., 30
Schürer, E., 127
Sebesta, J. L., 77, 80, 82
Shaw, B. D., 131
Sherwin-White, A. N., 189, 191
Sirks, B., 2, 83
Spawforth, A., 32, 85, 86, 87
Stahl, H.-P., 25
Stout, A. M., 81
Stuckenburch, J. T., 89
Syme, R., 28, 29, 44

Taubenschlag, R., 126

Thibault, J. C., 28
Thiselton, A. C., xiv, 151, 221
Treggiari, S., 19, 20-21, 40, 47, 49, 55, 57,
    72-73, 102, 113, 125, 126, 132, 145, 153
Turcan, R., 143

Van Nijf, O. M., 122, 150
Veyne, P., 20

Walcot, P., 123, 129
Wallace, D. B., 202
Wallace, R., 32
Wallace-Hadrill, A., 125, 137
Wardman, A., 34
Watson, A., 94
Whelan, C. F., 198
Wilkinson, L. P., 110
Williams, G., 45, 46
Winter, B. W., xii-xiv, 1, 7, 12, 62, 71, 77,
    88-89, 96, 112, 117, 122, 126, 127, 140,
    146-48, 154, 179, 183, 189, 194, 195
Wiseman, T. P., 34
Wood, S. E., 7, 34-35, 104, 181, 193
Woodhead, A. G., 127
Woolf, A., 33
Wyetzner, P., 103
Wyke, M., 22, 24

Zanker, P., 99
Zimmerman, R., 94

Index of Scripture and Other Ancient Sources

SCRIPTURE REFERENCES

Mark

10:42-45	199

Luke

8:3	202

Acts

1:23	202
6:1	128
11:27-30	128
18:7	91
19:31	201
20:20	149
24:17	128

Romans

9:3	201
14–17	203
15:5-6	203
15:8	198
15:25-27	128
16:1	198
16:2	194-96
16:5	203
16:7	200, 202-3

1 Corinthians

3:5	198
7:17	167
9:5	203
11:2-16	xiv, 11, 12, ch. 5, 122
11:17-31	115
11:17-34	91
11:20	96
12–14	115
14:34	93
16:1f.	128
16:7	201, 202
16:11	201
16:15	194, 196
16:16-17	195
16:17-18	196
16:21	201

2 Corinthians

1:8-10	200-201
1:9	200

Ephesians

5:22-24	167

Philippians

2:5	195

Colossians

3:18	167

1 Timothy

2:9	xiv
2:9-15	xii, 11, ch. 6
2:12	xiv
2:15	xi
3:8-13	120
3:11	120
4:3	120
5:11-15	12, 122, ch. 7
5:14	xiv, 120
5:15	122
6:3-10	120

Titus

1:1	147, 151, 165
1:2	150
1:6	163
1:7	147, 154
1:8	145, 151
1:9	151
1:10	148
1:11	147, 148
1:12	149, 151
1:15	147, 160
1:16	147
2:1	151
2:2	145

2:3-5	ch. 8
2:6	145, 151, 164
2:9-10	151
2:10	166
2:11-12	165
2:14	165
3:2	xiii
3:3	151
3:3-8	165
3:8	151

1 Peter

3:3	120

LITERARY SOURCES

Aeschines

1.19	181

Antipater of Sidon
Anthologia Palatina

7.413	81

Antiphon

82	132

Apuleius
Apologia

10	25

Artemidorus of Daldis

Oneirocriticon

2.30	87

Artemidorus Tarsensis
Grammaticus

1.45	150

Athenaeus
Deipnosophists

36c	154
186b-187a	91
188c	91
521b	44, 105
564c	94

Cicero
ad Atticum

6.1.24-25	23

Against Verres

2.1.94	176

Brutus

210	116

de Republica

2.37.63	50

Fam.

9.22	135

pro Caelio

2.68	22
20.48	68, 164
31	132, 136
32	23
35	23
38	129
49	132, 139

Clement of Alexandria
Educator

2.10.105	107
3.2.4.2–5.4	120

Cynic Epistles
Of Socrates

1.4	147

Demosthenes
Against Aristogeiton

93	156

Arius Didymus
Epitome of Stoic Ethics

11b	109-110

Dio Cassius

48.5.11	47
54.16.1-2	49
54.16.7	54
54.19.2-3	57

55.10.10, 14	52
55.10.16	47
56.2.5	53
56.3	160
56.3.3	53
56.3.6	53
56.3.8	53
56.5.2-3	53
56.6.5	53
56.6.6	53
56.7.1	53
56.7.2-4	54
56.7.6–8.1	54
56.10.1-3	54
14–15.1	57, 94

Dio Chrysostom

7.141-42	37
8.5	199
8.9	147
8.12-13	158
32.1	148
34.49	156, 158
64.3	82
74.10	164
75.8	184

Diodorus Siculus

1.27.2	119
12.21.1	44, 100
19.106.4	

Diogenes Laertius

7.175	62

Dionysius of Halicarnassus
Roman Antiquities

II.4.24	92
II.11.6	92
II.11.37	92
II.14.2	92
II.24.6,1	49
V.43.2.5	158

Diphilus

132	132

Epictetus
Discourses
I.24.3-10   89
II.10.15   101
II.23.4   89
III.22.23-24   89
III.22.69-70   89

The Encheiridion
XL   101

Felix
174.20   78

Aulus Gellius
Attic Nights
10.23   19, 41, 68, 152
12.1   111

Herodotus
Persian Wars
1.8   101
6.67   95

Hesychius
63-64   117

Horace
Odes
III.6.21-23   130
III.6.25-28   28
III.24.27-29   52
IV.5.21-24   50
IV.15.3.9-12   50

Carmen Saeculare
11-12   46
13-20   45
18-19   46
45   46
45-48   45
57-60   45

Satires
I.1.62-63   100
II.5.23-29   48

Isidore
Origines
19.2.5.5   82

Josephus
Ant.
5.256   159

Bell.
3.445   159
4.119   159

Juvenal
Satires
1.55ff.   28, 90
2.61   105
2.119ff.   78
6.242-45   179
6.405-6   136
6.448-56   114
6.458-59   104
6.501-3   104
6.592-606   137
6.593ff.   111
6.617   34, 104
7.266-67   49
14–16   78

Lalleius Paterculus
2.100.3   29

Lucian
Apology   112, 149

*On Salaried Posts
in Great Houses*
36   113

Macrobius
Saturnalia
2.5.1-9   29

Martial
Epigrams
2.39   100
8.81   106
9.737   116

11.104   20

Menander
The Arbitrators
262   135
575   135

Samia
299-300   135

Musonius Rufus
40, 8-23   63
40, 17-25   95
42, 5-8   64, 65
42, 24-25   114
42, 25-32   64
42, 1-9   65
42, 11-15   65
42, 24-29   66
42, 33-35   65
42, 54-58   114
44, 9-15   67
44, 18-22   70
46, 23-29   68
86, 10-29   69
86, 29-40   70
88, 1-6   70
88, 10   71
88, 17-19   71

Maximus Tyrius
30.5g   156

Nepos
Lives of Foreign Generals
Praef. 6   33-34

Ovid
Amator
37-40   27

Art of Love
2.7.45-46   27
2.14.5-9   27-28, 35-38, 110
3.747-808   27

Remedies of Love
357-62   27

Sorrows of an Exile
2.206-11   28
2.243-56   27

Tristia
2.212   100

Perictione
*On the Harmony of a
Woman*   74

Petronius
Croton
140   131

The Ship of Lichas
110   129
111   130

Satyricon
67   105

Philo
Conf.
262   157
179.4   158

Congr.
67-68   146

Det.
3.3   157
32-34   147
34   62, 134, 147
49.5   158

Flacc.
155.1   158

Fug.
35   151

Gig.
47.1   158

Immut.
53.1   157
64.4   157

Jos.
73.4   157

L.A. III
167   148

Legat.
7.4   158

Mig.
14.5   157

Prov.
2.55.7   158

Vit.
54   22, 153

Philostratus
Lives of the Sophists   116

Phintys
On Woman's Moderation
151ff.   73, 102

Phylarchus
Histories
25   44

Plato
Phaedrus
274b   92

Plautus
Cistellaria
36-37   22

Menaechmi
766-67   31

Mostellaria
690-97   31

Pseudolus
182   81

Pliny
Letters
5.16   106
10.96   196

Natural History
5.101   192
8.83   150
9.56.112   106
9.56.114   106
11.50   106
14.28.140-41   130, 152
14.89   152
14.141   28
37.6.17   106

Plutarch
Moralia
"Advice about Keeping
Well"
126b   71
"Advice to Bride and
Groom"
140d   137
138d   78
139b   24
139c   101
139d-e   103
140a   24
140b, d   20
140f   142
"Consolation to His
Wife"
609c   107
"How to Profit from
One's Enemies"
73c   95
80b   95
"Old Men in Public
Office"
792e   144
"On Brotherly Love"
490b   164

"Listening to Lectures"
37d   101
"Precepts of State Craft"
808e   92
"Progress on Virtue"
86c   150
"The Eating of Flesh II"
997c   71
"The Roman Questions"
267c   43

Lives
Aemilius 23   149
Antonius 10.3   118
Lysander 12.1   165
Lysias 20.2   149
Numa 12   138

Polybius
xiv.6.18.5-22.2   149
xxxvi.17.7   129

Propertius
I.1   25, 26, 127-30
I.5.59-60   26
I.5.67-68   26
I.12   25
I.34   26
II.6.41   26
II.7, 1-5   26, 46
II.8.13-16   26
II.16.11-12   26

Quintilian
14–16.1.1   116

Sallust
Catiline 25   23

Seneca, the Younger
ad Helviam
16.1   138
16.2-3   197
16.3-4   60
16.5   81, 101
17.4   61

ad Marciam
16.1   62

Brevitate Vitae
4.5   30, 51

de Beneficii
3.16.2   48
6.1-2   51

Moral Epistles
89.8   61
94.26   70

Sextus Empiricus
Outlines of Pyrrhonism
III.245   92

Sophilus
6   132

Soranus
Gynaecology
1.19.60   111
1.20   125
1.33   125, 132, 163
3.3   163

Strabo
Geography
4.10.16   150
4.18.20   150
9.2.4   94
9.3.11.17   159
10.2.22   144
10.4.17   150
10.4.20   160, 163, 165
10.4.22   144
14.664-65   184

The Suda
3.520ff.   56

Suetonius
Augustus
34   40, 48, 54
40.5   40

65   29
69.1   29
73   134

Claudius
25.9   187

Horace   45, 50

Julius Caesar
50.2   106

Tiberius
10   29
35   47, 56

Tacitus
Agriculture
4.2-3   116
21   164

Annals
2.50   140
2.85.1   24, 47, 55-56
3.25-28   51
11.27.1   78
13.32   18, 140
13.33.4   189
15.37.9   78

Dialogue
28   116, 161
29   161

Germania
19   82
19.2   136

Tertullian
On the Pallium
4   5

Theocles
Lyricus
5.40   92

Valerius Maximus
Memorable Sayings and
Doings

2.1.5	103
2.9.5	103
3.8.6	115
4.4	105
6.3.7	18
6.3.9-12	153
6.3.10	43, 82
6.3.12	43
7.7.4	137
8.3	176
8.3.1-3	66
8.3.2	177
8.3.6	180
13.3.8	18

Vitruvius
Architecture

Preface 4	116
6	116

**NONLITERARY
SOURCES**

Epigraphic sources
L'Année épigraphique

(1958) 78	182
(1965) 209	182

CIL

I.1221	19
IV.7698	27
V.8837	189
VI.10230	137
VIII.8123	159
XIII.1983	19

Epigrammatica Graeca

243b	138, 161, 168, 174, 204
272	162
497a	100

610	100

Epigrafia Greca

IV.445	198

Gortyn Law Code

2.3	143
3.45	142

IEph

3218	199

IG

VI.170	87
VI.209	87
VI.1390	86-87

IGUR

1239	200

IPerg.

II.604	159

Kent, *Corinth* VIII.3

128	35
199	90
265	194

Lex Col. Gen. Julia Urso

CXXXII	37
LXVI	37

*Monumenta Asiae Minoris
Antiqua*

iii.499c	165

SEG

XI.493	87
XI.498	87
XI.500	87
XI.626	87
XI.627	87
XI.629	87
XVIII.143	205
XXI.1121	192

Papyri
BGU

96	114
1052	126
1104	136

P.Haun. II.13	72, 73, 107, 109

P.Mich. IX.529	200

P.Meyer 20.23	132

P.Oxy. 2190	147

P.Ryl. 154	126

P.Tebt. 104	126

P.Tebt. 286	200

Roman Laws and Statutes

lex Coloniae Gen.	37
lex Fannia	103
lex Julia maritandis	40, 45-46, 50, 57, 84, 125, 137-38
lex Julia adulteriis	40-41, 43, 45-47, 49, 51-52, 54-55, 57, 84
lex Julia theatricalis	31
lex Licinia sumptuaria	103
lex Papia Poppaea	54-55, 57, 138

The Digest

3.1.1.5	178
3.2.9-11	138
9.9.20	84
16.1.1-2	93
23.3.44	44
25.4.1.10	136
47.10.15	82, 121
48.5.25	42
48.56.1	124